WALLACE
LEGEND OF BRAVEHEART
BOOK I

DEATH
OF A
KING

SEORAS
WALLACE

Published in 2019 by Wolf and Wildcat Publishing

Seoras Wallace has asserted his right to be identified as the author of this
Work in accordance with the Copyright, Designs
and Patents Act 1988

ISBN Paperback: 978-1-9999170-2-9
Ebook: 978-1-9999170-3-6

A CIP catalogue copy of this book can be found
in the British Library.

Published with the help of Indie Authors World
www.indieauthorsworld.com

www.facebook.com/InDiScotland

Wolf & Wildcat publishing
+44(0)7766 584 360
www.wolfandwildcat.com
www.facebook.com/Wallace.Legend
Clan Wallace PO Box 1305 Glasgow G51 4UB Scotland

Dedicated to the memory of my mother,
Janet Elisabeth McWilliam Wallace

The inspirational
"Wee Maw"
And all the precious wee maw's
around the world

Acknowledgements

Big thank you for the writing support from
my hard working family and friends

*

* *

* * *

Leili Wallace

Uliann Wallace

Jade Macfarlane

Matthew Costello

Surraya and Graham Healy

Kim and Sinclair Macleod

Jim, Ellen, Frank and Anna McGuire

Robert and Dawn Probert

Faolán Lee

Nat n' Arif

Rindy Bo

Pop and Dawn Reid

Rachael and Mairi Sutherland

Mary and Alain H'Alpine Eagle

Colin Turner and Mary McCluskey

Tasha Clark (Horsemaster Clan Wallace)

Satan, Fanny, Haggis and Lilly Wallace

Eve and all the family

And last but not least,

all the elders

o'

The Clan Wallace

Foreword

Traditionally the family of the name Wallace, since
before the 13c, has passed down family legends orally
for future generations, by the family
SEANACHAIDH
The Seanachaidh, the ancient storytellers of each
Clan family, grandfathers and grandmothers, would
often recite the legends to grandchildren at family gatherings
or as personal bedtime stories, ensuring the history and
personal account of the family of that name is passed down
each generation for knowledge,
inspiration and posterity.
WALLACE
the
Legend of Braveheart
begins with…

…Death of a King

About the author:
Seoras Wallace

After a career in the film industry spanning over thirty years, in such films as Highlander, Gladiator, Rob Roy, Braveheart Saving Private Ryan and many more. In 1997 following a serious horse riding accident, Seoras turned his valuable experience to becoming an author, and parallel to his professional life, Seoras' has also served as acting chief executive of the Wallace Clan Trust for Scotland.

"An experience like no other," said Seoras, "One of the constants in my vocation has been the revelation of private or secretive documents and accounts from many unusual sources that gave me a wholly different perspective of William Wallace that shaped him as a man who became a nations Iconic patriot and world hero in the eyes and hearts of many. At first I used to think that the information I witnessed was too incredible to be true, but when certain parts of that narrative repeated from different sources, another story from the academic norm began to emerge, also, growing up in a remote west coast village, that was extremely patriotic and nationalist, I was taught from the clan elders at an early age the family legend of Wallace, but that too did not match the publicly available narrative. On my many travels around the world, especially after the release and success of the film Braveheart, people would often say upon hearing my account, "You should write a book about the Wallace." "I have always replied that no one would ever believe it, but following my accident, I decided to leave the family legacy as a fact based fictional narrative for my family and future generations, almost as a historical bloodline diary. The epic account I have written about the Life and Legend of William Wallace has been an inspiration and brought to me a newfound love for the man, the people and the country he fought for. Many who have been test reading the epic series as it developed, have a constant response that stands out more than any other comment, "Seoras, I've researched what you've written, and it's true..." "My reply has always been... "Naw... it just fiction!"

The Maidens Gathering

Scotland March 1286: A harsh winter spike of thunderous storm clouds deliver a ferocious sleet squall against the formidable defensive walls of a majestic old castle, that sits proudly atop an extinct volcanic outcrop. The ancient stone fortress looms like a great brooding leviathan, perpetually guarding the old town of medieval Edinburgh from the darkest machinations of man and nature since time immemorial. Throughout the storm-lashed night, an eerie ochre glow from the many sentinel and brazier fires is cast against the castle walls like a bloody shimmering veil, transforming the burnished black Ordovician and grey Silurian stonework an ominous blood red, causing illusionary demonic spectres to appear in the darkened niches and crannies as a host of hells fire wraiths, stalking the unwary, preparing to steal their souls and take them to the bowels of the under-world. During a lull in the eye of the furious storm, thick yellowish smoke stacks escape through the towns thatched roofs from a multitude of peat and pitch home fires, like deathly grey smoky fingers, they reach up into the night sky to push against the unyelding clouds of thunder; then descend again to smother the old town as a sinister acrid smog, burning the eyes and choking the lungs of those unfortunates denied shelter from the myriad of inns, brothels and religious establishments that cling to the base of the outcrop. Slowly this acidic haze of man and nature envelops the ancient fortress like a great cloak, obscuring the tallest watchtowers and battlements, creating another mystical apparition, reminiscent of a giant Loth dragon crouching precariously upon the highest battlements to cast out its fiery sulphuric breath to protect Edinburgh's old *Dun Eidyn*, the Maidens castle, from evil intent. Inside the Grand halls and Royal compartments of Edinburgh castle, these other world senses give way to a warm and more cordial spirit emanating from a unique gathering of people, all oblivious to the maelstrom pounding the stone flagged roofs. Everyone in attendance has been brought together this night by the personal invitation of Alexander Canmore the King of Scotland, a noble son of the Dunkeld *Cruinnè* (Crooth-nie-Picts) dynasty. Under Alexander's guidance, the kingdom of Scotland is growing from a savage warlike realm on the fringes of civilisation into a major trading force in Europe.

"Glorious" Alexander is much loved by his people, who support his firm yet often benevolent leadership. His plan to progress the trading success of his realm is coming to fruition, due primarily to Scotland's successful wool, lumber and fish trades, underpinned by vital new connections with major economic power capitals of the civilised world. Delegates in attendance hale from major cities in Europe, bringing with them exciting new ideas, vital trade opportunities and most importantly, gaining Scotland direct access to the lucrative Mediterranean and Aegean transshipping of silks, medicines, spices and exotic goods, including a vast array of rare luxuries from the Nordic and Russo Scandia, European mainland, middle and far East. Many important luminaries from leading principalities of Christendom throng the chambers of the ancient castle, successfully creating many new commerce opportunities and trade agreements, linking Scotland with the highest-ranking Kingdoms of Europe and beyond. Musical accented harmonies seamlessly blend the rich European, middle-eastern and local dialects together as one orchestral song, all keenly bartering for the export and import of quality trade goods. Deals are struck for Scotland's famed hunting Mastiffs, greyhounds and falcons, wind dried meats, cured and smoked fish, hides, quality ingots of Highland gold, Strathclyde silver, precious and semi-precious Blue Sapphires, Cairngorm Garnet, Tourmaline and Amethyst. Also in abundance for trading is the valuable lumber produce from the great Caledonia forest, including *Alamhagh* (Alloa) *Mòinteach Raithneach* (Rannoch moor) *Lanarch* (Lanark) and *Gallghàidheilab* (Galloway) lead and coal. Wealthy traders anxiously seek out the extremely luxurious must-have items coveted by the religious and royal establishments of Europe.

Rare products from Scotland's great rivers and mountains are particularly cherished by the wealthiest traders; such as the precious pure blue and pink-hued fresh water pearls, tiny Lewisian diamonds, exotic garnet and romantically titled Fyvie Blood Red Ruby. Spirits are high this night, particularly as the Scots have secured a major shipbuilding contract for the famed Inverness and Aberdeen sea docks to construct warships and trade barges for the wealthy Florentine banker, signor Donato di Arnoldo Peruzzi, the economic mastermind behind the Florentine banking conglomerates. For the Scots to win this prestigious contract to build the finest modern ships in Christendom for the powerful Genovese sea-fairing dynasty, brings with it great accolades and acknowledgements from the international trading community, establishing Scotland as a viable and important trading partner in the family of trading nations and alliances of the world. The greatest prize for Alexander is the presence of Hanseatic Marshalls from Novgorod, Lübeck, Cologne and Visby. The attendance of these international dignitaries' at this gathering is to finalise details for Scotland's full membership of her east coast seaports into the *Varjag Skånemarknaden*, the lucrative herring markets of the *Liga Hanseatica*, the Hansa league, a powerful federation of merchant City guilds and mutual martial alliances dominating the Baltic and Nordic maritime trade routes of Northern Europe. The Hansa Federation is robustly extending its influence into the Mediterranean and beyond.

This radical allied community hales from many different religions, faiths and cultures, operating its own unique legal system where all members are equal before Hanseatic law, fostering progressive enlightened liberties collectively as free peoples, free from singular royal or religious authority. Uniquely in Christendom, the Hansa exists as a secular society, unshackled from any particular religious bias. The Hansa also employs its own mercenary army and professional naval fleet, created to protect individual diplomatic privileges and economic interests of all sovereign member city-states, should a single member be attacked, all members unite to protect the individual as one. Though Alexander is a hereditary elder of the ancient *Breathaimh Rígh* (Brehon Rígh – High Judge) and *Feinechan*, (Law givers), he favours the meritocratic, economic and social policies of the Hansa, where all members enjoy autonomy and imperial freedoms from royal imperial and religious authority. Alexander's vibrant seaports will soon become full members of the *Varjag Skånemarknaden* and Hansa, promising Scotland's future outlook to be the wealthiest of realms within the islands of *Albain*. (Britain) This is truly the dawn of a golden age in the history of Scotland, under the firm benevolent rule King Alexander Canmore III... Glorious Alexander.

Glorious Alexander

Alexander is tall with a powerfully built physique, distinct and handsome in his fortieth year and every inch a proud King of merit. His long red-greyish coloured hair is intertwined with gold braid and pleated back in ornately stylised plaits that sweep down and around his broad shoulders in a manner befitting his royal stature. His pointed beard distinguishes his *Cruinnè* (Pictish) origins... Alexander smirks as he sits contentedly at the head of a great feasting table, knowing that a glance and mischievous sparkle in his dark brown eyes still makes the court ladies blush and swoon. By his side, dressed in silken jet-black regalia adorned with the heavy silver chains of his religious order, sits the most powerful Cluniac Bishop of Glasgow, Robert Wishart. A respected cleric in his late forties; easily distinguished by his white cropped haircut and neatly trimmed white-grey beard. His smouldering hazel eyes gloriously accentuate his features. Wishart is also blessed with a handsome demeanour and is commonly known as a notorious philanderer who freely enjoys the delights of the fairer sex, much to the consternation of his pious peers. Wishart is also highly respected as the foremost religious leader and vociferous defender of Scotland's independence, in both religion and state. In his younger years, Wishart was a renowned warrior priest who fought valiantly beside King Alexander against several attempted Norse invasions. The erstwhile cleric had also fought for Alexander's father against powerful local Warlords, invading Danes, Jutes and Saxonach. In later years he represented Alexander at the council of Lyon, where he vehemently opposed the proposition for the conquest of the Holy land by perilous crusade. Although Wishart is but a few years older than the King, he has mentored Alexander like an elder brother since the beginning of their childhood friendship. As the years pass, Wishart has witnessed his friend grow from a reckless carefree young prince, into a strong, powerful and wise King.

Wishart too has good reason to be satisfied in Scotland's new-found strengths and prosperity. Everyone knows this well-liked cleric is the supreme spiritual mentor, not only to the King of Scots, but also all of Scotland. His courage, pride and dogged determination in maintaining the independence and religious autonomy of the Scots church, while working in partnership with the Scots crown estate, is the crucial cohesive force behind Scotland's progressive successes. His patriotic fervour ensures that the singular independence of the Scots as a sovereign and secular realm, combined with the strengths of Alexander as King, has brought a backward and viciously divided warrior society to the forefront of European trade, boding extremely well for Scotland's future prosperity. Alexander and Wishart sit together at the head of the royal feasting table discussing the achievements' of the gathering, when amidst the festivities, Alexander notices a knight of Scotland's realm enter the great hall and walk towards him. Wishart too watches the knight striding impressively across the stone-flagged floor with an obvious confidence and pride in his gait. Heads turn to look at the handsome battle scarred veteran of many campaigns, who appears similar in physique and displays familiar characteristics as the King, with his long blond brown hair tied back and plaited in a style denoting his high rank and station within the royal court of Scotland. This particular knight stands apart from most court dignitaries' with his exceptional tall powerful bearing and fine chiselled features. His attire of full body habergeon and rare guild crafted and riveted chain mail, cloaked by a full-length wheaten-coloured tabard and bordered by a display of richly dyed blue and white diced checks alternating down the flank of each tabard edge. The centre of his wheaten chest-piece tabard is emblazoned with a visually stunning coat of arms; an intricately woven turquoise blue-bodied gold-vein winged dragon, immediately identifying this powerful looking knight as the commander of the *Garda Bahn Rígh* (Queen's Royal bodyguard).

His armorial bearing also confirms this particular knight is from the house of the Wallace. Alexander looks directly at Wallace, who responds with strong confident eye contact, both smiling in recognition of each other's presence. Wallace halts by the side of the feasting throne and stands before his King. Alexander rises to warmly greet his faithful friend, personal council and loyal hereditary Commander of the *Garda Bahn Rígh*, bodyguard to the king's beautiful wife and Scotlands' Queen, Yolande. "Sir Malcolm Wallace..." exclaims Alexander.

Malcolm replies, "*Mo Artur.*" (My King)

Alexander continues, "Wallace my old friend, pray sit and tell to me that my sojourn here is at an end and all is prepared for my journey into the Norland wind this eve."

Sitting down next to Alexander, Malcolm thinks it proper to be addressing his King formally; despite common knowledge that Alexander's favoured trait is to be familiar. "I'll be tellin' yie this *Mo Artur...*" says Malcolm. "It would be better if you were to stay here in the castle this night, for terrible gales from the North Sea are soon to be upon us. And there's a maelstrom gathering over the old Kingdom of Fife."

Alexander sighs as he studies Malcolm's animated expression, predicting what he may say next; such is the intimate understanding of each other's character from a lifetime of friendship.

Malcolm speaks with frustration in his voice. "Ach, *Mo Artur*, if we are to be travelling safely this night and in good fare, we should be leaving now. But if yie really want ma advice… it would be best that we wait until the morn to be travelling to see the bonnie *Bahn Rígh*."(Queen).

"Wallace…" exclaims Alexander, "Yolande eagerly awaits my return and I'm as eager to be with her. You do know she's with child, and every day of my life as a mortal man, the sun rises in my breast to be by her side."

Malcolm frowns, showing his displeasure.

Alexander continues with a sigh, "Malcolm, you of all people should know what it feels like to be a new husband and father in waiting." Alexander stands up from the table and looks to Wishart for support. The Bishop, drinking lazily from a goblet filled with fine Burgundian wine, glances at the King.

A moment passes before he humorously raises an eyebrow. "Why do you look at me so Alexander? What would I know about one wife waiting…?" Wishart winks at Malcolm.

"ONE wife waiting?" emphasises Alexander as he sits back down bemused, and to gain a better more focussed look at his mentor and old friend. Wishart simply grins and continues supping from his goblet, his gaze turning once again to the gaiety and beautiful dancing girls on the floor of the great hall. Alexander turns his attention back to his Queen's body-guard, only to see Malcolm grinning at the obvious answer from Wishart. Once again, Alexander looks to this old-world religious cleric with curiosity and scrutiny. He ponders and shakes his head in mused bewilderment. *'Is Wishart jesting with me?'*

Alexander turns to speak with authority to Malcolm. "I shall be going home this night Malcolm, and that's the end of the matter. For to be here in this very fine but drafty old castle or to be with Yolande in the Eden of Fife, is not an option that merits any consideration... nor debate."

Malcolm sighs, he is aware from a lifetime's experience that the King is as stubborn and as obstinate as himself, or so he'd been told on many an occasion.

Suddenly Malcolm's attention is drawn to a commotion at the main doors of the great hall. He watches with hawk-like attention as a group of notorious *Gallghàidheilab Gallóglaigh* (Galloway Gallgael, Galloglass-mercenaries) dramatically enter the royal halls, appearing as bestial mountain men so alien to court protocol, and causing a momentary fluster amongst the more refined guests. These uncouth brutish looking men are tall, lithe and unshaven, their wild tousled hair and great beards are bedecked with small feathers, amber or silver orb amulets and finger-bone trinkets. The feared *Gallóglaigh* wear their magnificent woodland garb of mixed animal pelts and leathers as a second skin over their forest green *léine* (leenya), a pleated garment and attached bell-sleeved shirt, constructed from one single piece of woven-cloth, much-favoured by the King's hunters... and forest outlaws. Malcolm keeps a keen eye on the *Gallóglaigh* Chief, he watches him unhitching his longbow and quiver then pulling back the hood from his Highland bull-skin brat. (Cape) Malcolm smiles when recognising the leader of this pack of brutish humanity is his younger brother Alain, who immediately glances across the crowds to make eye contact with him. Alain acknowledges his elder brother then glares disdainfully around the great hall while releasing his heavy wet brat, causing it to fall noisily to the floor. Alain stands proud with his romantically named Wolf and Wildcat Hunters, now bawdily warming their bare buttocks in front of an enormous hearth fire. Alain Wallace is Alexander's' lead huntsman and master of the Royal hunting lodges in the beautiful fastness of glen Afton, situated on the northern edges of the vast Wolf and Wildcat Forest of Galloway Kyle and Carrick, from where he had travelled with his huntsmen to the King's feast a few days earlier, bringing fresh royal game for the gathering. Younger than Malcolm by a year, Alain is tall, lean and his facial characteristics display the sinewy rugged features of a mountain man, with deep weathered lines etched into his face, half hidden by a wild unkempt beard. His dark brown hair is hog-greased and cross-plaited down his back.

Unlike Alexander in his fine ermine lined robes, lavishly embroidered with gold and silver thread, and that of his elder brother Malcolm, who wears the stunning polished haubergeon, armour and surcoats, typical of a knight commander of Scotland's realm, Alain adorns the wild beast-like garb of the forest outlaw, a *léine* that drapes over the top of thigh-high kitten-pelt leggings, knee length ox-neck boots, weather-protected with thick leather grieves. On his chest, he wears a long sleeve bull neck-leather battle-jack, with small plates of iron embedded within for flexible armoured protection. Reaching halfway to his elbows from his wrists, Alain wears thick armoured otter-skin vambrace. On the floor, lies his thick heavy Brat, a winter mantle of Highland bull-hide, lined with a light felt coloured tartan, made locally from dyes accessible to his clan, certainly not the dress of a town dweller or any courtly knight. Alain cuts an equally impressive presence as that of his brother and is also identifiable as Malcolm's kinsman from the house of Wallace by his huntsman's jack, centred by a faded coat-of-arms, similar to that of his elder brother, differing only by his particular blue dragon holding in its two back claws, a clutch of five white shafted arrows with blue and white feather flights and golden arrowheads. This variation of the Wallace Coat-of-Arms signifies Alain's particular vocation is a rank commander of the Kings Archer bodyguard and a chieftain within the Clan and house of Wallace. This wild-looking handsome giant from Glen of Afton, terrifies the same court ladies who blush and swoon for the King, though not all the fair ladies withdraw, as could be seen by interested glances from some of the court roses, much to the chagrin of their more gentile husbandry.

Alain Wallace loves his King, but he's no lover of civilisation. His angst in court is that of a wild beast trapped in a cage, a sense that greatly amuses a sympathetic Alexander. Malcolm excuses himself from Alexander's presence then walks across the hall to meet with his brother, where they shake hands and warmly embrace. Alain enquires enthusiastically… "*Co'nas mo bràthair*? (How are you brother?)"

Malcolm replies with a grin, "*Tha mi gu math, tá* (I'm fine thanks).

Malcolm smiles and slaps Alain on the shoulder. "It's good to be seein' yie here wee brother."

Alain grins, "Aye… and its good to be seeing you here too." Glancing around the great hall, Alain glowers at the throngs of people, clearly unimpressed by what he sees. He looks at Malcolm. "Tell me, brother, when do we leave this awful feckin place?"

Malcolm laughs heartily then becomes a little more sombre. "We leave this eve, for the King wishes to be by the bonnie Yolande." Alain is surprised to hear this. He is about to enquire when Malcolm turns to speak with a *Ceannard a' Garda* (Guard Commander) "Ceannard, call out the *Garda Rìoghail*, (Royal guard) and make ready the King's horse troop. We ride for *Dun Ceann Orran* (Dogs head Castle - Kinghorn) this night." The Ceannard acknowledges Malcolm's order and immediately makes his way out the main doors, signalling two guards to follow.

Malcolm turns to speak with Alain and notices an exasperated expression on his face. Alain blusters. "Malcolm, you are feckin jesting with me?"

Malcolm replies, "I wish I was jesting yie Alain, but the King is stubborn as yie very well know, and his mind is set to be riding out o' here this night."

Alain shakes his head in disbelief. "I want to leave this place too, but ma *léine* and brat are sodden freezing feckn deadweights. Even I, in seeing this awful feckn weather thought to be leaving by the morn would be soon enough, but now you say that we're going to be travelling to *Dun Ceann Orran* later this night?"

Malcolm sighs, "Aye, that we are, but in fairness to himself being our *Ard Rígh*, (High King) would you be thinking different if it were yourself wanting to be going home to bonnie Mharaidh?"

Alain nods his head in agreement. "I reckon naw, I wouldn't be thinking different, though I do want to be getting' home to Mharaidh, but no' to be travellin' through the night in this shit…" Glancing at his brother, he enquires anxiously. "Surely Alexander will wait till the morn? It'll be a feckin miserable night to be travelling, and if this weather turns any worse it'll be nigh impossible to make any headway against the storms. Ah supped with the Moray and Avoch hunters earlier this eve down in the *auld toun*, (Old Town) they told me storms the likes of which they'd never seen before are raging all along the east coast."

Malcolm sighs. "I agree with yie brother, I've told the King we should be waiting till the storms pass, but he wont feckin be listening to good advice."

Alain shakes his head despondently, then notices something close-by. "A moment brother…" He turns and walks away a few paces, picks up a cask of whisky sitting in a corner then gives the cask to his Wolf and Wildcat Huntsmen, whereupon he instructs them to make their way home to their beloved Glen Afton. Alain knows his hunters won't be needed for the journey to *Dun Ceann Orran*. Bidding his kinsmen farewell, he turns to see an officer knight of Alexander's personal household approach Malcolm, with a look of obvious consternation written all over his face.

"Sir Malcolm Wallace, if yie please…" bellows the Knight.

Malcolm replies cordially, "Why Sir Richard Lundie, what can I be do doin' for you this fine night?"

Lundie frowns. "Wallace, could it be that you inform your brother to keep his raggedy savage heathens away from the Royal halls and our guests?"

Malcolm looks at Lundie a little bemused. "And why would I be doing that?"

"Well," replies Lundie, "just look at them, they are all mangy curs. And really Wallace, we don't want our guest ambassadors, visiting princes and imminent dignitaries to think we all live like…" Lundie pauses as though he is about to wretch, then says contemptuously, "THAT!"

Malcolm laughs to himself. He's no stranger to the effeminate snobbery of many court officers, though Lundie is extremely efficient and the king favours him, perhaps is even amused by him. Malcolm isn't really surprised at Lundie becoming flustered by the appearance of Alain and his men. It would seem that the Wolf and Wildcat Hunters are the vanguard for the antichrist legion of courtly bad fashion… in Lundies' opinion. Malcolm smiles, "They're here specifically awaiting our King's pleasure Lundie. But I've already spoken with Alain and they'll all be leaving shortly."

Lundie raises his eyes in approval. "My gratitude to you Sir Malcolm. I knew that at least you would understand." Lundie glances toward Alain, bares his teeth, scowls and tips his head back; then he looks down his nose towards the *raggedy* hunters. Alain observes the fanciful expression as Lundie flicks his hair to the side as he turns and walks away towards the King's table. Grinning, Alain shakes his head in muted exasperation. He thinks. *'It would sure be an insult to a woman to call him so, but there's something definitely odd about that one.'* Malcolm grins too, for they both know what Lundie is like.

Rejoining Malcolm near the fireside, Alain smirks. "Problems, big brother?"

Malcolm sighs as Alain continues. "I saw Lundie seek you out. Is it your oversized tackle hanging loose and dangling below your tabard that's way too much for Lundies' court sensibilities?

Malcolm looks at his brother with a cynical smile. "Aye Alain, something akin to that."

As the eve is drawing to a close, Alexander, and Wishart wander through the crowds towards the Wallace brothers, passing courtly gestures to guests along their route, untill finally, they reach Malcolm and Alain standing beside the great fire. Malcolm hands a large goblet of whisky to Alexander, who drinks it copiously then he thumps the empty goblet brusquely on a nearby table.

Alexander curses, "Thank fuck for that…" He licks his lips, savouring the peaty tang. Everyone overhearing his remark laughs, for Alexander has a reckless way of regarding his own rank that ridicules the delicate sensibilities of those who expect a more civilised discourse from him. The King's self-effacing humour in the privacy of close friends, has made many tough loyal men not only respect their King, his earthy ways make them feel that he is a also a man after their own heart, a man and King his people would follow into hell without a doubt or question if he commanded it so."Malcolm?" enquires Alexander.

Malcolm replies. "Aye, *Mo Artur.*" Alexander continues. "I require you be riding ahead of me this night and inform Yolande I'll be with her later this eve, or at the latest, I'll be with her by the early hours of the morn. I've only the Flemish traders to speak with then I'll be leaving. I should only be a few hours ride behind if you leave now."

Before Malcolm can reply, Wishart comments. "*Mo Artur,* you must be speaking with the Florentines too, for they're anxious to confirm Ambassadorial establishments in Inverness, Fife and Leith. Also, the Varjag Hansa Marshalls require your consent to be building a Kontor enclave in Berwick."

"Soon enough," replies Alexander abruptly, "Just let me confirm with Malcolm here everything regarding the detail of my journey." Alexander smiles, "If that's all right by you Malcolm?"

Looking into the resolute face of his King, Malcolm replies, "Aye *Mo Artur,* you have it your own way then. But don't be saying that I didn't warn you if you catch your death out there this night."

Wishart exclaims. "Wallace... that's a harsh way to be speaking to our bonnie King."

Malcolm continues in a gruff voice. "Well it won't change the feckin' facts none, however which way you dress them up." Turning to Alexander, Malcolm pleads, "*Mo Artur*, I reckon you should be leaving your journey till morn, or at least till there's a long break in the storm."

Alexander grins as Malcolm sighs, "I know, I know... this night you'll be by the side of your beloved *Bahn Rígh* come hell or high water!"

The two men look at each other as though bluffing at a dice gamble. A moment passes as Wishart and Alain look on in amusement. Finally Alexander enquires. "Well then...?".

Malcolm reluctantly acknowledges Alexander then both he and Alain turn to execute the Kings command.

Pausing to think for a moment, Alexander calls out, "WAIT! Hold that command..."

Malcolm and Alain look back. Alexander continues, "I was thinking, forget *Dun Ceann Orran*, I want you both to be looking to your kinfolk this night, go see to your family vittals at *Ach-na-Feàrna*, (Elderslie – Grove of Alders). I'll soon catch up with my cousin Duncan the earl of Fife, he travels North with lords Comyn of Badenoch and Moray of Avoch and Petty. They left but a wee while ago and they're taking the old Roman road towards *Stryvlen* (Stirling) they'll be crossing at the Brighaugh and heading north from there. I can easily catch up with them early at the Chas Chaolais ferry landings."

Alexander rests a friendly hand on Malcolm's shoulder. "Have no fear old friend, they always stop there awhile with Alex the local burgess at the Hawke Inn. Wouldn't it be so that Duncan, Moray and the Comyn have good cause to celebrate their deal with the Genovese? They'll be having a warming dram or two from the burgess' *craitur* (Whisky) before making their way to the lands of Fife and Avoch."

Malcolm sighs, "Still *Mo Artur*, it's no' a night to be travelling..."

Alexander glances compassionately at his old friend, knowing his loyal companion needs time with his own kin too. He says. "I'm aware you've pressing family business with Wee John... Am I correct?"

"Aye *Mo Artur*, you're right," agrees Malcolm. "It's true that Wee John is anxious and his bride to be, but..." Alexander interrupts. "Wallace, who would harm me? Scotland enjoys such new-found prosperity and we're a realm of many a happy creed are we not?" Malcolm groans as Alexander continues, "Look you Malcolm, we've fine whisky and rich French wine for our palette, good food in our stomachs, yet still you fuss and fret about me like an old mother hen. I'll soon catch up with Duncan, Moray and Comyn, and I've my squires' retinue at hand, so go take your leave. I have the lord's guard to watch over me."

Malcolm looks at Wishart vainly for his support, he says, "Will you tell him, Wishart?"

The amiable Bishop smiles, then he shrugs his shoulders and replies, "Me, I'll be going back to Glasgow this night, if or when true Tam arrives, so I cannae be telling the *Ard Rígh* here to be sitting on his arse in this old freezing castle when I'll be going to warm my cockles at the Bishop's palace near Glasgow can I?"

Appearing extremely pleased, Alexander speaks with a hearty voice. "There you have it Wallace, it's official. I'm going to be by Yolande this night and the journey sanctioned by the most imminent leader of our church himself."

The King grins boyishly having gained a religious blessing of sorts. Malcolm looks his old friend Alexander in the eye. They had fought many battles against Scotland's enemies, with the Wallace brothers' standing loyally by his side. Both Malcolm and Alain were badly wounded and their father

Billy Wallace had been killed, when as part of Alexander's personal bodyguard, they'd helped save the King's life from powerful Norse invaders at the battle of Largs many years before. This sacrifice has created a lifelong bond of brotherhood between them, a bond only blooded warrior's can fully and truly understand.

Malcolm says, "Ahm still no' happy, nor sure about this journey *Mo Artur.*"

Alexander leans forward and replies in a whisper. "Malcolm, I'm so feckin tired of these meetings and official functions, sometimes I think war is easier... And we've completed all the meetings with the trader's ambassador's and delegates." Alexander smiles as he continues, "Everyone is happy here Malcolm and I believe the subjects of this eve's negotiations may progress well enough without me now." He pauses then humorously he holds a cupped hand to his ear. "Would you listen to all this wonderful banter Wallace? Are you hearing all of this wonderful music? Look..." Alexander sweeps his open hand as though sprinkling the magical fairy dust of happiness throughout the great hall, "Can yie no' be seeing the joy in those that are left here to savour the nights festivities?"

Alexander pauses then gazes around the hall, giving Malcolm time to absorb the facts; then he continues with a parting observation. "Look see Malcolm, they're all as drunk as lords anyway. Well... all except you, Alain and sir Richard Lundie of course." Alexander desperately suppresses his own humour while sensing an ominously tense atmosphere coming from Malcolm's consternation. Alexander continues, "Well not this Lord." He winks at Alain who shares the humour of seeing Malcolm's courtly angst.

Deliberately shifting his focus away from Malcolm, Alexander puts his arm around Wishart's shoulders. "And you ma fine bonnie Bishop, what are your plans? I didn't quite hear what you said earlier with all this noise."

Wishart replies, "As I said *Mo Artur*, I'm awaiting the arrival of Sir Tam of Ercildoune…"

"True Tam?" Exclaims Alexander. "Is he to be coming up here this night?"

"Well," says Wishart, "if he can pull himself away from his mystical fairy Kingdom, aye, though more it's likely that he's intoxicated in one o' the toun Shabeens. (Town drinking dens). We had planned to travel to Glasgow then onwards to the black monks abbey of *Crios Rìoghail* (Crossraguel – High/Royal Cross) but since he is no' here yet I don't think I'll be seeing true Tam till the early morn now."

Warmly reflecting on one of his fond mentors, Alexander exclaims, "True Tam? Feck, I've no' seen him in such a long time. I surely hope he does come up to the castle this night, but soon though, for I would be sorry to miss him."

Malcolm smiles, "Aye, *Mo Artur*, he's some man."

"Aye, he sure is" agrees Alain. "I like him… even if he is off his feckin' head… especially when he scares the living shite out of the Christians with his seer's sight and prophecies."

A sudden tension immediately fills the air as Wishart glares at Alain with cold piercing eyes. The small group become noticeably silent, tentatively awaiting Wisharts response to Alain's words of sacrilege. The long cold silence becomes too much for Alain, who blurts out, "Fuck, I'm sorry Wishart, didn't I just plain forget you're now a Christian." For a few moments the tense atmosphere continues. Alain can feel his mouth dry up as the moments pass by like an eternity. The critical impasse breaks when Wishart laughs out loudly, followed by laughter from Alexander and Malcolm, who both slap a confused Alain on the back, much to his consternation, then relief.

"I couldn't keep it in any longer," laughs Alexander. "You should o' seen the look on your face Alain." Wishart laughs too; then he leans towards Alain, grips his shoulder belt firmly and pulls him close.

Wishart speaks quietly with conviction. "That's what I like about you Alain, serious to a fault. But you be heeding my words, you'd better not be shouting so loudly about true Tam, the *Fae* (Fairy folk) and the Christian faith all in the same breath master Alain Wallace o' bonnie Glen Afton."

With an indignant attitude, Alain enquires. "And why no'?"

Wishart, so serious by his thunderous demeanour, expresses in a firm voice. "There are important clerical people here this night Alain, and they might overhear your *Fae* talk... and you do know that the Christians are awfy sensitive and don't much like hearing Elvin kingdom nonsense in the same breath as their God."

Alain is becoming extremely uncomfortable at his own indiscretions. It isn't till the small party begin laughing at Alain's state of alarm does he realise Wishart has fooled him again. Wishart is, of course the most imminent Christian cleric in attendance, though religion is nonetheless an extremely serious and volatile subject in Scotland, as much of the remoter parts of the realm still practise the ancient faith of the Tuatha dè *Cruinnè-cè* (Companions of the universal Goddess) and follow the laws of the Breitheamh Feinechus. As with many other Nordic countries, Scotland has adapted to the protectorate of the global Christian community, but there are still occasions when Alain dawns the saffron cloak and emerald *léine* as an elder of the *Tuatha dè Cruinnè-cè* and a *Breitheamh-Rígh* (High Judge) Offering judicial and faith guidance to better the everyday lives of the country people in the notorious Wolf and Wildcat Forests of old Galloway, maintaining an ancient force of faith, judgment and law. Though more often now the *Cruinnè-cè* faith is coming into conflict with Romano-Canonical Law.

"Come Alain..." says Wishart "You've been in the Wolf and Wildcats for far too long ma friend. Where's your humour?"

Hearing Wisharts light-hearted tone, Alain feels relief. He says, "Wishart, you are one big religious feckr. Yie had me heart going there, no' just the once, but twice."

As everyone laughs, Alain thinks with some consternation on the humour of the moment in front his King and the realms leading Christian authority. He takes relative comfort knowing that Wishart is a senior *Breitheamh-Rígh*. But Alain hates the life of town and the royal court, in particular moments like this when he subordinates himself to Christian dogma for the sake of the greater good. Despite the charade, the Breitheamh Rígh forever hold silent and secretive bond and honour codes they share behind the face of the Christian religion, including Alexander, despite his outward trappings. These powerful men are all Tuatha De' *Cruinnè-cè*, *Breitheamh-Rígh* and hereditary Ceannard of the ancient *Garda Céile Aicé* (Queens immortal Guard). Warrior Guardians and servants of the female face of God on earth, represented by the *Aicé*, (Queen) the Mother, Wife, Sister, Daughter and Magda mòr, (Mother Nature).

Alain is brought back to the conversation when he hears Wishart speak his name... "Alain, you're a very lucky fella the Deity is our companion and no' our Judge, for if you had uttered those words in a Norman or Catholic court, I believe your big stupid arse would now be toasting over a white hot brazier, with the fat off your flanks keeping the dungeon pitch-lamps lit for months." Alain glances at his brother, then at the King, both obviously approving Wisharts words.

"*Ard Rígh*", says Wishart. "I was thinking that maybe I should go down to the auld toun and seek out true Tam, though I fear he's bathing in fine wine and *craitur* from the Leith dock Shabeens, which is unfortunate, as there is much to be doing that requires his unique wisdom. Then we need be getting back to Glasgow by the morn. Though I cannot leave willingly without him, I may have to do just that."

Alexander replies. "I'll send my guard to look for him, though they may have to visit every ale and cathouse in auld Edinburgh, for true Tam sure likes his comforts."

"*Tá*, (Thanks) *Mo Artur*, for I've a great deal of legal notary work to complete before I can think of leaving, and we need to be concluding the land rights dispute for the Temple Priory of Ballentradoch with abbot Abernethy. There's also the Varjag warrants we need to complete, granting the Marshalls permission in law to build their Kontor's in Berwick, Saint Johns Toun, Dundee Inverness and Aberdeen."

Alexander smiles. "Then I mustn't delay you, Wishart. But I'll see you soon enough, will I not?"

"Well," sighs Wishart, grinning at the King, "I'll be in attendance to bless the new prince or princess... not so far away now I believe?"

"Aye, not long to go now old friend." The two men shake hands warmly then Wishart bids his leave. Alain bids farewell to the king, but before he departs he turns to speak to Malcolm. He says, "I'm goin' out to have a wee word with Wishart brother, I'll catch up with yie at the kings stables."

Malcolm replies, "Aye, but don't you be too long if we're to be travelling this night."

Alain nods then he follows Wishart out of the great hall, leaving Alexander and Malcolm standing together.

Malcolm says, "I'll tend to your travel arrangements *Mo Artur*, even though ahm still no' happy about it."

Alexander nods his head, "I'll not be too long Malcolm, I must bid my friend Donato Di Peruzzi, the Flemish knights and all Hansa Marshalls farewell."

Malcolm takes his leave of the King as Alexander makes his way over to the various delegations to bid them farewell. The crescendo of the multitude and sound of music playing in the Royal Halls suddenly become very muted as the great oak doors close behind Alain and Wishart. They walk together a short distance then halt underneath a crossway, sheltering from the heavy downpour of rain and sleet. Alain savours the refreshing breeze as the crisp sea air caresses his face. He sighs, "Thank feck for that…"

Wishart grins as Alain continues. "I couldn't hear a feckin word in that place. Wishart, I ask yie, who could enjoy that madness in there?"

Wishart laughs. "Some of us must endure that madness Alainn, for the greater good." They stand together awhile sheltering under a castle crossway, watching thoughtfully as the stormy squalls begin to recede to a light drizzle to grace the chilly night. Both men stand in silence looking to the heavens, catching the occasional glimpse of the North Star shining brightly between the black clouds near the quicksilver ring of the moon.

Finally Wishart speaks. "Alain, will you walk with me? It's been awhile since we have had the time to talk alone as friends."

"Aye," sighs Alain, "It's been too long." As they walk through the castle grounds, they reminisce awhile, until Alain eventually stops the chatter. There are concerns and questions on his mind that perhaps only Wishart can answer. He enquires, "Wishart, there's something that has been bothering me for a long while now, and my words may not even describe the true feelings of my heart. But I seek your advice, as a fiend, and as my elder *Céile Aicé*. Will you be so free for consideration o' ma thoughts?"

Looking into Alain's eyes, Wishart senses deep wounds in his friend's soul. He enquires, "Is it about your sons?"

Alain is not surprised that Wishart knows his mind... He replies, "Aye Wishart, it is. It seems to me that the older I get the more I need my boys near me. Every day the hurt I thought had left me years ago, now returns to haunt me tenfold."

"Then tell to me what you're thinking?" enquires Wishart.

Alain replies. "I'm thinking that the pain of their absence is near to the breaking of my mind and my heart. Not a day now goes by without them in my thoughts nor the guilt that I feel. I don't know how the boys are fairing and I cannot be asking my brother, for shame engulfs me."

With an understanding tone in his voice, Wishart replies. "Alain, the last time I saw the boys they were doing just fine. But I do think its Malcolm you really need to speak with on this matter, not I. Though I can tell you more of young Alan's progress within the church."

Alain's eyes light up. "How's he doing?"

"Ah, young Alan," says Wishart. "Isn't he your eldest boy?"

"Aye, replied Alain. "Then there's William, the middle born, Wee John, and now of course, young Caoilfhinn (Kaylinn)."

Alain's face beams with pride at the very mention of Caoilfhinn as Wishart continues, "Well I'll tell yie, young Alan, he's doing fine as a chaplain..."

Wishart looks at Alain curiously. "You do know that he is been residing in the Cluny cathedral of Saône-et-Loire in France?"

Alain nods. "Aye, I've heard it so he is in France."

Observing Alain's sombre expression, Wishart says, "You've not seen him in awhile either, have you?"

"Naw, I've no' seen any of them since their dear mother died nigh on eighteen years ago. Bless her soul."

Wishart enquires, "And you don't keep in touch at all?"

Alain looks away. With sadness apparent in his voice, he replies, "Young Alan used to write me, but I could never find the words to return of a worth. Now such time has passed us by so quickly it's been many years since I have heard anything from him." Alain shakes his head. "You know me Wishart, I was never one for the skreevin' (Writing). Then the time between each muse from Alan got further apart, till eventually, all his communications stopped."

"Rest yer angst," says Wishart, "Alan's doing fine and well, you can settle your heart on his account, he's a credit to you and Brìghde, God rest her soul."

Alain looks at the ground in obvious emotional pain. Wishart continues. "I'll tell you, Alain, I've been keeping an eye on your other two boys who you also deemed for the priesthood." Alain looks at Wishart with hope in his eyes. Noticing the change in Alain's demeanour, Wishart continues light-heartedly. "Ah now, those two boys are something else."

Alain enquires with a curious smile, "Wee John and William?"

With mirth in his voice, Wishart replies, "Aye Alain, I think... naw, I 'KNOW' that priestly ways are not for them. In fact, I must tell you with less than a heavy heart, they are most definitely not for the cloth of the church... ever."

Appearing slightly amused by Wishart's comment, Alain enquires, "What's with the boys and the cloth? They've been attending your personal Cluniac chaplaincies for nigh on eighteen years, so what's their problems?"

Wishart looks at Alain, thinking long and hard he replies, "Alain, I've grave news I must be sharing with you."

His face showing concern, Alain enquires regarding this solemn statement. "What's this news that apparently grieves yie so Wishart?"

"Well," says Wishart, "It would seem to me that they're too much like their father."

For a moment, Alain is bemused, then he exclaims... "What?"

"Aye," laughs Wishart. "They both have a great fighting spirit, of that there is little doubt, but they show little faith nor respect for church disciplines. Nor is there any sign that they ever will acquire the submissive nature required to be loyal and faithful servants of the Church." Alain smirks as he runs his fingers slowly through his hair. Wishart continues...

"I've had them tutored in Paisley, Dundee, Dunipace then back in Paisley. Aye Alain, they're well-learned boys for sure, but they are a nightmare with their mischief and lack o' respect for the cloth."

Alain smiles, "I can understand them having a dilemma o' faith Wishart. Even I'm still confused and no' appreciating the new ways of the church myself. We used to be independent, but now, now you Christians all pull your forelock to some wee fella in Rome nobody has ever met."

Wishart's expression darkens, "Which brings me to a point of solemn importance..."

Sensing a lecture, Alain enquires, "And what would that be?"

Wishart's stern expression lets Alain know what is coming. "Alain, what I must say to you now is extremely important. I feel that some day, your very life may depend on the ears to your soul hearing my words. It's with utmost gravity I broach the subject and I say this to you as your friend."

Alain has rarely seen or heard Wishart speaking with such morbidity in his expression, nor such sombre tones in his voice.

Wishart continues, "Alain, You must be leaving the faith of the *Cruinnè-cè Céile Aicé* and mantle o' the Breitheamh Rígh behind you. Our ancient faith, like that of the Druids of *Chuimrigh* (Wales) and the Persian-Romano Mithras, has long since passed into history. We must now appear most civilised and embrace the Catholic faith."

Alain looks starkly at Wishart with the piercing eyes of a focused hunter. Feeling utterly betrayed by his mentor, Alain exclaims, "Naw not you, Wishart? I wont believe you've given up the honour o' the Breitheamh Rígh and faith companion of the De' *Cruinnè-cè*. Nor will I believe you could abandon that which we both hold so dear of nature's blessings and love of the Magda mòr." (Mother earth)

Looking deep into Wishart's eyes, Alain exclaims, "Naw, not you, Wishart? I wont believe that. You're still the venerated head of the *Céile Aicé*, the guardians of our faith. Do you dare say these base words to our beloved Alexander, and him being *Céile Aicé* too? How can you tell me our lives very meaning and the purpose of our existence is no more? What example is this Christian religion that rejects like base vermin their own *Aicé* of the seven veils?"

Wishart tries to interrupt, but Alain is incensed. "What about the betrayal of your Christian *Aicé* of Magdala Wishart? She who should be the true and venerable inspiration of your Christian faith, why do you tell me I must change my faith to another as easily as I change my brat? How can that be possible, when all I see from your adopted faith is a mere selective discipline of beliefs? I watch as your new-found religion thieves from or destroys' ancient faiths to suit the guile of your masters and duplicitous feckn priests, all who foster fear in the gullibility of the masses. Your new faith Wishart, believes in an unknown deity that requires no evidence of existence.Look all around you Wishart, what more evidence do you require to restore your faith in mother earths existence and her nurture of us in all that we see?"

Glancing at Wishart with disdain, Alain continues, "And now you want me to believe in something that cannot be proved? That's not faith Wishart, that's an unconscionable abuse of the *Anam Alain* (Beautiful spirit)" Wishart remains silent as Alain continues, almost in a rage… "Remember this Wishart, I've read all of your holy books, from the Coptic gospels to the Versio Vulgata of St Gerome, I cannot reconcile myself with the sickening hypocrisy of your Christian faith and the malevolent contrary actions that I have ever witnessed in its name, all blessed by these wicked servants in the name of your one true God. How could anyone have faith in that religion?"

Incensed, Wishart's face is almost purple with rage. He says, "Alain, do you not realise that Alexander himself, even though his heart is *Céile Aicé*, must accept the faith of the Catholic Church like his father and forefathers before him? He's demonstrated publicly his acceptance of the apostolic constitution and accepted the sanctity of the holy chrism upon his confirmation as a blessed prince of Rome. Otherwise Alain, we would all still be pricking our bodies blue, eating bird berries and still be in constant warfare with our kinfolks were it not for the unifying blessed grace of Christianity. Alain, we're now a civilised Christian realm… and much so the better for it."

Glaring at Wishart, Alain replies tersely, "You preach that we must follow this so called Catholicism that smothers our ancient ways, yet these self-important holy hogs from Rome feast freely on the meat of our ancient deities. These holy falsemen steal from the poor and distribute that wealth gained amongst their own elite, all in exchange for their own personal glorification while preaching self-denial, terror and damnation upon the masses. Wishart, these religious leaders you serve are naught but self serving sycophants who prey on the weak and simple-minded for nothing more than self aggrandizement and power."

Wishart places his hand on Alain's shoulder and speaks calmly, though inwardly he rages at Alain's lack of understanding of the necessary politics of religion and state. "Alain, please, I beg of you, I need you to understand… the way of today is so very different from our youth."

Alain scowls, "Aye, that may be so for you town dwellers Wishart, but life and faith for the mountain folk remains forever true and unchanging."

Wishart replies curtly. "Aye, Wallace, you who live your life as a free born mountain man who has no apparent need of civilisation. But you who also depend on that self same civilisation and our realms ability to protect you to live as that same free man. Listen to me Alain, to exist protected as equals with our neighbours' and thrive as a part a greater world, I need you to understand that our very existence depends on our attachment to the Catholic way. Acquiescence to the faith and our future good fortune is forever entwined and henceforth guaranteed." Wishart adopts a more salutary tone. "Alain, it's the path laid down for us and so ordained by the Catholic brotherhood, that we must walk in the protections of their collective freedoms, or we will most certainly perish."

"Freedom?" exclaims Alain. "I don't need this new religion of yours to live as a free man. We *Cruinnè-cè* didn't need it when the Romans and Saxons came with fantastical armies and weapons to conquer us, or when the Norse sent a thousand long-ships to enslave us at Largs where my father died fighting for our right to live as freeborn Scots. Naw Wishart, our collective faith in the *Cruinnè-cè* is what sent our enemies home with bloodied tails, not some priest in collusion with enslaving Norman fuckin' noble bastards."

Suppressing his anger, Wishart stands in silence as Alain sneers, "Even you must see this false King in Rome sends to conquer us an army of deceitful soft-spoken bitter-tongues Wishart. Naw... I'm *Céile Aicé* and I live by my companionship with the blessings of Magda mòr. She who rewards my faith and good stewardship of the land and the common beast with the gift of self-fulfilment. As *Cruinnè-cè* I am singularly responsible for what I see, touch, sense and smell, to nurture and be nurtured with nature around me. Unlike you Christians Wishart, I'll not relinquish my intellect to follow a single God I cannot see in base servitude and self-denial. Hear me well Wishart, we *Cruinnè-cè* take responsibility for our actions. As *Cruinnè-cè* and *Céile Aicé*, we don't lay false blame on others nor do we hide behind our faith as an excuse for our actions against others. Fuck that and fuck them all."

Wishart reacts with solemnity. "Quite a speech Wallace. You speak of Freedom? What type of freedom would you wish to talk about?" With anger evident in his voice Wishart continues, "Is it your own personal freedom Wallace, a freedom without consequence? Or is it the collective faith and mutually agreed freedom of the community that grants you that freedom?"

Alain senses the intense heat of rage emanate from within his mentor and old friend. Yet he can't understand Wishart's real meaning behind his words as he continues... "Think long and hard before you answer Wallace. Who protects your freedom? Do you think you may just take that precious gift you espouse like a base thief who cares for none other but himself;

then you taunt me with that same base theft? If you are that thief, what then becomes the freedoms' of that community who protects you, when that same community needs your protection by return? It is I and others like me who labour from within the community with it's growing arc of social justice that protects your rights to do as you please Wallace. Do you not rise with honour to protect our collective freedom as your father did before you? What special freedom is it that anoints you and enables your love and loyalty absolute to serve without question the needs of our King? If you are so independent as a free man Wallace, who gives you that freedom to choose? You alone?"

Alain replies hesitatingly, "Our King grants me that freedom…"

"Aye Wallace, my king, your King, the King of our community by agreement and by consent. Therefore, his law and his will is our law by collective approval. Alain, there is freedom in the Christian faith too, but this can only exist by the will of the common people and the faith of all who dwell in Scotland having a cordial relationship with the civilised Christian world."

Alain falters, while thinking of how to reply, Wishart continues. "Alain, have you not fought and bled in blind faith and trust beside our King for his freedom to rule us justly? Did not your father, whom I loved as a brother; did he not die protecting our King and the community of Scotland? Or is it not our collective faith that we live by and our common laws agreed through compromise that gives us our freedom?" Perplexed, Alain gazes into the eyes of Wishart. Even now, as he challenges his superior, he senses immense frustration and anger building inside both of them. He realises that if he claims dedication, belief and respect for his own ancient faith of the *Tuatha de Cruinne-cè*, like so many warriors still do, then Wishart is still the religious leader of that faith and knows he should be honouring Wishart by heeding his advice, despite the obvious religious trappings and strange words he uses from another faith. Wishart demands sharply. "Wallace, what's your answer? Where is your reply?"

Alain is at a loss for words, he mumbles, "I don't know...?"

Wishart's voice is calmer as he speaks. "Alain, you must listen to me. If you truly believe in our ancient faith then you must recognise what we must do now to survive in these turbulent and changing times."

"I don't know," sighs Alain. "It's difficult keeping up with all the fast moving changes in a modern world."

"Alain, for freedom to exist, without compromise there is no freedom. Consequently there will be no Scotland if we do not embrace the Christian Catholic faith in all its forms and the beneficial alliances gained with the other Christian realms it brings. You need only look to the merciless crusades against the Cathars of the Languedoc and to the Saracens of the Holy Land. Look to the present day at what's happening to the Jewry in England as an example of what our fate will be if we do not conform."

Alain realises that Wishart had just said. *'Our ancient faith.'* He knows in an instant that Wishart's heart is still *Dé Cruinnè-cè Céile Aicé*. These unguarded words slipped from Wishart's tongue calms Alain's temperament. It's a change that Wishart has noticed too, dissipating both of their frustrations to an apparent compliant understanding and acceptance in each other's words. A broad satisfied grin sweeps across Alain's face, observed by his religious mentor.

Wishart realises that he too can easily slip and reveal himself when speaking with an unguarded tongue. "*Geallach Quaich?*" (The equal moon) says Alain, with a hint of a smile.

Wishart laughs. "Ha, *Geallach Quaich* Alain… Aye right enough, we agree we see the same thing when standing together, yet each of us would describe what we see so differently as individuals, no matter how close we be."

"It's not easy?"

"It has to be my friend, for our very survival depends on it to be so. Not only for us but also for our children. As a freedom-loving Kingdom, everything depends on us keeping the old faith of Scotland a memory and accepting the faith of the new world Alain. Otherwise the hordes of religious invaders landing on our shores will be many, zealous, unrelenting and will surely destroy us and take this land we love so dearly as their own, use our children as slaves and defile our wives as Sabine whores."

There's a long pause, then Alain smirks, knowing he can break the heat from this contentious debate between them. He quips in mock surprise. "OUR Children Wishart? OUR wives?"

Wishart appears momentarily puzzled; then he laughs and replies with a grin. "Aye well, you've got me there Alain Wallace." Wishart laughs to himself, but his smile is not as big as the grin on Alain's face in catching his old friend with a slip of the tongue as Wishart had caught him earlier in the great hall.

"Alain," says Wishart, pointing a finger humorously. "Will you stop grinning at me like a court fool? You cannot be surprised at a Breitheamh Rígh having a few wives and some children?"

"Some children?" mocks Alain. "You mean there's more than one?"

Wishart laughs, "Many more than those blades of grass in that bonnie glen o' yours." Alain smiles as Wishart continues. "Listen to me Alain, you used to call an armbow a crossbow, didn't you?"

Curiously Alain replies, "Aye, we call it an armbow now because your Holy fella banned the crossbow, but it's still the same thing."

"Exactly," sighs Wishart. "It's the same thing for us all. By simply using a different name in order to survive, the *Cruinnè-cè Céile Aicé* must do the same."

Glaring at Wishart, Alain thinks this over-simplification unnecessary. It takes him all his power of restraint to hold down his resurgent anger at being spoken to like a child. He thinks… *'This what religious people do in order to win a debate. They throw out a lopsided analogy in the absence rationale, evidence, logic or even simple intellectual wit. Then they say its Gods Will.'*

Alain's thoughts are interrupted when Wishart speaks, "Alain, I'll be going to my compartments now for I'm so very tired and not as young as I used to be." A smile crosses Wishart's face, then he laughs. "And my mouth sometimes doesn't know the rest of me is so tired."

Alain acknowledges Wishart's willingness to lay this topic to rest. He enquires, "Will we be travelling back to Glasgow together?"

"No, I don't think it so, I must bide here for true Tam. But you're leaving later this night are you not?"

Alain replies, "Aye, we'll be leaving directly after the *Ard Rígh* departs for *Dun Ceann Orran*."

Wishart says, "It's been an eventful and trying few days ma friend and I must be retiring to my quarters soon. Will you be giving my warmest regards to your mother when yie see her, for she's a fine lady and a dear friend to me as you well know, and pass my regard to the Lady Mharaidh too of course."

"Aye Wishart, that I will."

"If time allows true Tam to clear his mind of the mystic ways and favours us by his presence, may we call in to the hand-fast of little John and Rosinn?"

Surprised by Wishart's request, Alain replies quickly, "Of course, it would be an honour if you and true Tam could make it in time for the tryst." Alain looks away and shakes his head almost mournfully, then glances back at Wishart. "I hope you understand, but I cannot bring myself to attend."

Sensing that Alain's pain will not find an answer in one night alone. Wishart replies, "I do understand Alain, believe me I do. I pray we may continue this conversation another time and I shall pray that you will find a solution that we will never have a need to talk of this again. Go see William and Wee John before the wedding, they need their father, not the church nor Malcolm, and that Alain, is sincerely what I believe is the true answer to your original question."

Reflecting on the kindness in Wishart's voice soothes Alain's heart. They have both been friends since childhood and party to all the joys and great sadness of life they've often shared. Only the grief that struck Alain when his first wife died had shut him off from everyone he ever knew for many years, but even during that period in his life had been part of the forging of their brotherly friendship.

"Before I rest my weary bones," says Wishart "I say this next to you for your own heart's healing Alain, otherwise, I fear all you will ever know is eternal torment."

"Go on then," says Alain.

Wishart continues, "Those boys of yours deserve your fullest attention Alain, and you surely do all deserve the loving peace it will bring. It's time to think of them and no longer about your own tribulations, that's your duty as a father, and that's ma final thoughts on the matter. Now Alain, ah must thank you for the discourse, but ah'll be bidding yie a fair night auld friend."

As Wishart disappears into the darkness of the castle vennels, Alain thinks long and hard about what's been said. He also thinks of Wee John's wedding on the morrow and can feel great remorse in telling Wishart that he had no intention of attending the wedding tryst in person. Too many years have passed since he had contact with his sons. Both his shame and his hurt have now grown into an entrenched habit that refuses to let him face his sons. But now, now he has a feeling that perhaps things may be a little different.

The Golden Teeth

Wandering aimlessly along the Maidens' castle battlements, Alain reflects deeply on Wishart's words and advice regarding his sons. Pulling his brat around him to keep warm, he laughs, thinking of Wishart's earlier remark that the boys didn't conform to the sensibilities and needs of the Church, he mutters to himself, *'They're too much like me...'* Alain smiles, thinking of when Wishart had tongue slipped twice, saying, *'Our faith'* then emphatically confirming he's still *Cruinnè-cè*. Perhaps Wishart was also correct when he said the circumstances of Wee John's forthcoming wedding to Rosinn could provide him with the opportunity he so desperately needs... *'Maybe...'* he thought as he pauses to shelter inside a guard alcove from the freezing drizzle. Alain notices the storm beginning to ebb a little more. He looks into the night sky, thinking the Gods of storm and thunder must be drunk and very angry, or perhaps just playing with all the little people on earth who scurry about seeking shelter from the mischievous deities, who stir this wild storm broth in the heavy clouds with their lighting rods, then spill heavenly life-giving rainwater to nurture Magda Mòr. Looking to the sky once more, Alain thinks... *'Should be good harvests this summer... then good hunts in the fall...'* Alain yawns and stretches his tired aching muscles, but the persistence of his guilt returns, causing him to reflect on his plight with his sons. He gazes over the castle battlements, looking down onto the thatched rooftops of the little township of Edinburgh then peers into the dark night towards the Bass Rock, a peculiar looking island standing like a gargantuan humpback guard in the sea just a few miles out in front of the old town and castle. But all he sees in his mind's eye are his sons as he remembers them to be so many years ago, when they were but infants. The memory saddens him, for the last time he held them in his arms as children had been so long in the past… now they're young men. He dearly hopes that time really is the great healer as his mind descends into turmoil thinking of another time when he gave his sons up for fostering to his brother, Malcolm. A time when grief, whisky, rage, anger, all of these things had torn his life apart. He thinks too upon how the long years since the death of his first wife Brìghde, has mellowed him.

Maybe the long time that has passed is also a reason that his abandonment of his sons has begun to fade. He thinks *'I have to find a way,'* then a rare warmth stirs in his heart as a feeling of peace begins to engulf him. Sensing this is an emotion he hasn't experienced in many a long year, much longer than he could ever remember, pleases him. Perhaps he feels the comfort of love embracing his heart as reward for at least thinking to seek out his sons and attempt reconciliation. He smiles realising he's enjoying this inner warmth that's making him feel so elated. Perhaps Wishart is right after all. Alain perks up, content in all that has passed between him and Wishart and his own clarity of thought during his solitary pondering in the guard alcove. Feeling elated, Alain senses he's closer to finding the real reason for his heart-breaking pain and dilemma as a father. It may be too that the birth of his daughter Caoilfhinn to his second wife has triggered a resurgent nurture in his breast? Smiling again he thinks, no matter what the reason is, it's a good feeling and greatly welcome. Rubbing his hands enthusiastically, Alain savours this euphoric feeling. This stirring and excitement of what could be, truly is small reward for his thoughts of extending his hand out to his estranged sons? Suddenly, he becomes aware of his surroundings when he hears faint shouts and the clatter of heavy iron horseshoes crashing about on cobblestones in the distance. He quickly focuses on his duties, composes himself then makes haste back to the great hall, only to find that the King has already departed. Alain hopes that Alexander will still be in the grounds of the maidens Castle.

Walking briskly through the dark claustrophobic vennels of the old castle, Alain follows the sounds of men and horses towards the source, till he arrives in a large cobbled court-yard at the south port of the castle, much to his relief, he sees Alexander and his squires grooming horses preparing for their departure from the royal stables. As Alain approaches Alexander, he sees he is busy currying the long black mane of his faithful horse, Areion, a mighty Arabic-Andalusia cross stallion, standing sixteen hands at the withers, looking so very handsome with the telltale Arabic wedge-shaped broad forehead and beautiful large eyes, typical of the exquisite Andalusia breed. A prolific horseman himself, Alain keenly observes the beauty of the stallion by following the lines of Areions' finely chiselled bone structure and beautiful arched neck. *Such a magnificent creature* he thinks as he reaches up and cups the stallion's ear, then he runs his other hand down the mane while scrutinising the perfect level croup, concave profile and distinctive high tail carriage of Areion.

"A very fine horse, *mo Artur*," expresses Alain. He shakes his head almost in disbelief at this perfect equine example then smiles in awe as he studies Areion. "Ach, *mo Artur*, those words I utter don't come close to describing the magnificence of this stallion." Areions ears prick forward. The stallion looks at Alain with his beautiful mesmerising black skinned liquid eyes, then nudges the King with his nose as though declaring to all… *'This is my King, my Alexander…'* Both Alain and Alexander laugh at this equine declaration; such is the telepathic gift that few are blessed with in a lifetime sharing the company of the horse.

As Alexander continues to groom Areion, he says, "Alain, I've a stable of these Arabian Andalusia crosses. They were gifted to me many years ago by an old Mamluk friend called, Qalawun."

Alain exclaims as he strokes Areion. "An old what?"

Alexander laughs, "Qalawun… a fine friend from another time from the lands of the Crusades."

"A Christian king?"

"No Alain, Qalawun is a great and noble warlord of the Islamic Caliphate, a true friend to me when I was in desperate need in the Holy land. Curiously though, many Scots found a greater bond with the people of the Caliphate than we ever could with some of our so-called Christian allies."

Shrugging his shoulders, Alain says, "Well whoever this fella is *mo Artur*, he sure does know his feckin horses." Alexander smiles knowingly hearing Alain's unfettered reply then reaches up and grasps Areions saddle horn firmly as a squire cups his hands under the arch of the King's left foot. As Alexander mounts his royal stallion, Areion immediately rears and raises high in the air and skitters about, causing sparks to fly off the stone cobbles from the great iron-shod hooves as he eagerly prepares to ride out. Alexander sits back in the deep saddle holding the reigns gently when he notices Malcolm exit the Blacksmiths forge and approach them. He calls out, "Malcolm, it's been a long ten days for everyone, therefore I have decided the *Garda Rìoghail* may remain here this eve and rest, they can follow me to *Ceann Orran* the morn."

A disgruntled Malcolm looks up at his King in dismay, but he is momentarily distracted seeing the majesty of the broad gold Crown circlet and nasal bar on the King's silvery-blue steel helmet. The inset golden circlet with tiny raised golden fleur-de-lis reflects the rich fiery glow from the braziers and blacksmith forges. Alain glances at his elder brother, who appears completely mesmerised by the magnificence of their warrior King as he sits astride his mighty warhorse before them. Malcolm continues to gaze at the King, so boldly attired in his light brown leathers and warm ochre ermines, with luxurious flowing wolverine mantles and Bear brats that drape lazily down the flanks of Areion.

Alexander's blue-steel state armour is beautifully garnished with intricate gold and silver inlaid knotwork, complimented with finely designed ornate grieves and vambrace also reflecting the forge glow. Holding the reigns lightly, Alexander trots and canters the soft-mouth Areion around the courtyard to warm and stretch his powerful equine muscles, in preparation for the long ride out to *Ceann Orran*. In Malcolm's imagination, Alexander fulfils the majestic characterisation of Gabrán macCenél pen Dragŷnn, y Manaan, the noblest hero King from the legendary Triads Gwŷr y Gogledd (Men of the North). Malcolm's love for Alexander is exemplified by this very epitome of the original warrior King's who once ruled the immortal *Garda Céile Aicé* of the *Tuatha de Cruinne-cè*. A noble King sworn by blood oath to protect the children of Titan Danu, armed spiritually with the *Garda Céile Aicé* virtues of Humility, Courage, Fearlessness and Selflessness.

"MALCOLM, are you with me," enquires the King.

Malcolm suddenly snaps out of his boyish admiration. "Aye, *mo Artur.*"

"Wallace."

Both Wallace brothers reply simultaneously. "Aye, *mo Artur.*"

Alexander laughs out loud as the two brothers look at each other. He smiles, then continues, "Malcolm, there's no need for the *Garda Rìoghail* to haul with me this night. I'll ride with my squires, look, see…" Alexander raises a hand majestically toward the heavens. "It's a full moon breaking through those black storm clouds. The mellow light of the *Gèallach* (Moon) will illuminate my journey. And before you say anything, I'm well aware you both should be attending Wee Johns la' Bainnse Fèis" (Wedding day Festival). Alexander leans contentedly on the horn of his saddle and looks up to the darkening skies once more. "And should it be the weather turns foul once more this night, I'll reside at one of the golden teeth of the Forth untill it blows over."

Malcolm mutters, "I don't like it at all when you ride out alone *mo Artur.*"

Observing the clouds in the night sky, Alexander dismisses Malcolm's concerns. "Ach you fuss too much old friend."

Suddenly, a voice calls out from the Blacksmith recesses as a short wiry man with a cropped white beard, wearing a skewed leather skullcap over short-cropped white hair, walks towards them. He calls out tersely, "Malcolm's right, *mo Artur…*" He approaches the small gathering while wiping greasy hands on his bull-skin apron.

Alexander exclaims humorously. "Leckie mòr Lynn…

master hammerer and personal sword maker to the King of Scotland... Where have you been this fine night Leckie? Why were we not blessed with your inspirational presence and fine dialogue at the gathering? Your witty discourse was sadly missed in the great hall of deliberations."

Leckie simply scowls, clears his nose and spits on the ground, "Aye right," The surly blacksmith continues, "Ah've been shoeing Areion and those other fuckin' horses, but ahm thinking now ah should never' o' done it, for that would o' kept you here safe in the Maidens Castle till the morn."

Alexander laughs hearing Leckie's court decorum, he says, "It's my will."

In the momentary silence of the stable courtyards, Areion appears magnificent, tacked in detailed Royal livery, finely emblazoned with the symbolism of a proud king of Scotland. The amply ornate caparison is padded with silk and jute felt, completely cloaking the muscular flanks of the mighty warhorse in a bold armorial display. Alternating on each quarter is lavishly embroidered the red rampant Lion of the King and the finely stitched symbolic silver embossed Unicorn of the Queen upon a saffron base. Gloriously flashing silver-wire threads complement the entire royal insignia. The caparison skirt tongues border the edges with two parallel blood-red lines interrupted with intricately woven red fleur de lyse. Mirrored on each side of the Lilies are embroidered green and purple thistles, truly a horse fit for a King of majesty.

Turning Areion one last time, Alexander faces his loyal men. He says, "*Soraidh mo càirdean.*" (A wish of happiness upon parting my friends).

Pulling gently on the reigns, Alexander turns Areion around in a sweeping motion, causing the caparison skirts to wave effortlessly as he spurs Areion and majestically canters towards the Castle South gate, quickly followed by four loyal young squires, all with their horses dressed as Areion. Each squire proudly holds a fluttering Royal banner or pennant high, representing the house of Canmore, the King and Royal house of Scotland. Alexander and his retinue soon ride through the castle gates to begin their long journey for *Dun Ceann Orran.*

Malcolm, Alain and Leckie mòr watch as the King disappears into the night. "Aye, he's a stubborn man our Alexander." groans Leckie.

"That he is," agrees Alain. "And behaving like a young buck with the bonnie Yolande."

Malcolm smiles, "Aye, she's a very bonnie lass right enough, both in appearance and in heart." Malcolm's good humour disappears. "We all sure do know what it's like to lose a wife, but to lose your whole family as has been visited upon our Alexander and be the personage you were prior, that takes a backbone of the finest tempre."

Alain says, "Aye, brother, it sure does. Our *Artur Àrd Rígh* deserves his time with Yolande though after what he's been through."

Standing beside the brothers, Leckie enquires, "And how are you Wallace fella's doin'?"

The brother's reply, "Fine… fine."

Malcolm enquires, "And you?"

Leckie glares at them. "Ahm too feckin busy to be standing here talking with you two feckin wasters when there's work still to be done." Leckie growls and mutters to himself as he marches back to the forge, waving a backhand to the Wallace brothers who both laugh as Leckie disappears into the fiery forge workshops.

"Nippy auld Bastard," grins Alain.

"Aye, that's Leckie mòr Lynn for yie." Malcolm looks at Alain. "Well brother, should we heed *Artur*'s words and be joining our families for the union of Wee John?"

"Should we really be leaving this night to journey home?"

"Aye," replies Malcolm.

Alain grins, "Then we're as foolish as our dear *Artur*."

Malcolm looks at his brother... then they both burst out laughing at the shared sense of understanding the King's haste.

Alain says with certainty, "Lets get away then, for we should always be considerate regarding our *Artur*'s fine example when it suits us should we no'?"

"I didn't think I'd have had to ask you twice brother."

Chuckling, they walk towards the Castle halls to say farewell to friends and guests, then they begin their long journey across Scotland to the west coast and childhood home of the two Wallace brothers.

High up in the castle battlements, no one notices a soldier putting a night blazon torch out on the castle wall then relighting it. He repeats the odd action six times, starting a relay of similar actions by men secreted on all roads leading away from the Maidens castle. Who would notice one torch over hundreds burning around the castle, blinking on and off during the dark stormy night over old Edinburgh.

Miles to the North, a large body of horsemen dressed in heavy layers of black-waxed mantles to keep the wild freezing elements at bay, are impatiently waiting as the cold biting gale winds of Scotland's east coast stirs their horses.

Suddenly a lookout sees something important in the distance. "Look, my lord... the light relay coming from the castle, it's giving us the signal. The Scotch King comes our way this night."

The leader of the horsemen is a knight wearing no obvious coat of arms that could identify him. He mutters, "He comes to us at last. We have waited months for this opportune moment. it will be a while before the Scotch King reaches us, so let us prepare."

***

Driving hard through the squalls, Alexander and his proud young escort of squires finally arrive at Chas Chaolais southern pier for the Forth River ferry crossing as North Sea gales bring in another relentless storm. Through the dark night, sleet and rain, Alexander can make out a cog barge fast approaching the boarding piers. As the barge closes on the pier, it will not be long before he can attempt the crossing and make the last part of his journey to be back in the arms of his beloved, Yolande. Slowly and cautiously, the barge eventually berths at the pier. The pilot jumps ashore and meets with the King, at the same time, a Burgess of the port comes out to meet with the group who incredulously dares to challenge the dangerous currents of the mighty Forth River.

The large well-fed Burgess struggles to see through the pounding rain as he approaches the group sitting on horseback, he calls out. "There'll be no river crossings this night. Only a fool would attempt the unthinkable."

Alexander clears the brat hood from his face and calls out to the Burgess. "Then I must be the biggest fool in all of Scotland old friend."

"*Mo Artur...*" exclaims the Burgess when realising its Alexander. The Burgess rushes over and rests his hand on the king's saddle-horn. "Surely you will not be a taking the barge across the Forth this night?"

Alexander sighs, "Not you too?"

The Burgess continues with his plea. "*Mo Artur*, this storm grows fearsome and is much too powerful for the barge to match the winds and currents of the mighty Forth Flow?"

Alexander replies tersely, "Does no one want me to be with my *Aicé* this night?"

The stout old Burgess wipes the rain from his eyes as he looks up at his King. They are old friends as the Burgess had previously been Alexander's personal cook before he retired years before to manage the Hawke inn. The Burgess exclaims, "*Mo Artur*, stay the night at my lodgings? Even the fish and crabs hide in fear of the coming storm?"

"If the bargemen are willing to ride the river dragon for me, then I'll make sure you're all well paid for your fears, my fine old Burgess."

Exasperated, the Burgess shakes his head. "Aye well..."

Alexander queries the bargemen. "Will you be the men who will aid me on my quest to see my *Aicé*?"

The barge pilot shouts back through the noise of the wind and rain. "If we don't delay and depart now *Ard Rígh*, aye... but yie should be getting aboard damn quick and no' be wasting any more time."

Alexander immediately guides Areion onto the wildly swaying barge as it bumps and drifts from the pier. Once on board Alexander calls out to the Burgess, "Has Earl Duncan, lords Moray and Comyn been and gone or are they still seeking shelter at the inn?"

"They've been and gone awhile now." Replies the Burgess he then points frantically to the west. "*Mo Artur*, the Comyn and Moray, they are old because they're wise. Your cousin Earl Duncan, he'll grow a little older too for they thought it best to take the long road north."

The squires finally board the barge then the pilot orders the tacking of a short sail as the Burgess calls out "They're going along the auld Roman road to Stirling to the brig o' Haugh, then they're cutting north over Ochil Snowdonia following the drove roads."

Alexander waves farewell to the Burgess who waves back, then he wraps himself tightly while making his way back to the warmth and shelter of the Hawke inn.

The crew push away from the pier with their oars and begin to make headway towards the northern shore across the Forth River. The lifetime experience and skills of the bargemen pulling and tacking every few moments allow the pilot to negotiate the powerful white-water currents of the Forth, where all others would certainly have failed. During the crossing, a heavy storm closes in, but despite the foul weather, Alexander can still see along the river, knowing that even in the darkest of moonless nights with the great coastal sentinel brazier fires lighting his way, it'll not be long before he's back in the arms of his beautiful *Aicé*, Yolande. Unexpectedly, the storm eases its fury a little as though the heavens are now cradling Alexander's wish to be travelling safely on his journey to be with his *Aicé*.

A squire approaches Alexander leaning against the cog gunnels, looking down the Forth River. He enquires, "*Mo Artur*, why do they call this the lands o' the Golden Teeth?" Alexander smiles as he recalls his same curiosity as a boy. He replies with a smile, "Well, it used to be called the land of the Dragons' Teeth, but the Christians changed that." Alexander points, "If you look along the great river in both directions, you'll see on each coast many Fort, Keep and wee fortalice fires, they are there to light the Forth River meanders for the night fisher folk, more importantly they're there to protect the great river from any invading armies attacking us by sea. Should any enemy dare to sail the river inland toward the citadel of Snowdonia at the very heart of Scotland, then their bows and sails must cut through the fiery reflection of the teeth, it's then they'll be seen by the night watch-guard. This way, all along these banks and shores, the 'Golden Teeth' have protected us since time and fire began."

The young squire nods his head in understanding.

"Look over yonder," says Alexander, "Look to where the Forth River narrows just past the salt flat headlands of Ceanncardine and Airth. The further inland you sail, the fire reflections on each side of the river seemingly closes all around you like a dogs jaw. Do you see it now? Each fire reflects and beams a long way across the surface of the water like a golden tooth. Now do you see that anything sailing this river at night can be seen cutting through the reflection of each fiery tooth?" The young squire strains to see the teeth as the King continues, "The further inland you sail, the more teeth close around your vessel, then it is the more likely you'll be seen."

Lifting his head up, the young squire exclaims with pride, "I understand what you're saying *Mo Artur*. But even if an enemy is seen, how can they be stopped?"

"Each of the golden teeth fires has guard keeps and watch-towers on the shoreline, and each of those has a small flotilla of Birlinns (long-boats) cogs and fire-barges. Their duty is to close in from both banks simultaneously upon any invader, just like the jaws of a ferocious hunting dog closing on its prey. If any invader who would cause us harm or malice did manage to sail inland by the river Forth, they would most surely never get back out again. At night, these soft yellow flames of the sentinel fires reflect a long way across the water surface, and will alert all our watch-guards of any enemy presence. Though it is a rough sea tonight, you can still see the fires still reflect upon the water surface, stretching almost from one bank almost to the other?"

Excitedly another squire replies, "Aye, now ah can see them, *mo Artur.*"

Alexander pauses as the other squires take time to imagine the King's words. Pointing towards Stirling Castle, Alexander says, "Now I want you all to look down the centre of the Forth in the direction of the Ochil Snowdonian hills, then look towards the great Abbey Craig and townships of *Dun Srivelynn…*"

Alexander observes the expression of wonderment on the squire's faces as he had himself displayed in the days of his youth. He says, "Well boys, I'll tell you, the ancient name for the castle beyond the Craig there was the Citadel of Marlynn (Sea-River) Snowdonia. It was once a sea fortress belonging to the auld Kings of Manaan and the original sanctuary for the relics of the Holy Rude, and also supposed dwelling place of Marlynn Pendragon (Warrior Chief) of *Henne Óg lyd*. A mystical warlord who protected the *Clach Claidheamh Mhanainn Ard Rígh* (Sword stone of the Mhanainn King).

A squire calls out. "Is that why the lands around Cambuskenneth are called the Marlynn Ideo o' Camelon?"

Alexander laughs, "Aye, that it is, son."

Another squire looks into the face of Alexander. "Dun Srivelynn? yie mean Stirlin' castle *mo Artur?*"

Alexander chortles, for he loves being the storyteller, but has had little time to use this wonderful gift since the deaths of his own children. He looks into the face of the young squire and smiles. "Aye son, I did mean Stirling Castle. Once upon a time the fortress there was surrounded by the north Sea." He points toward the Northwest source of the Forth River "Now look you in the direction of Stirling Castle, but don't look at the banks of the river. I want you all to think and use your senses... keep focussed on the centre of the river like I told you and soon your senses will show you the jaws and all of the golden teeth." Alexander pauses for the squires to focus. "Now then, can you see all the fire reflections on the water's surface taking the shape of a dogs closing jaw?"

A moment passes then the squires all shout in unison, "We can see the teeth!" The squires become excited on seeing all that the King has described.

Alexander points again. "Now, look away to the East towards the mouth of the Forth and the great sea."

A squire points excitedly, "I see it now, *Ard Rígh*, there's the teeth again!"

Another squire ponders curiously, "Ah, is that why the Kinghorn headland is called the Dogs head?"

"Aye, me boy," replied Alexander. "*Ceann Orran*, the dogs head. That's the old Gaelic name for the headland and Dun is the old word for a fort or castle as you would know it." Pointing to the southern headland Alexander exclaims, "Look to the bottom jaw of the dog away yonder and you will see the great glow above Edinburgh town caused by the Leith docks and castle fires. Can you see the both of Edinburgh and the Kinghorn headland fire glowing in unison?

"Aye, *mo Artur*," the squires call out collectively.

"Well, that fiery glow is why our enemies thought a fire breathing dragon lived in these lands, and the Golden teeth was its open jaws."

Alexander revels in telling these old stories to the squires, for it keeps their young minds free from thinking about the fearsome Kelpies that silently stalk the barge, waiting to pull them to a deep watery grave.

He continues. "Sometimes, you may only see things when you don't look directly at them, that's called seeing with your peripheral senses. Always remember this me boys, you have more gifts in your heart to be using than just the everyday ones you are familiar with. Your eyes see the present, but your ears let you hear the past." Savouring his role as a mentor to his young squires, Alexander's heart is warmed; it's been many long years since he had asked those same questions. He also knows the best way to inspire youth is by talking in riddles that they might discover and find solutions themselves. This is the mantle of his experience from his many years on this earth as a King, and as a father. Now he's using this gift to occupy the young minds of his squires on this fierce cold and stormy night.

A melancholy sadness comes to him, remembering when his sons and daughters once asked those same questions, but now they are gone and only their memories remain. He also reflects on his late wife Margaret, sister of Edward Plantagenet, the great King of England. Raising his head, Alexander looks down the great river Forth and sheds a tear for his first family, now gone to a better place…

Meanwhile, the experienced pilot and crew barely hold the barge in a nautical line and are thoroughly exhausted after fighting against strong currents and tides. The crew make one last effort with all their strength and skill, for they're now only a few feet from the northern pier and safety. Suddenly the barge is hit simultaneously by a large wave and squall wind, pushing the vessel violently against the northern pier-head to glance off the wooden piles, driving the barge broadside onto the beach. Areion rears high, Alexander quickly mounts and regains control of the magnificent stallion then effortlessly they leap over the barge gunnels onto the shore.

His young squires are not so fortunate as they mount and also try to leap ashore. The squires' horses, already spooked by the sudden collision, fail to clear the barge gunnels and topple into the dark shallows, throwing their young riders into the chilling River. Alexander quickly dismounts and joins the bargemen now wading into the Forth to catch and restrain the panicking horses while the drenched squires make there way ashore. After securing the horses, Alexander and the bargemen laugh at the state of his freezing, shivering young escorts, so proud and dignified moments before in their royal accoutrements and positions of honour astride their noble horses, dressed in all their finery and holding high the colourful banners of Scotland's king. Now they have the appearance of sodden wet kittens, looking so very sorry for themselves as they stand shivering on the freezing shore. Observing the sad little huddle before him. Alexander is finding it difficult not to laugh.

"Bargemen, take these youngsters to the inn and dry their poor wee souls as I have not the time to be nursing such fine young horsemen."

The Pilot replies, "Aye, *mo Artur*,"

Alexander turns to the squires. "And when you boys are fed, watered, dry and warmed, you're to follow on to *Ceann Orran*."

Pausing to pass the Pilot a bag of silver, Alexander glances at the condition of his fine warriors-to-be. With a knowing smile he looks to the barge Pilot, winks, then speaks to his shivering squires. "Well boys, maybe not watered, but when you're dry, warm, had some hot vittals and maybe some sleep, you may follow me on by first light of the morn. I must be leaving now to be home before dawn."

Mounting Areion, Alexander soft-spurs Areion onto the coast road and on toward *Ceann Orran*. He canters off alone into the dark night, unaware that deep in the woodlands above the north pier, sinister and hostile eyes are watching his every move.

"God is truly on our side," exclaims the knight as he observes Alexander canter along the coast road. "The King of Scots is alone, we must follow him to be of a vantage." He pauses before continuing, "You four men, I want you to stay behind, make sure those riders who accompanied the King do not follow. If they do, you are not to harm them, but by any method delay them as long as possible. If we are successful, you are to meet us here by our return." The knight scowls as he continues, "Mark my words all of you, on pain of death you will utter a word to none, do not speak to any we may meet. You must make sure no ears hear even a cough from any of you, for if any personage does distinguish your accents or dialect, we are undone."

Leaving the four men behind, the knight, along with twenty other horsemen, quickly speed off in the direction the King of Scotland has taken.

Riding fast and recklessly through the night, Alexander is relentless, but for such an experienced horseman and after travelling more than twenty miles at a fast pace, he knows Areion is tiring and needs a slower pace. With the weather once again turning into a ferocious rainstorm, Alexander reluctantly acknowledges caution is the fastest route to his beloved Yolande's bosom. With the occasional lights of the teeth guiding his way, he continues to maintain a steady pace on his journey toward *Dun Ceann Orran*. Occasionally riding at a gentle canter, Alexander is soon but a few miles from his home when he pulls Areion to a halt for a much-needed rest.

He takes shelter under the trees of a small cliff-face embankment, overlooking the mouth of the Forth River. As he waits for Areion to rest, he hears the feint sounds of cantering horses gain on him. Alexander peers through the heavy rain and darkness till he and the night-riding horsemen are no more than a few clothyards apart before they can be distinguished. The riders move their horses slowly forward and approach the King, some moving ominously to his flanks, blocking him in. Although Alexander has his back sheltered into the cliff face, Areion becomes skittish and agitated, nervously moving about trying to make his own space away from the closing horsemen. This sudden change of atmosphere unsettles the King as he struggles to maintain control of Areion. Alexander calls out through noisy, stormy gales as he pulls hard on the reigns. "Is that you, Moray?" He shouts, but there is no reply.

Slightly confused by the silence, Alexander calls out once more thinking it may be his cousin, Donnachaid (Duncan) the Earl of Fife, who'd left Edinburgh earlier with John Comyn and the Lord Moray, "Duncan, is that you?"

The lead horseman slowly pulls back his wet sodden hood, revealing himself to the King. Alexander is astonished when he recognises the knight. "Sir Humphrey de Courtney... I thought you were in Edinburgh with the English Ambassador?"

While waiting for an answer, men approach Alexander unseen from his rear flanks. Suddenly Alexander is violently dragged from Areion and thrown to the ground. As he struggles to stand, his sodden mantle wraps itself round his arms and legs, trapping his movements. The assailants renew their attack and force him to the ground, pinning and securing him from making further movements, but unseen by his assailants, Alexander has already pulled his Dirk (long dagger) from his belt. Freeing his left arm Alexander blindly strikes upward at lightning speed, plunging the fifteen-inch long needlepoint blade deep into the groin of his closest assailant. Quickly freeing his right hand from beneath the heavy mantle, he grips the assailant tightly by the throat while forcibly pushing the blade upwards in to the hilt, twisting it in the man's lower gut, in the hope the horrific screams of pain and terror from his assailant may momentarily deter others who would dare lay their hands on a King, giving him valuable time to gather his wits from this vicious assault. Holding on tightly to the assailant, Alexander uses him as a shield then slowly he backs himself and the wounded man into the security of the cliff wall behind him as the other assailants close in. Suddenly, Alexander jerks forward, throws the dying man behind him and launches himself headlong into his attackers, slashing one across the throat, catching another with a backswing across his head, slicing him open from temple to chin and cutting him to the bone.

As Alexander passes the third wounded man, he swings the dirk back, burying the blade deep into the man's skull. The other assailants are momentarily stunned by this astonishing attack by Alexander, but quickly they regain their wits and surround the King before he can make good an escape. Alexander hears orders being called out in English accents not to mark him, only to capture and secure him. He continues to fend off his assailants with all his skill and mastery, mortally wounding another attacker and seriously wounding another two, keeping the rest at bay while desperately searching for any potential gaps in the encirclement that he may run and flee into the dark night. Alexander feigns to stab at one of his attackers, the man avoids his strike by moving quickly to the side, Alexander sees his opportunity and instantly moves to make his escape through the gap, but the pommel end of a sword fells him from behind and knocks him to the ground where he's quickly subdued and securely bound.

"Do not mark him," screams de Courtney.

Alexander struggles to escape his assailants, but is momentarily stunned by another blow to his head. He tries to raise himself from the ground, but once again the pommel of a sword brutally strikes him down. His head feels as though it's exploding, his senses spin as a searing white-hot pain from the brutal strikes cause him to be physically sick. For the next few moments of uncontrollable nausea, Alexander lies in a daze on the wet bloodied mud, drifting in and out of consciousness.

Another few moments pass by before he regains partial strength and clarity of mind, enough to demand an answer. "De Courtney... what the fuck are you doing?"

The English knight replies calmly as he walks toward Alexander. "We do Gods work."

Alexander strains to see through the haze of pain and his blood filled eyes, he enquires, "Is it really you, de Courtney?" The knight does not reply as the small group gather around the King, ensuring he will not succeed in another attempted escape. De Courtney squats in front of Alexander, replying with a sneer. "It is I."

Alexander looks into de Courtney's eyes. "This is treachery you perform, de Courtney. I swear, this assault upon my person will cost you dearly."

De Courtney laughs and looks around at his men, then he replies, "Not so, Canmore, for whom shall know of it?"

Alexander looks into the eyes that scorn him, though the blood that trickles into his eyes impairs his vision, he is aware that evil intent looks back at him.

De Courtney scowls, "Do you really think that your mother's French blood, and now possibly a male heir by your French Capetian whore, that you would be allowed to remain on this earth to threaten my master?"

Alexander is enraged, confused and still struggling to break free from his captors. "What are you talking about De Courtney? Who is behind this base treachery? King Eric?

Adolphus? Who is paying you? Release me and we may resolve this madness, for if you do not…"

De Courtney grasps Alexander roughly by the face then speaks with venom in his heart to the Scots King. "Your father's alliance with the French once before threatened our holy Kingdom. Do you think we would allow that to happen again through you and your unnatural spawn of bastards?" Looking closely into the eyes of Alexander, De Courtney continues. "Canmore, we do not have time to discuss this with you. The sooner you join your heathen brethren the better it will be for my master."

An overwhelming shock of adrenalin pulses through Alexander's body as the realisation strikes home that this man means to kill him.

Uncontrollable fear electrifies every fibre of Alexander's being. With all his strength, he vainly struggles to be free of his bonds or find any way to escape this nightmare. Alexander spits out the words. "You cannot murder an anointed King de Courtney. This would be regicide, and God will surely make you suffer the eternal tortures of hell."

Moments pass by with nothing heard but the sound of the gales.

"But this 'IS' God's work, Canmore," sneers de Courtney "We are absolved of any actions we may deem necessary in defence of our liege Lord, God's chosen envoy on earth. You should be thankful you do not follow the same path as your sons, for you, this passing will be swift, more is the pity."

"NO!" screams Alexander. "I swear by all the saints de Courtney, your death will…" suddenly Alexander is forcefully pinned to the ground before he can finish his outburst. He's disorientated and devastated, hearing De Courtney's words is nigh incomprehensible, but he understands the gravity of the situation and realisation of the impossible. "You murdered, my sons?" whispers Alexander.

De Courtney laughs, "No, not personally, and your daughter too lest we forget. But not murdered Canmore. You don't think of drowning mangy kittens or bitches whelps in a millers bag as murder do you? And yes, we did assist your spawn to depart this earth, though I do apologise if you witnessed a slow death upon them, but needs must I'm afraid."

Alexander is in shock. His body begins to tremble with the trauma and assault placed upon him. Suddenly, he feels a sharp stinging pain in his face as de Courtney backhands him and laughs. For a moment, it appears there is a slight hesitation in the Englishman's thoughts.

This fleeting moment of hope is dispelled when De Courtney grasps Alexander roughly by the jaw. "Do not feel so alone, Canmore, you wont be the last of your breed to die. Think of your grand-daughter in Norway," de Courtney scowls. "She will soon be following you in death's footsteps."

Alexander rages, "I will kill you," as he struggles to break free his bonds. He almost gets to his knees before de Courtney smashes an armoured gauntlet across his face. Other assailants mercilessly force him back to the ground, brutally pushing his face into the wet, bloody mud. De Courtney glances at a burly yeoman standing above Alexander, who in turn, orders three others to position Alexander for his imminent despatch. One of the assailants grabs Alexander viciously by the hair at the nape of his neck, while another pulls out clumps of hair as he forces the King to his feet. Standing but unable to move, Alexander searches for any opportunity to escape when he's suddenly kicked behind his legs, forcing him helplessly onto to his knees. Three assailants hold Alexander securely in an uncomfortable kneeling position as a large man-at-arms aggressively clamps a hand tightly over Alexander's mouth and chin, then places' his other hand at the back of his head and holds him securely.

The yeoman then looks to de Courtney for the signal. "A moment..." says de Courtney.

Alexander's eyes are wide open at the realisation, the impossibility of what is happening and what has been said. Adrenalin and fear heightens all his senses; his awareness is ensuring a frighteningly acute understanding of his situation. He knows this is real, so very terrifyingly real. Unable to move or speak with a large brutish hand clamped over his mouth, Alexander is forced to listen to the sickening words of de Courtney. "Let that young squire over there do this mercy, for the youth of today surely doth need the experience."

De Courtney points at a young squire and beckons him. The squire rushes over and stands before de Courtney... "Ah, Marmaduke de Percy," says de Courtney, "you must show these old soldiers you have what it takes to firm their belief that the next generation is worthy of our noble cause."

Stammering out his words, the nervous young squire gasps, "What, me... You... you want me to do it?"

The soldiers' laugh while Alexander stares in horror at the scrawny feeble youth who is to be his executioner. Alexander glares to de Courtney, but the Englishman shows no interest in the King's plight, nor does he reflect any sign of mercy or humanity in his soul.

"Get behind him Percy," commands de Courtney. "Hold his head firmly with one hand, grab him by the chin with the other and twist as briskly, that should suffice."

The young squire nervously stands behind Alexander, placing his hands as he is bid. As his hands begin to tremble and shake, de Percy pauses and looks to de Courtney who quickly becomes irritated and impatient, he shouts at de Percy.

"DO IT, YOU FOOL!"

De Percy falters, then pathetically he wrenches at Alexander's head. A searing white-hot pain streaks through the King's neck and shoulders as de Percy's hands slip on the wet blood around the king's face, dispersing the force required and merely ripping muscles around the King's neck. Alexander struggles as his attacker's grip loosens for a second, but he's quickly secured. The older soldiers laugh and guffaw as de Percy places his hands back around Alexander's head, this time holding on tightly. De Percy looks to de Courtney who nods back for him to proceed with the murder. De Percy moves his feet apart and in a mighty movement, he wrenches at the King's head, but again he fails to break Alexander's neck.

De Percy calls out pathetically… "I cannot do it my lord." In a flux and frenzy, de Percy attempts several more times to snap the King's neck but fails with each attempt.

"Hurry, you useless fop." Commands de Courtney. Desperately, de Percy wrenches at Alexander's head, but with each vicious twist, Alexander feels his muscles tearing and tendons ripping in his neck and shoulders. With each and every failed attempt by this frightened ineffectual youth, it merely serves to magnify the horrific pain and the incredible thoughts of terror for Alexander. One more time de Percy whips Alexander's head around, sending unbelievable shocking pain akin to white-hot irons searing through every fibre of his being.

De Percy cries out, "He is too tough, his neck won't break."

De Courtney screams at de Percy, "Harder, you young fool, do you think it is your peg you're pulling?" Racked with pain, Alexander hears the older soldiers laughing at the young squire's feeble attempts to break his neck. After many more attempts, de Percy halts, leaving Alexander in excruciating pain. He gazes into the darkness in the vain hope that Moray, Comyn or Duncan would come at the last moment and save him from this hellish nightmare, but he's quickly brought back to reality as the searing pain shoots through his body one more time.

De Percy grabs Alexander and tries to break his neck once more, but cannot subdue the King of Scotland. "I can't do it, he wont let me," cries De Percy in despair, much to the continued amusement of the old soldiers.

"Enough," barks de Courtney in a rage. He stoops to look Alexander directly in the eyes."We have no more time to waste with you Canmore."

De Courtney glances at an older Yeoman who steps forward and grips Alexander firmly by the head and jaw, then he viciously wrenches at the King's head… a sickening cracking noise is heard by everyone, despite the noise of the storm. The Yeoman throws Alexander face forward onto the ground where his body immediately begins involuntary shuddering and flaying about grotesquely in its death throes. The Yeoman puts his foot under Alexander's shoulder and roughly kicks him onto his back to ensure that his neck is truly broken. The yeoman smiles when he sees Alexander's head flop over, dragged by the weight of the torso.

Both de Courtney and the Yeoman each put a foot firmly on Alexander's chest to still the violent spasms in his moments of death.

A misty blue veil begins to converge over Alexander's eyes as he feels the icy fingers of death squeezing and clamping his heart tightly, as though trapped in an ice cold vice. His mind drifts from terror to his love Yolande and their unborn child. As the great sleep pulls him from this life, Alexander whispers quietly, "Mo gradh (My love)." Almost fifteen minutes pass before Alexander succumbs.

De Courtney thinks he hears a whisper. "What did he say?"

The Yeoman replies, "I didn't hear anything my lord, probably just his last breath."

"Never mind," says de Courtney. "Fortune has been good to us this night, so much easier than we could have hoped. Our master will be immensely pleased at this night's work, Alexander dead and no risk or link to us, eh? A good job well done don't you think de Percy?"

Before de Percy can reply, De Courtney issues orders. "Throw the body from the cliff... No wait, hold that command, put Alexander back on his horse then drive them both from this cliff edge. It shall provide a proper scene for Alexander's retainers when they find him."

De Courtney looks at the murdered King of Scotland, satisfied that his mission's work is done. He calls out a command. "Get Alexander on his horse, now. And pick up our dead and wounded then secure them on their horses. We will dispose of them later. Now, we must finish this mercy and leave this scene with haste."

The assassins quickly tie their wounded comrades and secure the dead bodies to their horses and make ready to leave. Others secure Alexander's body upon Areion. De Courtney orders his men to herd the stallion towards the small cliff edge to push him over the steep rocky incline. The assassins cautiously encircle Areion who is extremely agitated "NOW," commands de Courtney.

The assassins shout and wave their swords and mantles, driving the horse and lifeless rider ever closer to the cliff edge. Areion, his black eyes open wide in confusion and terror, kicks, snorts and whinnies, rearing on his hind legs wildly flailing the air with his front hooves, trying desperately to escape the cordon, but he cannot break free from the menace of the assassins. The King's loyal stallion wants to fight as this beautiful war-horse has been trained to do by his master, but no signs or signals would be coming from his lifelong companion. Areion continues rearing and kicking, valiantly trying to fight off the menace that's enclosing this magnificent horse and his King, but to no avail. The assassins securely encircle the great horse ever closer, denying any opportunity to break free.

De Courtney screams, "Hurry you witless fools, we must finish with this business and be gone from here before dawn breaks."

His men redouble their effort, frantically waving their cloaks and swords while screaming in the face of the great warhorse, forcing him towards the cliff edge. Areions' hooves are torn and bleeding by the power of his own strength ripping at the rocks beneath his hooves as he tries to escape. The stallion continues fighting for his life as though in battle with his King, but finally he's beaten back till there is no more purchase left on the cliff edge for the mighty horse. Areion rears up one last time, ferociously kicking forward, but his hind hooves slip over the cliff edge.

Soon the assailants see their opportunity when Areion pauses for a second, appearing almost bewildered. As one, the assassins rush forward while avoiding being struck by the great war-hooves. With one last effort the assassins manage to push the mighty horse and his dead King over the edge of the small cliff. As horse and rider stumble and fall, De Courtney and his men rush to the cliff edge and watch as Alexander and Areion tumble down the rocky cliff, striking razor sharp outcrops, spinning and bouncing like rag dolls, till finally, their lifeless bodies lay deathly still on the sands of the shore bed. Areion, whom Alexander had named after the divine wild black stallion of the star Gods, carries his beloved King to eternity.

Glancing to the horizon, de Courtney notices the stirring of a false dawn. He orders his men to mount, it's imperative they make haste to Leith docks near the port of Edinburgh.

While the storm continues to pound the land with heavy sheet squalls, it allows the assassins ride back to the Forth river crossings undetected to take the barge ferry back across the Forth River and make speed to Leith. Halfway across the Forth River, de Courtney's men overpower the bargemen and pilot with lightning speed and determination. Promptly they push the ferrymen partly over the gunnels of the barge holding them secure, forcing the face of each crewman into the sea one by one, till their heads are fully submerged underwater. The ferrymen kick and struggle but their fight for life is hopeless. They hold firm till they're overcome and drowned.

No witnesses can ever be found that could implicate de Courtney, or that he and his assassins have ever been in the area. Laughing, de Courtney says, "The foolishness of sailing a barge against nature's wild and untamed spirits would be the obvious and apparent cause of the ferrymen's demise."

His yeoman enquires, "What shall we do with the bodies of our men?"

"Strip them and throw them overboard. The crabs and shit-eels will do the rest."

The yeoman enquires, "And the ferrymen?"

"Throw them overboard too, they'll find their own way home."

As the vessel reaches the shore a few miles east of the southern landing dock, the English assassins disembark, leaving the barge to drift freely on the tide, completing another scene that would be accepted as a terrible but tragic accident. De Courtney and his men make haste and soon arrive at Leith docks where other conspirators await their return to board a single sail freighter, discreetly tethered amongst many other foreign ships, waiting to carry the assassins away from Scotland and on to their final destination of Tilbury docks near London.

The captain of the ship greets de Courtney as he boards, after a few brief words, de Courtney orders the captain to take him to the masters cabin, where he quickly writes coded notes on small pieces of waxed-velum, then attaches them to messenger pigeons.

Sensing another presence behind him, de Courtney grips his dagger and swiftly spins round, he gasps aloud, "Brother le Jay.... What... I..."

Le Jay sweeps back his Black Malte Templar mantle and speaks, "I observed your duties for our Master de Courtney; you acquitted yourself very well."

A nervous De Courtney exclaims, "You saw... I mean... you were there?"

"Of course," replies le Jay, he continues, "Our Master does have trust in you, but only by degrees you understand, I was there to observe there were no mistakes. When next you return to Scotland, you will find me at lady Christiana's house of Esperston in Midlothian. We have chosen men waiting for your next mission in Scotland billeted in the Commanderie of Ballentradoch."

De Courtney replies humbly, "Yes my lord." Le Jay abruptly leaves the cabin. A shaken de Courtney returns on deck as the ship slowly pulls away from the Leith docks under full sail. True dawn begins to break over the horizon as de Courtney releases the pigeons to carry the coded messages to his master.

He feels an enormous surge of elation, he knows that the presence of Sir Brian Le Jay, Master of the English Templar's, Edwards personal henchman and political assassin, had been a warning, for none who makes the simplest of clandestine political errors on behalf of Edward Longshanks, lives long enough to tell the tale.

De Courtney watches the birds fly south toward their final destination. It will take less than a day for De Courtney's master to receive the news... King Alexander III of Scotland is dead.

LONGSHANKS

O ver a thousand miles from Edinburgh, another international gathering has been called upon the orders of the King of England, Edward Plantagenet. Famed and renowned throughout Europe as a shrewd political statesman, skilled in the arts of politics and fearless in the execution of war. Edward is also revered as a brilliant military tactician and highly respected warrior King of tireless stamina. Universally known as 'Longshanks' a moniker descriptive of his tall slim physique with exceptionally long thin legs.

Currently, the King of England resides in his ancestral home in the picturesque Château de Plantagenet near the Cathedral village of St. Jean d'Angely, southwest France. Edward sits impatiently at the bedside of his beloved Eleanor of Castile, holding in his arms his two year old prince, also called Edward. The mighty king of England demonstrates a side to his nature and character not known to most as he rocks back and forth on the chair, humming a lullaby. Using his finger, he gently dips the tip of his finger into warm maid-milk then lets the essence fall to his fingertip. Teat-like he feeds the young prince while his mother sleeps peacefully, but young Edward begins to cry incessantly for his mother's milk.

"He has strong lungs like his father," says a voice from the bed.

"Eleanor, my dearest… you are awake," exclaims Edward. "Please forgive me, I did not mean to disturb you."

Queen Eleanor has lost little of her Castilian beauty, even though she has mothered sixteen children to Edward, but now she lay gravely ill while gazing lovingly into her husband's eyes, she smiles weakly. With outstretched arms, she beckons to Edward that she wishes to hold their son.

Edward cradles the young prince with one hand then glances at Eleanor. With his other hand he lovingly sweeps her long, black, silvery gray hair away from her brow, "You do not have the strength, m'lady, would it be that I may command one of the maids in milk to nurse the boy and save your strength?"

Eleanor eases back her gown, revealing her full swollen breasts of motherhood, beckoning the young prince to suckle. "We have lost many children at birth my Lord, we shall not lose this little one. My milk is still the purest of elixirs to quell this noisy prince."

Edward passes the young prince to his mother, whereupon the child eagerly suckles at his mother's breast. Edward puts his arm around Eleanor's shoulders to comfort his ailing wife; then he holds her gently while watching mother and son bond through the nurture of suckle. Edward smiles, for he's never lost his feeling of enchantment in seeing a child nourish at his mother's breast.

Both doting parents are lost in the moment when a loud knocking on the chamber door interrupts their few rare moments of peace as a family.

"A MOMENT!" Edward calls out tersely. He turns to look at mother and child, only to be met by the exotically beautiful dark eyes of Queen Eleanor gazing back at him. In all their forty years together, none of the love they both cherish so dearly has lost its lustre.

"Go Husband," says Eleanor. "The world needs you now, but do not be so concerned, we shall both be in good spirits by your return."

Edward alights from the bed and stands over his wife momentarily then stoops and kisses her lovingly on her brow; then says, "My love..." Straightening his great ermine cloak and bib, Edward walks to the door of the chamber. As he opens the large ornate oak door, he reaches out and picks up his royal circlet, resting casually on a chair-head; then he looks to his beloved Eleanor. Sensing his gaze, she looks up and smiles for her husband, reassuring him that all is well with her and the young prince.

He leaves the apartment and is met by his younger brother, Edmund, Duke of Lancaster. Edmund enquires, "How fairs good Queen Eleanor?"

"This warm dry and fruitful land fairs better for her health than she may otherwise acquire in England."

Edmund sighs, "It is good to see M'lady flourish so."

Edward nods in agreement. "The royal leechers' advise most emphatically that we should reside an in-determined number of years in these climes for her to recover to full health."

The Plantagenet brothers talk freely as they stride down the long white marble corridors, lavishly covered with the finest rugs of Persia and decorated in abundance with swords, pole-arm and shields from the Angevin Plantagenet family history. Many battle trophies, weapons, flags and pennants of wars past are also placed on each wall between the pitch burning lanterns leading away from the private royal compartments at the heart of Château de Plantagenet.

"What news do you have for me?" asks Edward.

Edmund hesitates then he replies "The Royal messenger has arrived from Paris sire, from the court of Philip. It is by his royal command you must attend his court personally to pay homage and deliver all unpaid taxes to his treasury. Philip insists that you attend his pleasure no later than one month from now at the royal Château of Fontainebleau, or regretfully, he will be obliged to command chartres de annex to recover all your jurisdictions. This will include all territories and titles to Burgundy, Nantes and Normandy, which he will seize as punitive compensation for your taxation gratuities overdue to his exchequer."

Edward does not flinch nor waiver, though Edmund is in no doubt this news has incensed the English King. Ever the master of diplomacy, Edward contains his anger as the doors are opened for him to the great banqueting hall of the Château de Plantagenet. Upon entering, he sees that many of his allies and friends of the Northern Brotherhood have gathered there in anticipation of attending the diplomatic confirmations at the Château de Fontainebleau. Heralds blow their trumpets announcing Edwards' arrival. Everyone turns and graciously welcomes the King of England.

As he walks through the throng, Edward cordially acknowledges all the ambassadorial delegates in attendance, and many of those are family relatives or staunch allies who have spent the last two years formulating 'The Great Cause' A plan to take over Northern Europe and free it from the Catholic yoke, include replacing Philip of France with the all-powerful Edward as Magnate Supreme. The purpose of this particular gathering is to confirm alliances from as far afield as Scotland to Constantinople in regards to creating a new territorially defined landmass under the control of the Brotherhood of Northern Kings. An alliance of Kings, Magnates and Princes whose intention is to rule northern Europe with Edward Plantagenet reigning as magnate and overlord supreme, entirely free from Vatican influence.

A luxurious feast of exotic foods and privileged tasting of rare white Tuscan Chianti mountain wines especially imported from the villages of Gaiole Castillina and Radda near Florence ensue. The glorious fare is served, fostering an atmosphere of privilege befitting the imminent status of this powerful international alliance of thrones. Edmund sits to the right-hand side of Edward, leaving the left-hand seat beside Edward vacant, permitting a controlled stream of invited representatives and imminent magnates to take their own personal time to lend the King's ear in private. Only the most imminent guests could take this seat beside Edward 'Longshanks' Plantagenet.

The evening wears on with Edward continuing to be the perfect host and ear to his privileged guests. "A successful evening sire?" enquires Edmund.

"Yes, Edmund, it is," replied Edward. "Soon though we shall retire, for we must discuss the detail of the Great Cause in chamber. Decisions made these next few weeks will change England's fortune so, and in the fullness of time brother Edmund, the world will look back on our endeavours and immortalise us for our courage."

Behind Edward, stands a Herald who announces, "Lord de Lucca of Venice sire…"

Edward goes taught in the face. He glances at his brother Edmund; then speaks quietly, "I suppose all bodies of the finest strength require a blood sucking leech on occasion."

Edward laughs wryly, then turns to see a small portly man, distinctly Venetian in features and fashion of wardrobe, waiting courteously to be invited to sit on the privy seat of the King.

Edward greets de Lucca with open hand. "My dear Lucca, how good it is to see you."

De Lucca bows graciously. Edward insists, "Pray sit by me."

The small portly Venetian bows once more. "My Lord." He then sits at the King's left hand side.

"De Lucca," smiles Edward. "How unexpected to see you here this eve. Have you heard the news?"

De Lucca enquires curiously, "To what news do you refer my lord?"

Edward smiles then says, "My taxes and duties have been a great success, I have your requirements in my London exchequer."

De Lucca smiles; pleased to hear Edward's words. As fare and wine is placed before him, de Lucca replies, "For that information sire, my masters shall be eternally grateful. The Riccardi and the Florentine Bankers are most anxious that your understandable desire to secure your father's territories in France may have caused you to oversee repayment of your loans. And I may add my lord, the interest on your realm's mortgage."

Edward glares at the Venetian who quickly placates the English King. "But their confidence in you personally has never faltered sire. Particularly upon hearing of your rigorous fiscal policy currently employed in your recent conquests in Wales and Ireland, now under your gracious and benevolent rule. And of course my lord, my masters are extremely forti-fied by your forecast of expected revenues from the wool, fish and timber trades from those same dominions, which does foster confirmation in my masters faith in you."

Grudgingly, Edward nods in approval.

De Lucca continues ominously. "Sire, I must beg your indulgence, what I say to you next is most certainly based only on scurrilous rumours."

Edward glares at the hesitant Venetian with eyes of pinpoint focus. "Pray continue."

Coughing and clearing his throat, de Lucca continues, "My Lord, should you be considering a campaign against the King of France or any other for that matter, the bankers of Riccardi would not be in a position to finance such a venture. They have also instructed me to inform you that they cannot furnish you with further monies or gratuities till all previous debt and interest is deposited in full to their treasuries. Sire, they do advise most emphatically that you consider an extended period of peace, which will allow you to build a handsome reserve of your own."

Edward displays no apparent reaction to what de Lucca said, but inside he is seething as de Lucca continues. "The new King of France is now a very important client of my masters, as Philip has intimated he no longer wishes to pay the extortionate interest on loans from the bankers of the Vatican. It is for this reason in having such imminent clients as yourselves, that my masters advise the practise of diplomacy and trade, rather than war, may be a better solution for our two most respected clients."

Edward is almost beside himself with rage, but keeps control, he says, "Why Lucca, exactly what I was thinking. In fact, I should have informed you that I have been considering a union of marriage with my son Edward to Isabella, the daughter of Philip, bringing our two crowns together in union."

De Lucca sits back in the chair with a mild look of surprise. For many years, he has been servicing Edwards' personal debt as well as that of England's exchequer, and witnessed on many occasions the ruthless execution of duty and tactical genius practised by the King of England.

De Lucca enquires, "My Lord, I thought the union was planned betwixt your son and the grand-daughter of the King of Scotland?"

"Ah," sighs Edward. "Prudence, dear Lucca, both the Maid of Norway and Scotland will come to me in due course. After much consideration I believe this alternate marriage union proposal with Philip is more of a diplomatic prize. I am satisfied that through marriage, not war, the Angevin Plantagenet bloodline will soon inherit the throne of France by this union. And the promise of this marriage will surely be more pragmatic and satisfy your masters that uniting the house of Angevin and Capet to be honourable by this gesture."

"Extremely unexpected news my Lord," remarks a surprised de Lucca.

Smiling at this play with the important little Venetian, Edward continues, "I would not strive to vantage over young Philip by making war. Though I am very aware he still smarts from the calamitous and ruinous enterprise of his father's Arogonese crusade. It's universally known that his antagonistic view of the Holy Father is occupying his mind more than any thought of war with England."

"True," replied de Lucca. "It is common knowledge that he blames the interference of Pope Martin for the loss of his father's army and Fleet, but Philip inherits the largest home army in Christendom, and his contribution to the treaty of Anagni between Pope Boniface and Charles of Naples was certainly an astute move thought impossible by most, yet he alone proposed a formula and that broke the political deadlock. A significant achievement for one so young and inexperienced, most certainly it was a solution appreciated by my masters."

"Bah," exclaims Edward. "It may have been Philip's hand that signed the treaty Lucca, but it was his late father's almoner Guillaume d'Ercuis that guided it from the shadows."

De Lucca sits back, sups some wine, then he speaks. "It's true sire that Philip is young and impetuous, and he is causing uproar with the Holy Father. The Pope has already issued a Papal bull, the Clericus Laicos, to stop Philip from absorbing any church property into French Crown estate. In retaliation, Philip has halted the exporting of silver, gold, valuable exports and all revenues destined to Rome upon which the pope does depend for his Crusade against the Moors."

"This young King is wise beyond his years," says Edward smiling. "Or an impetuous fool to be snapping at the Holy Father's heels."

Shaking his head, De Lucca thoughtfully places his goblet on the table. "Who knows how this may end my lord. Philip has already imprisoned the bishop of Palmiers; now his Holiness has summoned thirty-nine French bishops to Rome for an emergency synod. Philip in turn, commanded the bishops not to attend, but they defied him and have already fled to Rome."

Edward looks deeply into de Lucca's eyes. "I have heard it so. And what was Philip's response to this public defiance of his authority?"

"Philip promptly confiscated all of the disloyal Bishops properties and monies. He has demonstrated openly that he has no love to grace, nor shower his Holiness with French assets or support my Lord." De Lucca glances cautiously around him then whispers, "I also have heard that Philip is raising finance from other sources to build a new navy. He intends to combat the rising influence of the Hanseatic Varjag and Genoese fleets. He has already financed a substantial increase of his formidable army sire, and its common knowledge the most powerful Duke's Bishops and bourgeois of France fervently and enthusiastically support his assembly of these forces. My spies also inform me that Philip is set on regaining Majorca and Sicily to French jurisdiction, to achieve this, Philip has negotiated new alliances with the Brotherhood of Mediterranean Kings."

Placing his fine wine goblet on the table, Edward enquires, "What is to become of us de Lucca? We have the Berber and Arabic host uniting against the Catholic Crusades, the Mediterranean brotherhood of Kings uniting with others unknown against Rome, now the Holy Father is alienating Philip and our northern Brotherhood of Kings. It is no wonder that his imminence is all a flutter."

"Ah my lord," sighs de Lucca. "I cannot answer that question, as the Bankers who fund war are the only ones who gain from war. Their sons, unlike you princes of Rome, never see a battlefield, nor risk their own lives. All they ever risk, are the notes of debt so easily recovered by interest and recouped from the victor, and of course the seizure of goods at rock bottom prices of the vanquished. Bankers will never lose profit my lord, they never have and they never shall."

De Lucca becomes aware that Edward is staring at him curiously upon hearing this comment about bankers.

De Lucca quickly changes the subject, "I beseech you, my lord, do show great restraint when actions appear to set England and France against one another. You both do maintain and provide the largest armies in northern Europe, therefore the greatest force for stability or destruction too."

"Restraint?" queries Edward. "Philip has let it be known that if I, as Duke of Aquitaine, do not pay extortionate taxes on my holdings and submit to him recognising him as my superior, he will be obliged to seize all my lands in France. And you ask me to show restraint?"

Suddenly Edward's rage ceases as he smiles. "But to this restraint, I do most graciously acquiesce and bow somewhat to his French wind. I grant you that by return of taxes he does say that he will forgive my indiscretions and restore my lands by good grace after a period of penance. But I am also aware Philip faces extensive financial liabilities de Lucca. His building of a new army and fleet must surely be draining what little inheritance he has left. I ask you, if Philip attacks my fleet in French harbours or his army and militias force incursions into my territories, then do tell me, what restraint should I then show?"

De Lucca is pleasantly surprised to hear Edward speak so openly about his concerns of war. "Forgive me sire, but I must be quite blunt as you are forthcoming, but what are your true intentions in regard to Philips summons?"

Edward ponders a moment, then he replies, "I will visit upon him due homage."

De Lucca is again astonished to hear this.

Edward smiles at de Lucca, then leans towards him. "I should inform you, in your confidence of course, that I have been approached by your rivals the Frescobaldi banking conglomerate of Florence. The Bardi and Peruzzi bankers have also sent delegates too, and I do admit, they are offering very competitive incentives, and both propose interesting charters of finance. Pray do tell me of what will happen if Philip withholds monies from both Riccardi and the Pope? And what if his Holiness recalls all Vatican capital loans from your Riccardi masters?"

De Lucca knows Edward is using subtlety in preparing for the imminent loan and re-mortgage negotiations. He replies, "Yes my lord, it is true that overtures from the Vatican indicate they may recall their loans, but what of your northern neighbours, my Lord? While you live so perilously close to bankruptcy, it is rumoured the Scots treasury and trader banks harbour unimaginable wealth. What will you do if the proposed alliance between the Varjag traders and Scotland's eastern ports comes to fruition? And what if the Scots join this burgeoning Hanseatic Federation, this new European union, they will then be beyond any possible control by England?"

A chilling glance from Edward causes de Lucca to think it prudent to pass information rather than question such a powerful King.

De Lucca continues, "My lord, I've also heard the Scots are negotiating to make alliance with the Genoese and propose to fund a new shipping enterprise on the main European and Mediterranean sea trading ports with their fleets. It appears the shrewd Scots are methodically expanding their enterprising horizons to include the lucrative middle-east ports with the Pisan traders of Constantinople and Tunis. This will give them direct access to the Silk Road merchants and by-passing all your ports of taxation." De Lucca sees the discomfort broaden across the face of Edward. For a few moments De Lucca thinks he's perhaps gone to far in antagonising the King of England, then Edward laughs. Both men laugh, recognising the unspoken words and implications in their moments of debate is mere gamesmanship, based loosely on fact and what could be.

They converse awhile longer, till amicable agreement appears to be the outcome, leaving both de Lucca and Edward very satisfied. Finally, it is time for this privy meeting to end. De Lucca pushes back his chair, stands and bows in respect to Edward. "My Lord, I must now leave for La Rochelle to depart on the first available high tide and fair wind with the good news of our agreement for my masters. I…"

Edward interrupts, "My dear Lucca, stay awhile longer. I invite you and your train to rest in comfort in one of my finest lodges. You must direct your thoughts to the pleasures of this beautiful province, for I believe they will be a welcome distraction to the hustle and bustle of travel. And please, do take any number of wench's or boys you may see about my household for your personal pleasures, for I surely would be a poor host should I not treat you as my most imminent of guests."

Uncharacteristically, Edward puts his arm across Lucca's shoulders as he continues, "You would save much on your own expense of lodgings and travel if you accept my humble offer. And come the morn, my dear Lucca, I insist you use my personal horse-guards to escort you to La Rochelle."

De Lucca, revelling in the attention Edward bestows upon him, graciously accepts the hospitality, he kisses Edwards hand then retires.

"More good news brother?" enquires Edmund.

"Well," says Edward glancing at the frivolity of his guests. "It was not all bad news."

Edmund enthusiastically asks, "Did you talk about the rebellious Jews and Irish?"

"No Edmund, but the Irish will give us no trouble, and as for the Jewry... I have plans for them."

Edward takes a long sup of fine Chianti wine pressed from his own vineyards; then he speaks quietly to Edmund.

"First it was the Irish, then it was the Welsh, next we will deal with the Jews, then finally, my dear Edmund... the Scotch. That's the order of elimination my dear brother for the final conquest and domination of Albain."

Edward's thoughts are disturbed when the herald announces, "Sire, the lord chief justice to the royal Bench of England, grand master of Château le Val, Robert le Meschin de Brix, (De Bree) Lord of Essex and Guisborough."

Standing by the King's privy seat awaiting an audience is Edwards' old friend, Lord Robert de Brix, once a loyal and faithful General of Edward's armies and former Lord chief justice of the royal law bench of England, now retired at his family château in Normandy.

De Brix defies his year's expectations in physique and certainly that of his peers and contemporaries. He is renowned for being fearless in battle, council and a trusted friend to King Edward, and unquestionably loyal to the house of Angevin Plantagenet. Smiling upon seeing Sir Robert, Edward stands up, opens his arms and welcomes his loyal friend.

"Lord Robert, my Lord chief justice, how good it is to see you here this eve."

De Brix replies, "Sire, I am simply now Lord of Whittle and Guisborough. You know well sire that I retired from that position many years ago."

The two men look at each other and laugh, both know a dedicated and loyal man never retires his hand truly from a position of power, only a fool would think it otherwise.

The friendship between Edward and De Brix goes back to a time when Edward was a young prince, first meeting during the English barons rebellion nigh on thirty years prior, where lord Robert played a major part in freeing Edward from the captivity placed upon him by the King's own Godfather, Simon de Montfort. From that point in time they became firm friends. De Brix also fought valiantly for prince Edward during his attempted relief of Acre in the holy land and stood at Edward's side during his coronation. They had fought many campaigns and battles together over the years, culminating in their last adventures shared, being the subjugation of Ireland and Wales. Such is the unswerving loyalty, keen intelligence and dedication of de Brix that Edward honoured him by establishing him as the first Chief Justice to the Royal bench in England's history. The informal greeting between

Longshanks and de Brix is very uncourtly by their embrace, but all present are aware of the special bond fostered over a lifetime's companionship between these two powerful men. Lord Robert has not only the ear of the king, more importantly; he's uniquely in receipt of brotherly friendship from Edward.

"Pray be seated Lord Robert," insists Edward with a genuine expression of friendship. He continues, "Dear Robert, you have served me well as you served my father before me. Had you not intervened and taken up arms with your army of Scots levies during the Barons rebellion, I may not have kept my head, far less the throne of England."

Shaking his head as he takes his seat, Brix replies. "Sire, my life has been fulfilled in your service as it began with your father Henry."

Glancing round the great hall, Edward speaks with a solemn tone, "My Lord Robert, I have urgent need of your considerations and experience. And should you fulfil my need, as I have no doubt that only you can, there will be great profit in these endeavours. And of course, a generous reward for your ever-growing family, for I shall grant you more lands in North of Hampton, Northern England and possibly more estate in Scotland and Ireland."

"But, Sire," splutters de Brix. "I need no reward other than that of being in service to you, but more importantly, what is so pressing that requires my attendance specifically?"

Edward waves his hand, implying the subject of reward is not for debate. "I must leave for Saintes on the morn to make preparations for an audience with this upstart Philip. I require you to enforce absolute rule over the disputed territories and Northwest border-marches with Scotland. Lord Robert, you are my only choice for this delicate matter."

De Brix nods in understanding, contemplating his King's request.

Edward goes on, "I require you to see to your estates in Scotland, and you must use your title as lord of Annandale, from there you will take control of the border marches with Palatine authority. You will base your official activities in Carlisle castle and from that place, I desire you to secure absolute fealty and servitude from my northern subjects. Everyone from the Northwest English border lands with Scotland, all of Cumbria and as far south as Wrexham. Sir Robert, I know of no other man I may entrust with such a valuable charge as this."

Appearing concerned, de Brix enquires, "Sire, do you fear insurrection from your subjects? Or is it an insult from King Alexander and the Scotch?"

Edward laughs aloud. "No old friend, not the Scotch. It's my northern subjects. I am informed the Northern barons are sorely vexed at the increased taxations upon the export of wool I must place upon them. But with you by my side and the Scots behind you as before, I feel there would be nothing from those lands that would concern or distract me in my enduring search for peace while here in France."

De Brix nods in approval. "I understand, sire. I'll return to my estates in Scotland to expedite your command."

"Good," says Edward. "You are to apply extreme diligence and assume your position as my Northern paladin lord at your earliest opportunity."

De Brix has no hesitation. "I'll leave for chateau de Andres immediately and organise a sail for England forthwith."

Edward beckons a scribe standing in the shadows with sealed charters held firmly in his hands. The scribe passes the charters directly to de Brix as Edward continues, "I want you to take these charters with my writs and seals. When you arrive in London, show them to lord Cressingham at the exchequer. Draw from my treasury whatever monies and bonds you require for this expedition. Then you must meet with chief justice, Ralph de Hegham and my most imminent law lords, Gilbert de Thornton and Sir Roger le Brabazon. They will furnish you with all legal writs to make this a lawful venture."

Lifting his head after scrutinising the charters, de Brix nods in approval.

Edward looks at his old companion. "All is in order Lord Robert?"

"All is in good order sire." De Brix picks up the charters then bows his head, demonstrating acknowledgement of his task without further question.

Relaxing for a moment, Edward notices a teenage boy standing in the shadows behind de Brix. He enquires, "And who is this strapping young lad Lord Robert?"

De Brix smiles as he proudly pulls the young lad round the side of the chair to meet the King. Edward notices the immense pride shining in de Brixs' eyes as he continues, "This is young Robert, my favoured grandson."

Edward commands, "Come here boy."

The youngster walks from behind his grandfather towards the King of England. Edward reaches out and places both hands firmly on the youngster's shoulders and looks into the boys face. "Look at you," exclaims Edward. "Haven't you grown tall since I last saw you?" Edward scrambles the young-ster's hair, much to young Robert's chagrin. Edward studies the character of the boy. "So this is young Robert then? He has the look and sprightly gait of his grandfather in his young limbs, I'll warrant you that, Lord Robert."

De Brix smiles as Edward continues. "And what age are you now young Robert?"

Robert glances toward his grandfather then looks at Edward. "Nearly fifteen summers, my lord."

"Would you like to be a knight of my court when you are grown up into manhood young Robert le Brix?"

Young Robert puffs his chest out with pride and clenches his fists by his side like an old soldier, gazing with piercing innocent eyes at the King of England, he replies with the arrogance of youth, "My name is not young Robert sire... I am Robert the Bruce."

Choking on his Chianti, Edward laughs heartily at this budding young soldier of Christendom. He exclaims, "Robert Thee Bruce, is it?"

Edward strokes his beard once more, admiring this fine spirited youth and his obvious temerity. Edward exclaims, "My, my, Robert Thee Bruce... I'll warrant that you certainly know your name and birthright young sirrah. I certainly wont be forgetting you."

Edward looks to his friend, de Brix, and smiles. "You have a fine young leopard in the making Lord Robert. Perhaps you may let me have him as squire now he is of age."

Completely surprised, de Brix replies, "Sire, that would be an honour I could never repay..."

"No, lord Robert," remarks Edward while waving his hand. "I sense in this boy great things to come. It would be a privilege to assist him on his road to greatness." Then Edward suddenly turns his attention to more serious matters. "Lord Robert, It is imperative you reinstate your Scotch title as Lord of Annandale and employ all you deem appropriate to quell sedition in my northern marcher lands."

"Yes my Lord," replied de Brix. He continues, "By using my Scotch levies, this will bring any malice from your Northern subjects upon the Scotch, rather than the crown estate."

"Precisely," replies Edward. "And your eldest son Robert, he is now titled the Earl of Carrick I believe?"

"He is Sire," replied de Brix.

"And he may assist you?"

De Brix replies, "He will sire."

Edward sits back, pleased by this response from de Brix. While supping wine together, Edward studies young Robert le Brix. He casually enquires, "Is it true the boy's father was held prisoner by lady Maroc of Carrick... and she would not release him till he married her before God?"

De Brix is somewhat embarrassed by this question. Before he can reply, Edward continues. "Lord Robert, you must tell me more about your Scotch estates. It has been too long since we talked of your family and your affairs in Scotland my old friend."

The two men talk a while longer, until it is time for de Brix's departure for Normandy then to the border marches between Scotland and England and assume his Scottish title as Lord of Annandale and palatine lord of Cumbria. De Brix retires from the King's privy seat and departs.

Edmund, who has been listening while gnawing on a roasted leg of swan, enquires, "A satisfactory ear with de Brix my Lord?"

"It was," replied Edward. "For such a disciplined, intelligent man as de Brix is, his only knowing what he needs to know and feeling that what he knows is all there is to know, provides me an extremely loyal and effective practitioner of his soldiery arts indeed."

Looking around the banqueting hall, Edward smiles then he continues, "De Brix has skilfully outlined to me in great detail the military strengths, weaknesses' and allegiances of all the Scotch-Norman nobles."

"And he will play his part in the Great Cause?"

"Yes, Edmund, de Brix is the perfect soldier. He will continue to be very useful to our Great Cause when he is fully informed of course, of that I am certain."

"A loyal man?"

Edward grins, "He is Edmund... and that young Grandson of his... I like his cut Edmund. One day he may be to my son prince Edward as his grandfather has been to me. I certainly will not be forgetting that youngsters name."

Edward laughs to himself thinking of the spunk of the youth as he mutters to himself..."Robert Thee Bruce..."

Laithe Bainnse

The success of King Alexander's trade gathering has been the main talking point between the brothers, Malcolm and Alain, as they travel through the stormy night toward the west coast. It's been a long arduous journey before the two weary brothers are within sight of *Ach na Feàrna*, home of Sir Malcolm. Both are tired, wet, hungry and completely unaware of the dramatic events about to unfold. Their spirits lift upon seeing the smoke rise in the distance from the morning fires of the *Ach na Feàrna* baile beag (Small hamlet).

They pull their horses to a halt then sit back in their saddles for a moment's rest. "Alain," says Malcolm, "Is it no' about time you made your peace with William and Wee John?"

Alain looks at his brother then enquires curiously, "Have you and Wishart been talking?"

Malcolm looks back at Alain bemused by his comment. "Naw... Why do you ask that?"

"Ach nothing," replies Alain. "It's just that he was saying something similar last night about the boys."

"Well then, all the more reason. Do yie no' think that it's about time you reached out to them? Especially on this day of days."

"Malcolm, I've been thinking on it for so long, I simply don't know how to be going about it, or what I would do or could say to the boys by way of an explanation. Sometimes I feel it's maybe a subject best just to be left alone, then perhaps not."

Malcolm is surprised by this response but says nothing in reply. The brothers sit exhausted, breathing in the crisp early morning coastal air while observing the beautiful scenery of the western Clyde seaboard. They gaze westward as the morning sun beats down the meandering path of the winding river Clyde as its dark green waters flow in spate towards the great Irish Sea and Minch peninsula. The glorious scenic mountains in the distance of the north and west coast highlands, form a breathtaking hazy outline of pastel blues and greys, set in vivid contrast to the fresh light-green dew topped grasses and brown budding tree branches of the springtime colours surrounding *Ach na Feàrna*.

Malcolm notices his brother is deep in thought. He gently nudges Alain's horse, causing him to look up.

Startled, Alain enquires, "What's happening?"

Malcolm looks to his brother. It's obvious something is still greatly amiss in Alain's soul. Malcolm thinks it is time to say something... anything that may bring Alain back to the family fold. He asks, "What's happened to you, brother?"

After a moment's hesitation, Alain replies with anguish in his voice. "I don't know... When I married the lady Mharaidh (Vaari) a joy returned to my life. When she bore us a daughter I felt elated, but then followed a great sadness as I thought of ma boys. I have a desperate need to be seeing them Malcolm, but I've a gut feeling it's too late to be a family that could include them. Fuck, I know it's wrong to think that and I know it's my responsibility to take the lead, but I didn't know how too, I don't know how too? For me to be neither their father nor them to be my sons I fear a soul torment and opportunity lost for all time."

"I understand brother, but this anguish of yours must be the left in the past. You've got to be creating a future that you and the boys want and need and do it now before its too late."

"Malcolm, I tell to you that these thoughts grieve me and burn in my heart with a pain that grows stronger each day. The only thing I do know with any certainty is that they must love you dearly as their father. But for me to reconcile with them... I don't know? Brother, I think I'm cursed."

"The world is changing, even for our King who's has lost so much, his wife, his children... likely more than we could both ever imagine." Nudging Alain playfully, Malcolm continues, "We saw him last night didn't we? He's like a spring lamb once again and we see how his enthusiasm and vigour affects the whole of the realm through his enlightened spirit. Our Kingdom is growing and thriving under his stewardship Alain, as will the spirit of William and Wee John under your guidance as their father. It's time brother..."

Alain stares intently at the palisade walls of *Ach na Feàrna*, then he mumbles an inaudible half-hearted response.

"Alain, for fuck's sake, everywhere, every part of this realm is alive with a fresh and thriving spirit, the likes of which I have never seen or ever known before. I see the bright light of optimism throughout our realm, even in your eyes wee brother. And look at you now, in all these years you've never spoken to me of William and Wee John as you've spoken of them these last few moments."

Alain smiles upon hearing his brother's words. They continue to talk until the stirring of their horses breaks the conversation. Their tired horses hang their heads low and are restless to be fed. The brothers squeeze their horse flanks and nudge them onwards. Malcolm is pleased hearing his brother's thoughts of reconciliation, he knows its time to force

Alain into acceptance. "I notice your sour face just cracked a wee smile there brother," he says.

"Aye, that may be so," replies Alain.

"And you say Wee John is growin' up to be an Ettin (Giant) like William?"

Malcolm laughs, "Aye, that he is, and Wee John is to be getting married to auld (Old) Stephen ua H'Alpine's beautiful daughter Ròsinn o' Connaught this fine day too. Do yie remember Auld Stephen at the Battle of Largs?"

Replying with a wry smile, Alain says, "Auld H'Alpine… it's his daughter and Wee John to be hitched? Feck I didn't realise it was Stephen's daughter. Aye Malcolm, I remember him. I fair liked Auld Stephen. Do yie remember the Irish clans that fought with us that day against the Norsemen? Amazing folk and braw (Brave) fighters, they Irish are surely just as our own people from the mountains and forests, no' tied into this soft town living. And be correcting me if I'm wrong, but the ua H'Alpine's are *Céile Aicé* and Garda nan Erin *Bahn Rígh*?" (Guardians of the Queens of Ireland) Malcolm exclaims.

"Alain, for feck's sakes, where's your head been for nigh on twenty years? And don't be mentioning the *Céile Aicé* again, did Wishart no' tell you about this?"

Malcolm pauses, thinking it best not to prod his younger brother's feelings too much, for this conversation about his sons is also an enlightening revelation to him. A discourse he never thought he would ever have with Alain. Nevertheless, it is one that has long been hoped for in the Clan of the Wallace. Alain glares at his brother while Malcolm is unsure of which way this conversation is about to go, then Alain's face shows care that Malcolm has also not seen for many years.

"Tell me, Malcolm, how are the boys doin'? Tell me about them, what are they up too?"

Relaxing a little, Malcolm grins. "Well, young Alan is fine and he's living in France as yie know, but William and Wee John, they're so like you, it's like I've been living with two of you all over again. They're so feckin' wild. They get into fights and forever chasing the fisher and crofter girls instead o' doing their studies and chores."

Alain laughs as Malcolm continues. "They're always getting beatings off the priests then shrugging it off as if they had just been a tickled by a wee feckin' midge (Gnat), much to the annoyance of the priests I might add."

Both brothers laugh, then Malcolm says, "Alain, they're growing into fine young men, and something they're both born to do is the hunt, aye… they're both great hunters for sure. I'm certain there are none in the realm who could match their eye and aim with the longbow, especially young William. Jaezuz that boy is as strong as an ox and can put an arrow through a church door guard square at a hundred cloth yards. And let me tell yie this too brother, I should know as I've had to pay for those same feckin' doors on more than one occasion when Wee John's arrows didn't make it through the guard square." Alain laughs heartily.

"The two of them fair take after you, Alain. You should be proud of them, for they're both like yourself in so many ways, aye, the seed doesn't bounce far from the root o' the feckin' tree right enough. Mind you, brother, it's obvious to everyone who knows the pair o' them that town life is not for them, far less the priesthood. And you can believe they don't get that twist from me."

"It sounds like they might like life around the lands o' Glen Afton and the Black Craig."

"Aye, ah reckon they would enjoy the glen living, and more so the freedoms of the Wolf and Wildcat Forest for sure.

Another thing to tell yie is that Leckie mòr has taken the boys under his wing these last few years and that has been a great vantage to the boys."

"Leckie mòr?" exclaims Alain. "Auld Leckie, fuck, doesn't he just hate everybody and everything except you and our King? Ahm sure that auld fecker eats sour sea salt and drinks spinster pish for breaking fast and supper. Look at what he was like last night, good eve, goodbye, fuck you two and that was it."

Malcolm laughs. "Ah know, I thought he'd never stop his talking."

The brothers chuckle merrily, thinking about the character of Leckie mòr.

Alain says, "Do you mind when we were young and auld Leckie used to grab us with those feckin big hands of his for stealin' his apples? It was like getting crushed in a giant vice. Mind you, that auld bastard could fight like yie wouldn't believe. And now you're telling me he's been training the boys to fight and likely educating them to be making fine weapons?"

"He sure is,"

Alain shakes his head happily, for he likes what he's hearing. "How did it come about that auld Leckie took them under his wing?"

"Ach they often travelled with me when I was on duty call for the bonnie *Aicé* o' Alexander. Leckie was training young prince Alexander when he spotted all the boys fight training together. He also saw in their friendship something special, so he brought them all together for the trainin'. Though they soon found out as we did, that a belt around the lug (ear) from Leckie was like getting belted on the side o' the head by one o' his feckin anvils. So it was rare they made the same mistake twice."

After a few moments' of mirth, the brothers reflect upon the mention of the young Prince, and also the sadness in his passing. Malcolm says, "Aye, a terrible time it was when the young prince died."

"I heard it was awful suffering for the young fella."

Malcolm shakes his head. "His body was a mass of sores and he bled from everywhere yie could think off. We considered putting him out of his misery but he finally expired after a month of the most excruciating suffering I've ever seen. It was the same curse that took his wee brother too. Alain... I don't know how the King kept his wit after losing his two sons so young then losing his daughter and his wife too."

Painful memories return to Alain, "I could no' suffer that much pain in my life Malcolm, naw, not again. To be losing your weans in such pain and suffering."

Malcolm looks hard at his brother. "Maybe therein is the warning yie need Alain, starin' yie in the face. There's still time for you to reconcile with the boys, and time is precious."

Alain nods thoughtfully. "You're right, I know it's for me to make the effort, and may it be so the boys can forgive me my actions caused by grief. Maybe they will once they are old enough to understand."

Looking up from their deep conversation, they realise they are now only moments away from entering the gates of the home of their youth, *Ach na Feàrna*.

"Why don't yie come in Alain? Seoras Dáithí (Davy) Bryan n' Joanny, our cousins, are all here from the Galloway. And the boys are here too, your boys."

Alain shakes his head with obvious uncertainty etched all over his face. Malcolm persists with softness and a care in his voice, "And Wee Maw would just be so happy to see you in this fine humour."

Looking into his brother's eyes, Alain says, "Aye, yie reckon?"

Malcolm knows Alain yearns to meet with his family but he still remains frustratingly hesitant, fearing rejection from those he loves.

Alain thinks about meeting his mother, to try and explain. 'No I can't,' he thinks.

He knows he isn't ready but Malcolm interrupts Alain's thoughts. "Wouldn't Wee Maw's wee heart just soar like an Eagle if she saw your big stupid face? And mind that the auld dear is no' getting any younger."

The two brothers sit on their horses, pondering awhile. Malcolm watches his brother closely as Alain thinks long and hard when Malcolm nudges his own horse forward, "Are yie comin'?" Malcolm looks at Alain with as impish a grin a forty something year old man could muster, daring his brother to say yes.

Alain hesitates, and loses the moment. "I cant…"

Becoming frustrated, Malcolm persists… "Alain, for fuck's sake, the King's son was no different in the loving of his father than that of William and Wee John have for you, would you deny them that? They miss having you their real father in their lives. Don't yie think it's about time to open your heart to the boys and stop thinking about yourself?" He continues forcefully, "Surely it's about the boys and what they need, not you frettin' about your feelings."

Alain thinks awhile longer, then finally he replies, "I cannie do this Malcolm. I still feel such shame in my heart and just don't know if I'm ready."

Malcolm retorts. "Do you not think that the boys might be ready? Is it no' a father's duty to be putting the care of his children first and to be putting your own feelings behind yie? Why don't you at least try? They're good boys and have always spoken with pride of their father, Alain Wallace, the great Hunter of the King. The mountain man who leads the Wolf and Wildcat hunters o' the Kyle and Ettrick forests. You Alain, you are their pride, no' me. They're young men now and I think they would..."

"ALAIN WALLACE!" A mighty voice hailing from some mythical giant cause Malcolm and Alain to immediately look toward the gates of *ach na Feàrna*, there they see standing in front of the huge wooden gates of the fortalice, a tiny frail looking white-haired woman with her fists tucked into her waist like a demonic little fire-stick, with a ball of white cotton wool hair, looking as a shocked mop placed upon her head.

"Wee Maw," exclaims Alain, "eh... Mother..."

Malcolm grins then punches his brother playfully on the arm, saying in a mock taunt, "Well, Alain Wallace, the great hunter o' the Wolf and Wildcat forest, there's no going back for yie now, trapped by your very own big mouth. Haha... and unless you want to see our Wee Maw chasin' yie all the way back down to the Black Craig... And before yie start objections, we both know that there's no' a defensive strategy created that would keep that wee terror from your gates, no' even wee Graham your mad arsed bodyguard."

It isn't till Alain sees Malcolm grinning, does he realise the mourning for his first dear wife Brìghde, has now well and truly passed. The two brothers pull together in warmth as brothers do when words cannot express emotions or sentiment.

Wee Maw calls out to them."Will you two boys stop a huggin' and a kissin' like wee girls at a corn dolly Fèis and be getting yourselves over here right the now, and give your dear frail mother a hug."

Dispelling previous concerns, Alain dismounts quickly and

walks with giant pace steps towards his mother. As Alain and Wee Maw meet for the first time in nigh on twenty years, he reaches out and picks her up like a light sheaf of the finest corn.

"Put me down, boy," demands Wee Maw, "Or me auld coarse bloomers will be falling off me for all the world tae see."

Alain lowers his mother gently to the ground from where she immediately reaches up and pulls him close with such a passion, she may never let him go for fear of losing him again, forever. Her embrace for one so small and frail is strengthened with all the love and nurture a mother has for a long lost son. "I love yie son…" she whispers as she clings to him. "I've missed yie so much and it hurts my auld heart to think that yie are still grieving for Brìghde."

Alain feels tears of pain and love's emotion flood his heart. Quite unexpectedly, he senses Wee Maw is gently sobbing as she huddles her face into his neck. They hold each other dearly, losing all sense of time. Alain says "Maw… you need to ease your grip on me a wee bit… I cannae breath and ma back is killing me."

Wee Maw grins as Alain drops gently to his knees where he can look his mother straight into her steely blue eyes. She tugs her son by his beard then gently she wipes away a tear falling on his cheek. Alain says, "Mother…"

Before he continues, Wee Maw pulls him to her bosom in a mother's loving embrace, thinking on the long twenty lost winters since the passing of Brìghde and seeing her painful death giving birth to Wee John. She remembers when Alain became so demented by the loss of his dearest Brìghde, his stewardship of Glen Afton going almost completely to ruin, as did his life and health. Alain remembers it was Wee Maw and Bishop Wishart who saved William and Wee John's plight, by taking them from Crossraguel abbey and bringing them to *Ach na Feàrna*, where Malcolm and his wife, Margret, reared the young Wallace brothers while he mourned deeply.

Eventually, it came to pass that the families agreed, as was the norm in Scot's culture, that the sons and daughters of a bereaved parent would be fostered and brought up by other Clan or family members as their own. Malcolm's wife Margret had nurtured and breasted both the boys as their surrogate milk-mother, sealing the bond between them as a complete loving family.

Alain and Wee Maw continue their embrace, both lost in their own thoughts of the past till Alain regains a little of his calm. He looks into his mother's eyes, trying to find the words. "Mother..." but struggles to express his thoughts.

Wee Maw smiles, "I know, Son... yie don't need tae be saying anythin'." Wiping the tears from her own eyes with her cooking piny, Wee Maw regains her infamous composure.

Stepping back a pace, she gently grips him once more by his giant beard. "So what's this then?" Before Alain can reply, Wee Maw states in a loving flurry, "Look at yie son, have yie no' been eatin'? And yer far too skinny for your age."

Tucking her white-knuckled little fist into her piny, Wee Maw wags a finger in his face as she continues with her loving tirade... "C'mon into the kitchens son, I'll get some good fine break fast made up for yie. Do you still like porridge, fried eggs, pancakes, scones, bacon, haggis, black n' white puddin'? And there's kippers n' smoky haddies as well, son... do you want kippers n' smokies too?"

Wee Maw doesn't wait for a reply. Alain is getting fed and wouldn't dare refuse a feed from the notorious Wee Maw. Regaining a sense of his surroundings, Alain sees that Malcolm has quietly walked the horses into the corrals, leaving him and Wee Maw to bond. He feels his mother's love like he was the little boy of old. Alain walks with his beloved Wee Maw toward the entrance gates with his arm around her shoulders, when two young men walk out from behind the gates.

Alain stares curiously at two tall strapping youths. Both in their late teens and well over six foot tall, handsome and proud looking young men, with physiques matched only by the finest royal longbowyers of the King's lead huntsmen from the infamous Wolf and Wildcat Forest. Alain notices their long blond-brown hair is plaited and tied back in the same style as his own. Their sharp keen features are that of the *Cruinnè Cè*. The young men stare intensely at the stranger. A Moment passes with the two groups looking at each other when Malcolm returns to the gates bringing with him Alain's cousins Dáithí, Joanny, Bryan, Seoras, their wives nephews and nieces who stand beside the two youths.

Malcolm walks forward and puts his hands on the two young men's shoulders as Wee Maw calls out to them. "Boys, your father has come home tae see yiez, c'mon over and welcome him back."

The two youths immediately run over to their father and pull him close in embrace. Alain is momentarily stunned. This is not the reception he thought would ever greet him. The maelstrom of thoughts, emotions and feelings are almost too much when Wee Maw calls over, "Right you three, I want you Alain, and you two boys to be away to the sweet grounds (Grave sides) and be showing your respects to the memory of grandfather Billy, and to Brìghde, your dear late mother. And all you boys, I'll be shouting for yiez when your breakin' o' the fasts are ready. Now, away yiez go."

As Wee Maw turns to enter the gates, she bumps into the rest of the grinning family, she steps back and wags her finger at them. "And would yie look at the rest o' yiez, anybody would think yiez had never seen your brother and Uncle Alain before. C'mon you lot, for there is plenty to be doing." Wee Maw leads the Clan back into the baile beag as Alain, William and Wee John walk to the graveside and spiritual Yew tree of Big Billy, the boys' grandfather and Alain's late wife, Brìghde, William and Wee John's mother.

They have much to share and talk about this magical morning as they approach the graveside of their mother. Wee John enquires, "Have yie come for my Haun-Faus Fèis (Hand-fast festival) Dá'?"

Alain grins. "Aye, that I have son… if you'll be having me welcome in attendance?"

Wee John opens his mouth to reply, but nothing comes out. Uncertain regarding his silence, Alain looks at Wee John with trepidation; Wee John exclaims, "Are you jesting me Dá? William, will yie tell me I'm no' dreaming and that our father is here with us?"

William replies with a big smile, "Yer no' dreaming brother."

Wee John whoops and grabs William by his shoulders, then shouts out loudly, "This is going to be the best day o' ma life."

"And you, William," asks Alain. "Are you fine with me being here too?"

William beams. "Dá, ah' tell yie, I'm with Wee John, if you're here for the Haun-Faus, then this will be one o' the greatest o' days here we've ever had."

William and Wee John gaze at Alain with enormous grins. Alain is dumbstruck. He had thought and often feared that meeting with his sons would be full of acrimony and bitterness, justifiably coming from them. He had also thought he would have to be defensive while trying to explain what he couldn't rationally express. But no, he can only find the innocence of love and kindness emanating from his boys, as though they had never been parted. He couldn't quite grasp why they were so open and happy to see him, and without any reservations. Suddenly a wave of shame creeps into his consciousness for all the years he has missed seeing them or being with them, years of not being there to guide them as they grew up from children into fine young men.

The guilt is near overwhelming Alain as they walk from the sweet ground and sit under the shade of the Wallace tree, where each of them touch the ancient Yew tree on passing, to the memory of a good wife, mother and also that of their grandfather. They all sit a while with nothing being said. The pain tearing through Alain's heart and mind at that moment is nigh unbearable as he thinks of another time when his dearest Brìghde was alive and the future seemed so bright. Now this moment he has feared and dreaded for so many years gone by is real, here and now. Alain fights back a sob that goes unnoticed by his sons. "Boys, I don't know if I can ever explain or justify to yie both my actions after your mother died. I feel so shamed now in not being there for you as you grew up. I'm so sorry that I cannot replace those years... and the way you have both greeted me this morn has me almost at a complete loss for words."

"Naw faither," say the boys together.

Wee John continues, "I still cannae believe that yie're here with us at all."

William puts his hand on his father's shoulder. "Dá, we may no' understand why it had to happen, but we're clan, and uncle Malcolm never ever took your place in our hearts for he always reminded us of who we were and where we came from. He always talks about you, telling us stories o' when yiez were young. He said to us that some day we may understand."

Alain wrings his hands then looks across the Clyde as

William continues."Dá, what we need you to be understanding is, no matter what has passed, we're happy in our lives, and we wouldn't have it any other way. What has passed has made us the men we now are, and no matter what the cause of it, your decision, your sacrifice, we could only ever honour you as our father, for our life has been good."

Wee John joins in. "He's right Dá, everyone in the Clan said that we were wild and unkempt, always getting into trouble, but fair like you and nobody ever would mess with the Wallace boys. And why did the folk say this to us Dá? Because they said we were just like you and Uncle Malcolm when you were our age. So tell us Dá, how could we dislike such a fine example to be set before us?"

Alain is so surprised by the words from the boys, he doesn't know if he should laugh or cry. "Boys I'm so very sorry." he reaches out and embraces both his sons close to his heart, "I cannot scarcely believe this." He almost chokes on his words. "I hear what you say boys and I could not have wished for finer sons. Feck, I don't deserve this."

"Ach Dá..." sighs William. Alain looks at them both then he enquires. "Will we be making this day the first day of the rest of our lives?" Both William and John gaze at their father with pride and joy.

William says, "Yie had better believe it Dá,".

Wee John laughs, "Aye Dá, for we sure do believe it."

This day of reckoning Alain had feared for many long years has finally arrived, releasing years of pain from his heart. To be having each other in the same company and fulfilling dreams they had all wished for but had never dared hoped for.

Father and sons sit and talk long into the morning, eventually they are interrupted when Wee Maw approaches them. "Will you three be wanting your vittals?"

Alain stands up and embraces his sons once more; then he looks at Wee Maw who winks back at him. William claps his hands together and rubs them gleefully, "Aye, ah reckon so Granny."

The two brothers set about playfully pushing and shoving each other as they run toward the Bothies (Shelter - cottages) and on towards the famed kitchens of *Ach na Feàrna*.

Wee Maw smiles as she looks up at Alain. She says "Would yie be looking at the life in those two young bucks, those boys are as happy as we are this fine day."

Alain shakes his head. "I cannae believe it Maw, I mean, I feel like it's all just a dream." Mother and son embrace, then clasping arm in arm, they walk toward the house to break fast with the rest of the clan.

On approaching the famed kitchens of Wee Maw, Alain sits down outside the main house to remain alone and take in everything that's happening. As Wee Maw is about to enter the house, she stops and turns, remembering something important. "Alain, yie must be meeting young Rosinn o' Connaught, she is the most bonnie wee Irish princess yie ever did see, and to be wed to Wee John later this day."

"Maw," exclaims Alain. "There's something I need to be tellin' to yie… my wife, Mharaidh, she will be so angry with me. For years she has been saying to make my peace with the family and that we should all be together again as a clan. Now I am here and she and little Caoilfhinn are down in Glen Afton so far away."

"Awe," sniffs Wee Maw. "Bonnie wee Caoilfhinn, when will I ever get to see the bonnie wean?"

Alain didn't see Wee Maw wink knowingly at Malcolm, who approaches with an old friend.

Malcolm taps Alain on the shoulder. "Brother, I would like you to meet someone."

Alain turns from his momentary daydream to see old Stephen ua H'Alpine standing before him… "Ua H'Alpine," exclaims Alain as he jumps up to embrace his friend of many years.

"Whoa, now just you steady on there Wallace, its no' us that is getting wedded yie know." Auld Stephen laughs and continues with a grand smile. "Come here me boy, sure I'm just messin' wit ya."

Auld Stephen pulls Alain close, then he grips him by the shoulders and looks at him proudly.

"How long has it been old friend?"

Auld Stephen ponders, "Not so long after the battle of Largs I'll be thinking is the last time we met."

"That must be nearly twenty odd years since Largs."

Auld Stephen replies with a grin. "Aye Alain, that's when I saw you last. And if I mind right, it was when you were but a boy and being so badly wounded wit' a big scratch on yer arse and you were sayin' some mighty fine and wonderful things about them there Norsemen that day."

Alain laughs and reflects on the time that has passed between them, then he exclaims, "Twenty odd years since, feck it's hard to believe."

It's then that Alain notices a beautiful and slender auburn haired young woman standing close behind Auld Stephen. She has the fine upstanding bearing of noble Irish woman-hood. So beautiful in the flowing silks and fine linens of her wheat coloured wedding dress, intricately embroidered with the finest of Irish knot-work. Her long soft Auburn hair plaited down her back entwines with the sweetest of spring-time flower posies.

"Alain," says Auld Stephen with a smile, "Sure now, I'd like to be introducing to yie here, me wonderful daughter, Ròsinn. Your very own daughter-in-law by the end of this day I'll be thinkin'."

Alain reaches out, beckoning the young woman to come close. "My... Let me see you."

He looks into the eyes of young Ròsinn. His heart soars with pride while gazing at her beauty, "Ròsinn, you are the most beautiful Irish rose that I've ever seen. I am so genuinely honoured that you and Wee John are to be wed. And ever since I had found out it was yourself, a bonnie princess from such fine Irish blood, I didn't know till I met you just how much I had really looked forward to this moment. Wee darlin', I cannot begin to tell you what this means to me and how proud I am of both you and Wee John."

Ròsinn blushes a little as her father affectionately puts his brat around her shoulders. Just then Wee Maw comes rushing back out of the main house. "Now Ròsinn bonnie darlin', we cannae be letting Wee John see his bride-to-be before the Haun Fèis. Now c'mon wie me, lets get you back to Uliann and Aunia before Wee John sees yie."

Wee Maw and Ròsinn leave for the bride's lodge while Alain, Auld Stephen and Malcolm sit down at an old oak bench where they talk eagerly about the forthcoming ceremonies planned for this day.

Alain is so engrossed in all that is happening he hasn't noticed William approach with a young wild and unkempt looking stranger..."Dá," says a voice from behind him. Alain recognises William's voice and turns with a smile, relishing the unfamiliar but much welcomed use of the word 'Dá' from his son. He sees William standing with a young man of similar age but slightly smaller. His style of dress is vaguely familiar to that of the Galloway Ceitherne, (Kern-apprentice warrior) and *Gallóglaigh* Wolf and Wildcat huntsmen. This wild looking young man stands beside William wearing a long saffron *léine* with large draping sleeves covered with a sleeveless patched goatskin top jack, all held tight and body central with a large ornately designed silver *Cruinnè* clasp fixed to his belt, from which hangs an intimidating long broad dirk. His hair is long, auburn-black, tousled, thick, parted in the centre and appears as though it has been immersed in bacon fat. Alain notices the glint from fabulous Irish jewellery of silver and amber adorning the young man's attire, a handsome youth with the soft facial hair growing but not yet reaching full maturity.

"Dá, this is Stefán (Stephen) of Ireland, Rossins' elder brother."

Alain's eyes open wide as he responds. "So this fine fella is your son?"

Auld Stephen replies proudly, "Aye, that he is… or so I have been told."

His son offers out his hand to Alain in friendship. "Madhainn a' bha Alain, s' *Co'nas* a tha thu? (Good morning, Alain, and how are you?)"

"*Tá*, tha mi gu math, s' *Co'nas* a tha thu s'fhèin Stefán óg? (I'm well thanks, and how are you, young Stephen?)"

Stephen continues with an impudent smile. "Well it's a good morning to ya, fadder-in-wedded-law-to-be."

Alain laughs as Stephen proudly keeps on shaking hands with him as a new-found kinsman, and keeps on shaking Alain's hand with a wondrous disarming smile and never-ending iron grip of Alain's hand.

"Me name is Stefán ua H'Alpine… but I prefer to be called Stephen of Ireland, for there is no other as deserving of such a foin name at all from that wonderful island but me'self, oi'll just be letting ya know that."

Alain laughs at the humorous intensity emanating from Stephen 'OF' Ireland. Eventually Alain manages to pull his hand away with an equally big smile at the brass of this young

Irishman. "Well. It's a fine welcome to you too young Stephen … of Ireland."

"That's me boy," quips Auld Stephen proudly. "He'll only be shaking the hands o' those fella's that he likes."

Alain wrings his fingers, waiting for the return of the blood supply. "Well I am sure glad he likes me for he has the cocky pride in his heart passed on from his father."

They all laugh and sit down to reminisce and talk of good times past and good times to come. As the conversation continues, an intensely happy Alain hasn't noticed an ornately decaled bow-wagon pulled by two fine grey Garrons escorted by four mounted *Gallóglaigh* warriors arriving through the gates of *Ach na Feàrna*. The wagon and horsemen eventually halt close to the doors of the main house steps, where the guards dismount and reach into the bow-wagon to help the occupants alight. Malcolm nudges Alain.

He turns to see why Malcolm has interrupted him, suddenly he jumps up from his seat as though struck by an arrow."Lady Mharaidh?" Alain gasps then he exclaims, "What the…"

Wee Maw quips, "Alain, before you catch all the flies in Pàislig (Paisley) with your big open gob, should yie no' be rushing over and making a fine *Ach na Feàrna* welcome for your bonnie wife?"

Standing motionless in another moment of bemused wonderment, Alain turns quickly toward everyone sitting at the table, "Please to be excusing me, but there's my bonnie wife and daughter and I…"

Alain's head spins with the onslaught of emotional upheavals he's experiencing this day. Lady Mharaidh is a noble heiress and descendant of King Uchtred, chief of the great and powerful Clan Scott from the ancient Kingdom of Galloway, Buccleuch (BaKlew) and Bellendean. Mharaidh is in her mid thirties and holds a natural regal and gentle poise with her long blonde hair plaited tightly behind her head and flowing effortlessly down her back in court fashion. She waits anxiously, peering through the busy gathering to seek out her husband of nineteen years since.

"Away yie go…" says Malcolm. Alain is flummoxed, "But what's Mharaidh doing here? I mean, how did she know?" But he doesn't wait for an answer as he rushes over to greet his wife to his childhood home. Alain welcomes Mharaidh with open arms and embraces her with great affection. Alain, smiling with glee, looks lovingly into Mharaidhs' sparkling hazel eyes and puts his arms around her slender waist. "Mharaidh… how did you know that I would be here? I mean… I didn't know myself, I don't understand?"

Mharaidh replies, "I've been in contact with your mother awhile now my love. Though I thought you would be with Alexander this day so your mother and I decided that I should represent the Wallace of Glen Afton at the wedding of Wee John and Ròsinn. I had no idea you would be here, but I'm so glad that you are." Alain kisses Mharaidh passionately. She looks into his eyes, "Oh Alain, my love, I had hoped in my heart that you would be here."

Once again they embrace and kiss passionately, when a child's voice calls out from the rear of the wagon…

"Dá."

Alain looks into the eyes of Mharaidh. "Is that…?"

Mharaidh calls out to the bow-wagon. "There's someone here to see you Caoilfhinn."

Just then, two heads pop out the front of the wagon from behind the ornate hemp cover. Katriona, the kitchen maid from the King's lodge of Glen Afton, is holding Alains precious six-year-old daughter in her arms. Caoilfhinn reaches out with her tiny hands for her fathers loving embrace. Stepping up to the wagon, Alain lifts his daughter and holds her so dearly. Mharaidh puts an arm round Alain's waist as he gently sweeps the long blonde curls of Caoilfhinns' hair away from her face. Stepping down, Alain says with joy, "Come Mharaidh, you must meet with the family."

He taps his beautiful daughter on the tip of her tiny nose. "And you me young fawn, you are going to be meeting your brothers, sisters and your Granny this day."

As the Wallace family of Glen Afton turn to meet with other family members, Alain notices William and Wee John standing only a few feet away. "Boys, this is Lady Mharaidh, my beautiful wife, and this little gem here who is trying to hide behind me is your little sister Caoilfhinn."

Malcolm and Wee Maw watch from a distance at this unexpected but long overdue family gathering. A teary eyed Wee Maw says, "Ah, wish yer Dá dear old Billy was here tae see this day son."

Malcolm, also with a tear in his eye, enquires, "Should we go over and join them Maw?" Wee Maw replies, "Come on son, ma poor wee heart is thumping out o' ma chest to be seeing ma bonnie grandchild."

The Wallace Clan settle into one of their finest Clan family gatherings in many a long year.

* * *

A different atmosphere is about to be brought home at *Dun Ceann Orran*, the castle of their beloved King Alexander, and that of his *Bahn Rígh*, Queen Yolande. Early that same morning, as the Wallace brothers had ridden into *Ach na Feàrna*, King Alexander's squires had ridden into the gate-house of *Dun Ceann Orran*. The Ceannard na *Garda Rìoghail* enquires of King Alexander's whereabouts. The confused squires tell of what happened the previous night and of Alexander's insistence to ride on alone, despite advice to the contrary. They insist that he should already be here. Panic quickly sets in and spreads throughout the castle as the King is nowhere to be found, nor is he residing at one of the Golden teeth fortalice's, as word would have been sent to Queen Yolande.

The mid-afternoon skies are laden grey over the east coast of Scotland as the gales and storms have died away and an early March sun begins to break, casting golden shafts of sunlight through the cloud canopy. Yolande, desperate with worry, repeatedly walks back and forth to look through the small windows of her apartment in the Dun of *Ceann Orran*, but she sees no sign of her love. Her maids in waiting are fraught with concern over Yolande's angst at the absence of her beloved Alexander, on this, a day that should be filled with the celebrations of her birth day. The Queen has already heard the news from Edinburgh by carrier pigeon that Alexander had left the previous night. She is desperately anxious and deeply distressed that her husband has not yet arrived at the castle. Since they had met and married, not a day has passed for them not to be in each other's arms. Alexander and Yolande are very much in love and she is now with child. The Castle Ceannard calls for the *Garda Rìoghail* to assemble immediately. One hundred men divide to search for the King to establish that all is safe and well with him, but the deep concern on the faces of the King's loyal men could not be hidden. Search parties hurriedly leave *Ceann Orran* as everyone fears that something must be amiss.

Search parties begin to scour the land in all directions, messengers are sent to every Keep, Inn and fortalice along the northern bank of the Forth river to locate the King, till finally late in the afternoon, the broken lifeless body of Alexander and his great war-horse Areion, are found on the shore bed at the foot of a small rocky cliff embankment, not far from *Dun Ceann Orran*. It appears King Alexander has died in a horrific riding accident, brought about by his haste to be with Yolande. A needless death, due only to his reckless disregard against all advice not to ride out in such dangerous weather conditions… this is what everyone believes. It appears the tragedy of love and such yearning to be by his pregnant wife, has caused the death of the beloved King of Scotland. Glorious Alexander is dead.

Far from *Dun Ceann Orran* and unaware of the tragedy, the wedding of 'Wee' John Wallace and Ròsinn nic H'Alpine begins with all gathered to witness the vows of love to be pledged. Wee John stands proud and handsome in his dun-brown *léine*, embossed in delicate golden knot-work and emblazoned edges with symbols of wild geese and deerhounds embroidered delicately on his wide hanging bell-sleeves. A mantle brat of wolf-skins adorns his back and shoulders. On his chest-piece is sewn the symbol of the Wallace clan of *Ach na Feàrna*, a turquoise blue winged dragon in particular circular a style, inlaid with gold-vein thread. Holding firm in the dragon claws is an embroidered silver Claymore of the *Garda Rìoghail*.Soon, Ròsinn appears and walks towards Wee John as the most beautiful of Elvin princess, in her long silken-linen dress of warmest wheaten-cream colours, with meticulous knot-work designs in emerald and sovereign siller green pastels blessed on every quarter. Her hair is beautifully interwoven with flowers and crowned with a posy of dried bluebell, rose and lily. She wears a flowing light muslin veil that covers her face, fastened with long silken ties that flow gently in the warm breeze as she walks effortlessly to stand in front of Wee John.

As the young couple hold hands and stand before the two elder Breitheamh Rígh, Auld Stephen ua H'Alpine and Wee Maw Wallace, who wear ancient honour attire of saffron coloured cloaks and emerald green *léine*, befitting those of the ancient order of *Cruinnè* orators, signified simply by party coloured Anam Crios (Spirit Belt) around their waist, a broad band of honour that denotes their standing of authority and respect within the *Cruinnè-cè* community. Now it is time to conduct and sanctify the union of love between Wee John and Ròsinn, by the authority of the Breathaim Rígh of the Cruathnie faith. The hand-fast begins as Wee Maw and Auld Stephen tie the young couples left hands together with two Anam Crios gifted from each family. The young loving couple walk and stand within a *Cruinnè* Quaich, a small circle of stones filled with Lilly flowers and broom, symbolic of their universe. Curiously in the centre of the circle of the tryst sits an empty churn. The spiritual circle is for none other than the loving couple, for when they speak or are spoken too, it is from within their universe of union from which they will reply or make statement as one, for they now see everything differently from all others. This special place is for them alone which none may enter except by the invitation of both. As they hold each other's left hand, Wee Maw begins…

"Is it before all that you wish to begin this sacred commitment of Love and never ending union?"

Wee John and Rosinn reply together as one,*"Aye we do."*

"Do yiez pledge your hearts and souls to each and no other, sharing all that is divine between you, inviting protection from the spirits of earth, the winds of the North, South, East and West? And do you both welcome willingly the gift of protection offered by the presence of the earth and wind spirits and the approval offered freely by your elders, ancestors and all who

gather here to witness this day?"

They reply, *"Aye, we do wish this blessed gift."*

"Then may the wind spirits bless this union with these gifts so willingly accepted in your heart, mind, body and soul. With the rising of each sun, the knowledge of growth together will be found in the sharing of this love. Bless this union with the gifts of the Sun that brings the warmth of heart's passion to your loving union and to brighten this love that lights and warms the hearth and home. Bless this union with the lantern of the full moon to light your way in times of darkness, bathing your sleep in the gentle caress of purity, that you may both wake with the gift of peace and wise as the night birds. Bless this union with the gifts from the passions as the deepest commitments of the sea and the grandest loch. May you both gain fulsome hearts from the swift and ever flowing excitement as that of the fast flowing river, in that, your love be eternally cleansed, replenished and refreshed as the purest cleansing of our rivers created from the heavens above. Bless this union with the gifts of the Earth as the firm foundations on which to build your home. The fertility of the fields to enrich your lives with children, and a home built with the strength of oak, to which you may always return."

Auld Stephen bids the wedding couple *"Will you cause each other pain?"*

Rosinn and John *"We shall."*

"Is that your intention?"

"No."

"Will you share each other's pain and seek to ease it?"

"Aye."

The ceremony continues awhile longer confirming all the oaths of marriage till finally, Auld Stephen grins. *"And so your love is sanctified and honoured by all. Now, will yie both hold out your left hands."*

Wee Maw takes from around her neck two golden cords then loops them loosely around the outstretched wrists of both Rosinn and John. She asks of them, *"Will you share in each other's laughter?"*

Rosinn and John reply with great smiles and giggles. *"Aye, we will."*

Auld Stephen, as the Breitheamh elder, ties the knots in the cords as the hand-fasting ceremony continues, till all the wedding vows are complete.

To conclude the wedding ceremonies, Auld Stephen now speaks. *"John Wallace and Rosinn nic H'Alpine-Wallace... It is time to mix the waters of union."*

The symbolism of this bonding is to be enacted where Rosinn then, followed by Wee John, must pee in a bucket, much to the amusement of everyone. It is a vow task that is slightly easier for Rosinn than Wee John as she squats discreetly in her skirts, after which Wee John has to hold the bucket close to his privates, which causes him great consternation, much to the silent mirth of all the guests.

Eventually, John completes his task of union. Wee Maw is handed the bucket by the betrothed and proceeds to swirl the contents... *"In the spirit of love, if any here can separate this gift then they may separate this union, and if so, now is the time for you to step forward and speak freely. If none are here to do this separation, then all blessed is their love as Anam Chara* (Soul Mates) *and blessing of the Anam Alain* (Beautiful Spirit)."

Wee Maw pauses a moment, looking round the guests, solemnly giving everyone a warning look. When she appears satisfied none would dare to step forward, she continues the blessing with a joyous smile... *"May you both live in a loving union for one year commencing from this day. And should you both or only one finds that true love is not to be found in each other, nor for each other, nor a child be born of your love, then you each may return home with blessing and honour."*

Wee Maw proudly states, *"Ròsinn Wallace and John Wallace… may you share great and everlasting love together. May you desire to always love and support each other, strengthen each other in times of sorrow, share times of gladness, and be companions to each other for eternity. By the presence of love in the hearts of each of you, from the deepening love you both share… you are now husband and wife. By my authority as Breitheamh Rígh of the Cruinnè-cè…You may now kiss."*

The young lovers meet with their first wedded kiss as Wee Maw wipes a tear of joy from her eyes, using Auld Stephen's *léine* sleeve. Everyone cheers, for now it's time for the happy couple to proceed with the final act of union. Wee Maw and Auld Stephen invite the wedded couple to step out of their own universe and join the families to walk in procession to the great Yew tree of *Ach na Feàrna*, where each may tie a single end of their individual golden cord to a branch, as did their ancestors before them. Next, they tie the hanging ends together in a tight knot while reciting their personal oath of the Anam Alainn. Wee John puts the silver ring of the moon goddess on the finger of Ròsinn. She then places a golden band of the Sun God on Wee John's finger.

Wee Maw says, *"As the Sun and the Moon rises each day for eternity, so shall they, as man and wife in the eyes of the Clan, Magda mòr and the eternal Aicé."*

The knots of the hand-fast have been tied, Rosinn and Wee John both have peed in the bucket of love, the pipers are giving it their finest playing of music and both the ancient Irish and Scots Clan's of Wallace and H'Alpine are united by this marriage, enjoying a day that both families have not had in many a long year. As early evening comes and as the sun begins to set, everyone is spread around *Ach na Feàrna* enjoying the festivities. The boys are sitting at the feast table when William nudges his cousin Malcolm óg and speaks humerously to Wee John...

"What's up with your face, wee brother? Yie would think yie would be so happy with a new wife so blessed and bonnie in looks and nature as Rosinn? Is it because it took yie awhile to pee into the love bucket?"

"Naw, its no' that," replied Wee John.

Curious, William enquires, "Then what is it that ails yie, brother? What's making your face se' sour?"

Wee John, sounding slightly bewildered, replies, "I was sittin' beside Wee Maw and Rosinn, well, more like they talked, I listened. Then I heard Wee Maw giving Rosinn her wedding day instructions, and yie know what Wee Maw is like with the *craitur* in her?"

William smiles, "Aye?"

Wee John continues, "Ah heard her telling Rosinn that having' a new husband was like having' a new bow and arrow."

"And…" enquires William curiously as the rest of the table listen intently.

"Well," sighs Wee John, "Wee Maw said we're both fine kept outside o' the Bothie, for she said to Ròsinn that the day will come soon enough when she would eventually just want tae shoot both of us? But I don't know what she meant?"

Everybody roars with laughter except Wee John, who in a drunken innocent voice, enquires, "What did she mean William?"

With tears of laughter rolling down his cheeks, William replies, "I'll explain it to yie later ma bonnie Wee John." William throws his arm around the neck of his drunken young brother, now shedding emotional tears, much to the mirth of all. Wee John continues his sorrowful outpouring, his voice broken by sobbing.

"I wish big brother Alan could o' made it here for the wedding too William. Especially with us and Dá getting together like this." Wee John pauses for a drink, then he enquires, "What made him go tae France?"

"Ach, John, I suppose it's because of the monks o' Paisley priory and Crossraguel," says William. "It's their particular faith that he follows. They're Cluniac priests o' that order o' religious folks and they're based away in some place called France. Here... d'yie mind they priests were always good tae us John, well apart from the beatings."

The two brothers laugh, then William exclaims, "Would yie be looking at that." He nudges Wee John and points over to the old yew tree.

"Feck," exclaims Wee John. "Now that sight has been a long time a' comin'."

"Yer right John, a long time."

The young Wallace brothers gaze toward the sweet ground of their ancestors to see Malcolm, Margret, Alain and Mharaidh sitting underneath the great yew and oak trees. The symbolic affinity shared between the Paisley and Glen Afton Septs of the Wallace Clan is the ancient belief of burying their people near a Yew or oak tree, which fuses the spirits of the people interred there with nature. The ancient followers of the *Céile Aicé* and *Cruinnè* Cè understood the unbroken connection with their ancestors by honouring the strengths of the Yew and Oak, which in turn feeds from and gains strength from the bodies fluids returned to the earth amongst the tree-roots. William and Wee John watch as their elders touch the wood of the trees, in memory of loved ones of the house and Clan of Wallace... for future good fortune."

The Sennachaid

Malcolm, Margret, Alain and Mharaidh sit under an ancient Yew as the sun finally sets over *Ach na Feàrna* in the sweet grounds of their ancestors. No-one talks as each privately reflects on times past while watching the small fishing sailboats meander through the straits and Ynchinnan (little islands) of the River Clyde, bringing home their catch for the markets in the morning.

Malcolm sighs as he observes the idyllic scene. "Ach Alain, it's been a great day..."

"Aye," agrees Alain, "It's been a day I never dreamt possible,"

Malcolm nods contentedly. "It's been good to see your old self back here too Alain, and to see you and the boys all here together, well..."

Alain interrupts, "Malcolm, I cannot be thanking you enough, and you too Margret, Wee Maw... yiez have sure brought the boys up well, and for me to get a second chance o' coming to peace with them? This is nigh unbelievable." Glancing at the scene along the Ynchinnan, Alain continues, "The boys genuinely understand what I could never express about my actions after the death of their mother. They seem to grasp the reasons as to why I couldn't face them. Feck, I was so wrong, yet they've made me feel so proud too."

"Aye, brother, yie should be proud o' them, they're great lads. A wee bit on the wild side though..."

Alain appears puzzled as Malcolm continues, "Aye, they are sure like their father right enough."

Everyone sits back to gaze peacefully at the Clyde when Alain frowns and clasps his hands anxiously. "Feck Malcolm, I reckon I've made such a mess of everything, I should have done something long before now."

Margret and Mharaidh sit quietly listening to the brothers' talk, then Mharaidh speaks. "Alain, you did what Magda mòr meant for you to do, now look at you this night, you're beaming with delight, we all are. It's like everyone here has just seen the most beautiful rainbow and discovered the biggest pot o' *Fae* gold in all of Scotland. It's like both the boys said, the past has been the making of them, and the morrow brings a new day like the first day of spring for all of us, as one big happy Clan."

Smiling, Alain nods his head in agreement. He says, "Their mother would be so proud o' those boys as she looks across the sea from Tír nan óg ("Land of Youth-Otherworld"). Brìghdes' heart will be warmed as she watches over us."

Margret looks at Alain then says, "And Aoibheann (Aivan) too."

Startled from his thoughts, Alain offers an immediate apology. "Oh, Malcolm, Margret, forgive me. I was no' forgetting Aoibheann, I… I meant, awe feck, I'm sorry, I was selfishly thinking of myself there."

Malcolm replies, "Ach, that's all right Alain. When Aoibheann passed away giving birth to Aunia, both Margret and I were blessed to find love in each other so soon afterwards. I reckon all of those we've loved that have gone before us, sure do bless the love we've found as mortals upon this earth."

Margret smiles as Malcolm puts his arm around her shoulders. "We now have a most beautiful family me darlin', and as with Alain's Angel of love that chose him a course of happiness with Mharaidh, I've been blessed with such love with you my dearest."

Hearing Malcolm's romantic words, Margret smiles and coyly looks away, then she notices William and Stephen following a group of giggling milking girls like a pair of thirsty bloodhounds on a trail hunt. She calls out. "Boys, come over here the now."

William sighs. "Awe, Margret," Stephen mutters, "Feck and Bolloks." The boys saunter over to Margret reluctantly, whereupon she says, "Now, the pair o' yiez, I want you both to be getting all the weans from the Hop." (Dance – Party)

Before she can finish, William moans, "Awe naw, do we have too?"

Ignoring the sullen complaint, Margret continues, "You're to be calling in the weans for eve vittals; then afterwards we'll be sitting around the late evening fire in the main house for the telling of great legends from Wee Maw, and…"

"Wee Maw?" interrupt Malcolm and Alain, both amused.

Margret corrects herself. "Your grandmother," She smiles as she continues. "Right boys, be away with you and fetch everyone from the Ceilidh that's no' a' hoppin' (Dancing) or guzzlin' (Drinking) over to the great hall for vittals, then we can hear tales of legends past from your grandmother."

William asks. "All o' the folks at the Ceilidh?"

Margret laughs. "No William, just be fetching the weans and the older ones who can't be dancing, or those who've sore ears from all that noise."

Stephen enthusiastically enquires, "Can we be asking the milkin' maids too?"

"Aye, that would be fine," says Margret. "Only so we may keep an eye on you two young bucks."

William and Stephen happily go about their duty while the elders make their way back toward the great house of the clan. Mharaidh also leaves the sweet grounds to prepare the sleeping compartment for her Caoilfhinn and Alain. Everyone else walks slowly towards the main house chatting of good times past.

Alain enquires, "Can I be asking of you both what I consider may be a thorny question?"

Malcolm looks at Alain. "What is it brother that's a burden to your thoughts?"

"I need to know if what I'm thinking is right by you both, but more especially right by the boys?"

Margret replies, "Alain darlin', you can ask us anything."

Alain continues with slight reticence. "I want to ask you about William, Wee John and Ròsinn... I mean, I'd like to be asking them to come back with me and Mharaidh to Glen Afton."

Alain tempers his nervousness while waiting on a reply. He asks nervously, "Am I being selfish? Do you think I may be asking too much?"

Linking arms with the two brothers, Margret stops walking and pulls the meandering trio to a halt, noticeably holding back tears as emotion wells up inside her. She looks thoughtfully into Alain's eyes as the three of them are held quietly in an eternal magical moment, a moment that only parents who know the purest form of love and nurture for their children could ever understand.

Alain wonders, "Does this silence mean yiez think it's a good idea? Or have I just asked the worst question in the history o' mankind?"

"Oh, Alain," exclaims Margret as she slaps him on the shoulder in mock anger.

"A good idea then?"

Margret commences walking and pulling the two brothers close, almost dragging them toward the great house. She replies joyously. "Of course it's right to be thinking so Alain Wallace, it's a wonderful idea."

Alain looks to Malcolm, "And what do you think brother?"

Malcolm shakes his head. "I've no' seen such a smile on Margret's face since last I gave my all in the nuptial crib and going far beyond the call of a husbands duty, and wrecking my auld back in the process."

Again Margret blushes as Malcolm puts his finger gently under her chin and gazes lovingly into her eyes. "But it was all worth it me darlin', to be making you my dearest Margret, a very happy woman with such a bonny smile?"

Now it's Malcolm's turn to receive a loving slap from Margret as they approach the doors to the main Keep. "Does that answer your question, brother?" he asks.

Alain, Malcolm and Margret are still laughing as they enter the great hall, where they're surprised to see many of their kinfolk are already seated.

Alain exclaims "Feck me, they're all eating their vittals like it was the last supper."

The noise, happy sounding banter and speed at which everyone gulps down their food is so that each may finish quickest to be seated closest to the famed storyteller to hear every word, confirming Wee Maw's stories are legendary and not to be missed. The main room soon fills with family and kinfolk while Wee Maw tends to her matronly duties in the kitchens. Everyone is chattering and laughing loudly, children are running about, shouting and squealing, causing familiar family gathering mayhem.

Margret calls out to Malcolm over the bedlam. "You'd better get some order over these ruckus weans Malcolm, or they'll end up burning the hoose doon."

Malcolm sighs, "Aye, dear." He walks over to the mantle head of the great fire, turns to face the joyous madness and calls aloud in a thunderous voice, "HERE COMES THE PRIEST!"

Everyone immediately stops what they're doing... horrified at what they'd just heard. Malcolm grins, "And now that I have gained your attention... the greatest Seanachaidh (shaunn-achie - storyteller) in all of Scotland will be here soon weans, so I want you lot be settling down peaceably."

As the children settle down, Malcolm gleefully rubs his hands together then he enquires, "So what fine story would you all like to be hearing?"

The family audience clamour and shout in a cacophony. "Tell us about the Normans, tell us about the Romans and the Saxonach, uncle."

Malcolm óg waves his hand in the air. "Tell us the story how you, grandpa Billy and Uncle Alain fought the Norsemen single-handed at the Battle of Largs and how yie both saved our Artur Ard Rígh (High King) and then the whole of Scotland."

While Malcolm ponders the variety of diverse requests, the children continue yelling and screaming with delight and in anticipation. Malcolm confidently raises his hand with authority as the master of his household and commands. "Right, RIGHT... QUIET!"

But much to Malcolm's dismay and Alain's amusement, none of the revellers, both young and old, take any notice and continue the mayhem. Exasperated and red-faced, Malcolm scowls at Alain then he calls out in a gravelly thunderous voice as though he were commanding soldiers on a battlefield. Malcolm growls again with great authority, "SILENCE!"

In an instant, nothing could be heard as a deathly hush quickly descends following his command. Nothing is heard except a slight whistle of wind blowing eerily outside the small window of the great hall. Malcolm looks around the room, amused in seeing all the excited and expectant young faces before him. He growls at the top of his voice, "That's enough noise from you lot."

Alain leans close to Malcolm and whispers, "We saved the King at the battle of Largs did we... AND Scotland too?"

Malcolm chuckles. "Of course we did, brother, don't yie remember?"

Both brothers laugh at Alain's apparent forgetfulness, then Malcolm looks to his youngest son. "And what story is it that you would like to hear gentle Andrew, since we're all celebrating your day too?"

Andrew replies, "Tell us the story of our name Dá, what does Wallace mean? Where does the name come from?"

William joins in, "Aye, will Granny tell us where we get the name Wallace?"

Alain, with a knowing wink to Malcolm replies, "Aye, brother, we want to hear the story of the Wallace."

The brothers exchange looks, gentle Andrew's request brings back memories of when they'd often asked for that same story when they were young.

Margaret says, "Gentle Andrew, away and be getting your grandmother. Tell her it's time for her special story."

Young Andrew springs up from the large bearskin rug lying on the floor in front of the fire to go fetch Wee Maw, Granny Wallace.

Without warning Wee John punches William on the muscle of his arm with such dead-force it knocks him off his seat. The noise of William clattering onto the floor brings immediate silence in the grand room.

"Right you two," growls Malcolm, "Yiez are young men now and yiez should be past all o' this punchin' n' a kickin' each other when yiez think I'm no' looking."

Alain keenly observes the interaction between his brother and his sons and feels a pang of jealousy that another man should have such intimacy with his boys.

But the distasteful feeling quickly dispels when Wee John looks directly at him and enquires "Dá, isn't it fair to be hookin' ma brother for kickin' ma shinbone earlier in the day. And isn't it right to be pickin' ma own time to do it?"

Delighted at the seamless joining of father and son, Alain feels enormous pride upon hearing these words, despite their long years apart. "What does your Uncle Malcolm say?"

Wee John pauses to think a moment. "He says that's what you used to do?"

Everyone, including Alain, laughs at Wee John's innocent reply. "Well your uncle Malcolm is correct, though yie must be picking a time when you know you won't get caught."

"Excuse me?" exclaims Malcolm, feigning indignation while trying to mask a grin. "It was YOU who used to be a' punching and kicking ME first."

"Yie mean like this?"Alain punches Malcolm on the arm, much to the approval and respondent laughter from the gathered clan. The room is in a great state of mirth, enjoying the continuing humorous antics of Malcolm and Alain, seemingly at odds with each other as Wee John and William had been moments earlier, then Uliann and Aunia enter the room with flagons of milk mixed with warm honey and berry juice for the children, they also carry a churn of Wee Maw's very own 'special' craitur (Whisky blended with Honey). Mharaidh and Katriona soon follow through the door with little Caoilfhinn in hand between them and proceed to sit beside Alain, whereupon he picks up little Caoilfhinn and sits her on his knee.

Everyone settles down and prepares for a night within the nurture, comfort and warmth of the entire family, when Wee

Maw enters the room with gentle Andrew in hand. Tension mounts as everyone waits impatiently for the famed story-teller to commence this wonderful night of legends. A night of telling tall tales of heroes, heroines and battles past.

Wee Maw stops in front of the fire, raises the tails of her long skirts and warms her bum while she looks curiously around the dimly lit room, then Wee Maw begins to talk in a wispy storytelling voice. "Is it the legend o' the name Wallace yiez will all be wanting to hear then weans?"

Everyone calls out by way of a noisy reply, "AYE GRANNY."

Wee Maw continues, "Then it will be the story of the *Aicés* yiez will be wanting?"

With mounting excitement, everyone calls back "AYE GRANNY!"

Wee Maw scrutinises everyone while roasting her backside by the fire, she sees all the children huddle together in expectation and excitement. "Right then," says Wee Maw, "I'll be wanting yiez all to settle down, and nobody is to be interrupting, talking or shouting."

Wee Maw pauses then points a bony finger, "And no fighting… especially you two, William and Wee John, do yiez hear me?"

"AYE, GRANNY," calls out everyone in unison.

Wee Maw puts a cupped hand to her ear, then in a loud and grumpy voice calls out, "I didn't hear yiez!"

All of the family giggle laugh and shout even louder. "AYE GRANNY!"

Everyone settles down, clustering around the great fire then they fall silent as Wee Maw gives Malcolm the infamous 'look'.

"Jings!" exclaims a flustered Malcolm. "Tha mi duilich (I'm sorry.)"

He quickly jumps up from the best seat in the room, Granny's 'throne'. Wee Maw grins as she takes her seat upon the throne, then replies politely, "Se' do bheatha" (You're welcome).

Malcolm proceeds to sit beside Alain and Mharaidh, everyone laughing at his apparent fluster while Wee Maw settles herself comfortably into 'HER' seat, then she wags her finger at Malcolm. "Yie might be a father and Sir Malcolm to this brood that's looking on son, but you and your brother are no' yet too old to be getting paddled across ma knee."

Everyone laughs and shouts joyously, witnessing this rare chastisement of Malcolm and Alain.

Wee Maw points. "Right then, I'll be wanting no noise weans, especially you Wee John, don't be punching anybody or twistin' your brothers tits or its straight off to yer crib yie'll be going."

Wee John moans, "But I'm twenty odd summers of age granny."

"Ròsinn…" commands Wee Maw with authority, "Will yie be taking seriously to the duties of a wife this night and beat that big lump Wee John to make him behave." Wee Maw suddenly changes her demeanour and flutters her eyes at Ròsinn, she says, "Yie must start darlin' as yie mean to go on." Ròsinn blushes as Wee Maw continues, "And you be minding now bonnie darlin', that big lovable lump of trouble over there is all yours now."

Wee John put his head into his hands and mutters, "Feck's sake, now there's two o' them."

"Little John," barks Wee Maw, "Do you want me to be sending you to your crib right the now?"

Everyone struggles not to laugh at Wee John's predicament. Wee Maw gives Wee John the 'look', enough of a look to silence the rest of the room instantly. The whole family fear the dreaded 'look' from Wee Maw's steely blue eyes. Better to obey this little matriarch than suffer her chastisement.

Ròsinns' alabaster-like cheeks flush a little more as she turns to speak to Wee John, employing for the first time her new found 'look' of matriarchal authority. She pats the seat gently by her side and commands in a sweet Irish lilt, "Sit nigh, Sean beag (Little John)"

Wee John responds in sullen servile obedience, the whole six feet three inches of him. He walks meekly over and sits beside his new bride, relieved he's escaping Wee Maw's glare while remaining uncertain as to the real threat behind this new 'look' from Ròsinn. Though he hadn't noticed that she too is desperately trying to suppress her laughter like everyone else.

The glances shared between Wee Maw and the rest of the family takes all their combined effort not to laugh out loud at Wee John's submissive acceptance to wedded bliss. Wee Maw pats Ròsinn on the lap and quips, "That's ma girl."

Everyone giggles except Wee John.

Wee Maw gives everyone the 'look' as she clasps her hands together then leans forward in her chair, glowering at all the eager faces of her kinfolks. This fiery little lady could scare the fiercest of warriors by a single matronly glance from her sharp clear steely-blue eyes, and everyone knows it. Wee Maw prepares for the storytelling by coughing and clearing her throat then she swallows a large amount of her own special honey flavoured *craitur*. Margret, now finished with her chores, enters the room and sits beside Malcolm, putting her arm through his and linking arms with Alain and Mharaidh. Wee Maw Wallace will soon begin to tell the legendary story as her grandfather had told her, as had been customarily passed down each second generation. Malcolm and Alain glance affectionately toward each other, for they had heard this legend often and it had inspired them both as children. The implications of the legends told by Wee Maw had matured in understanding and purpose for them both as they had grown from boys into men. These important family legends are paramount and inspirational to fathers, husbands, mothers and wives who long for the day they would pass this story to their grandchildren.

Finally, Wee Maw begins another of her legendary story-telling nights…"Right weans, what will yie all be doing to bring the little hush fairies into the room so they too may hear the story?" As one, the entire family begins the secretive breath-call to welcome in the good Sìhd (SHEE - Fairy-folk) "Shhhhhhh…"

The children nervously look to the doors and windows to see if the fairies are responding to the call. Again, they collectively breathe aloud, emitting the gentle sound that imitates the legendary Sìhd beating their little silken wings. One more time, the family beckon the fairy folk to enter and share the warmth, "Shhhhhhh…"

Satisfied the *Fae* folk using their invisible cloaks have entered the room, an eerie silence descends upon the clan as shadows and light from the fire reflect and dance around their faces. Everyone brings a collective focus on Wee Maw, the great Seanachaidh of clan Wallace.

Moments pass, till not a sound can be heard. Malcolm and Alain chuckle at the intense concentration of the weans, then slowly, deliberately, almost eerily, everyone turns their gaze from Wee Maw to stare at Malcolm and Alain. The two brothers in turn look at Wee Maw and almost jump out of their skins.

Wee Maw gives them an evn more intense version of the 'look.' Then turns her head away with utter disdain etched on her face and looks back toward the clan, who wait in eager anticipation.

She smiles, then begins her legend in a slow whispering voice... "Now weans, a long time ago... a very, very long time ago, when this ancient land was named Caledonia and Dragons lived in the rivers, great bears and bull-wolves roamed free in the mountains, there lived five ancient tribes. Now weans, these tribes had their quarrels like any other big family, but they always came together as one when threatened by outsiders. And in this story, I'll be telling you of what happened when the biggest army in the whole wide world threatened an invasion of our lands. Far, far away, there was a race of people called Romans, and their King was called a Cesar. Now this Cesar's fella's army was the biggest, fiercest, scariest army that the whole world had ever known. They had fought and conquered almost everyone there ever was, till all that was left to conquer were the five little tribes just north of Hadrian's great big wall... namely, us."

Wee Maw looks at Auld Stephen and smiles. "And our dear cousins the Irish of course." Everyone grins as Wee Maw acknowledges Stephen the elder, who politely smiles and nods back.

Wee Maw continues. "When the five tribes heard these Roman fella's were approaching our land with evil intent, the *Cruinnè* sent their *Artur* and *Aicé Ard Ríghs*' (High kings and Queens) to a very special place where they would plan what to do. And weans, I'll be calling them all from now on, 'The Chiefs'." Once again everyone nods in acknowledgment as Wee Maw continues, "Now these Chiefs would travel to a little place called An t-*Àrd Rígh* (Airdrie) the gathering place of Chiefs. From there they would travel North through the dense Caledonian forest all alone, till they came to small moorland above the Forth River. It was there that they stood before a great round Stone house in the middle of a high moor, called the Hwit raun Ærne (White round house) a very sacred place for our ancestors, where the ancient deities would only allow the Chiefs to meet."

Wee Maw pauses. "Any other who dared to enter that place of special magic was met with… DEATH." The children gasp and huddle closer together. Wee Maw tries hard not to laugh as she continues. "Aye, it was there the chiefs would discuss anything that threatened the peace of the five 'Island' tribes of Caledonia. Now weans, imagine this, the ancient Hwit raun Ærne had an wondrous outside curtain wall, made from the finest of white polished granite, fringed with thousands of white sparkling amethyst. It had a great dome roof completely covered in bleached white human skulls, exceptin' for a wee hole on the very top to let in the moonbeams. And so polished were the outer walls of this fabulous structure, it appeared as though the Hwit raun Ærne was constructed by the fairy folk, made entirely with winter ice. On a full moon night it glimmered and shimmered, like a magical glowing shooting star that had gently fallen to earth for a wee rest." Wee Maw stops for a nip of honey *craitur*, before continuing.

"On a full moon, the sheer moonbeams would flow through the wee hole in the roof and through slim high-wall arrow slits on the outer curtain walls, illuminating the interior of this very mystical place. When the time came for the Chiefs to enter the great roundhouse, each Chief would go through one of five separate arched doors, vaguely illuminated by luminescent swirling emerald green morion and glimmer-dream fairy crystals. The first thing the chiefs would see on entering this special place was black jet walls cloaked with thousands of shimmering purple and white amethyst quartz crystals. They would look up at the ceiling to see embedded dark Sard, Garnet and Cairngorm gems inlaid with countless tiny honey coloured amber and pearl orbs, all hanging on silver-wire threads, appearing as the grandest map of all the stars in heaven you ever did see. Well weans, these magical wee stones were there to help clear the Chiefs minds for them to be making right and proper decisions, for these gemstones created a magical impression on the Chiefs by instilling a feeling in each of them, like they were inside the womb of mother earth.

"The entire place sparkled as though the very universe blessed the *Arturs* or *Aicés* gathered there. For it is known from generations past, aye weans, as far back as bonnie Lilith and the bonnie wee angel Sammy himself, that the Hwit raun Ærne is the mystical magical wedding chamber built by the original *Fae* for the first *Aicé*, Gunn a' Bhar and the first *Artur*, Áeonán mac Áeonán." Wagging her finger, Wee Maw takes a large refreshing drink of her *craitur.* "Now weans, after entering this special place, you would follow a magical path along a floor made from the finest black-polished Jet, inlaid with a beautiful knot-work maze of a million tiny golden specs, reflecting like the still dark water surface in a blue sea dragon's cave. Each *Aicé* or *Artur* in turn would walk the maze to one of five alcoves carved into the inner wall and lined in purest of white marble. The lower half of the alcove is dressed with ornately carved Oghamic scripted human leg and arm-bones, with a purple woolsack cushion to sit upon, creating a most comfortable throne. Each Chief sits securely with their back deep into the alcove to protect them from harm, and none may sit in shadow. They face each other around a great circular stone wheel that lay flat as a table, called the Tablet of Adoration, held aloft by eight pillars of human skulls and leg bones, all steeped in white-lime mortar and inlaid with fine detailed knot-work... Each skull's eye sockets is embedded with white crystals centred with rare heavenly blue sapphire or a blood red Fyvie Ruby.

"So weans, the Chiefs when entering the alcoves each would draw their Brands (swords) and dirks (daggers) then slide the keen blades deep inside a specially carved channel set within the girth of the Tablet of Adoration, with each blade edge and tip safely contained, leaving only the hilts and quillons visible. This was so ordered in the event of a disagreement or insult between the chiefs, each would have their backs covered, which meant it is always best to talk out your differences eye to eye. If it were necessary, the Chiefs would draw their swords from the stone tablet, but only in defence, and only under threat of death as a result of another breaking oath. Aye weans, there would be terrible consequences for any Chief who drew their weapon with malice from the sanctity of the tablet. Their fate would be instant delivery to a better life by the remaining Chiefs." Wee Maw has another sup of her drink.

"Aye, The Tablet of Adoration... Some say this great stone tablet was used for a human sacrifice, known as the 'Gift' by the flesh-eating *Cruinnè* healers, the Duine lighiche (Medicine man) or Bean míochnú" (medicine-woman)," Wee Maw pauses with a wry smile, "But before the message from the Gift could be read, the Duine lighiche and Bean míochnú would drink the first drops of blood from the gifted ones, then after much life-force blood-letting and the final reading being satisfactory, the Duine lighiche and Bean míochnú would eat the wee fella's brains." Wee Maw stops for a moment chuckling quietly to herself as the children huddle ever closer together, mortified at the thought of human sacrifice and cannibalism. She takes another long sip of her favoured *craitur* then continues... "The tablet of Adoration is inlaid with the finest of gemstones, moonstones and has a latticework of deep-cut interweaving channels of the most sublimely crafted knot-work. Oghamic script is carved into the great tablet forming a many-layered maze of endless words of magic. The tablet is also bevelled and channelled from the centre to let blood from the gifted ones run down to the edges then over the lip towards the floor, where five churns collect the life force. For it is said weans, that whatever way the human blood from the sacrificial gift would run through the channels, the ancients would interpret then accurately prophesy the future." Pausing for another sup, Wee Maw says nonchalantly, "Then the Duine lighiche and Bean míochnú would eat the rest of the vitals of the gifted one to celebrate, and add another bonnie skull and fine set o' bones collected for the special place... Then there came one fine day in particular, a Duine lighiche and Bean míochnú caught a wee Roman scout fella. After he gifted his blood, liver and spleen, the signs said the five tribes should prepare for war, as these Romans were bringing us a terrible thing called civilization, and these Roman fella's sure intended us to have it, whether we wanted it or not."

Gentle Andrew interrupts, "Is the roundhouse still standing today Granny?"

Wee Maw refrains from giving such a sensitive wean as Andrew 'the look'. She replies graciously, "Aye Andrew, some of it. The Hwit Raun Ærne fell to disrepair and ruin soon after Christianity arrived, and didn't those wee Christian fella's just no' go and strip it clean of its beautiful ornamentation. But what they were really after was the Anam Alain (Beautiful Spirit) that it held within its walls. They Romans n' Christians held a similar belief to our Anam Alain, but they called it the 'Numen' That's a belief which holds that spirits of great energy inhabit all places, objects and living things. These Christian fella's thought to steal away the Anam Alain contained within the Hwit raun Ærne to be blessing a Catholic church called the Casa Candida near Bo'ness. Similar to one still standing away down in Galloway, but the foundation remains are still there to be seen. The local folk called it the stane hoose on the moor and there's a wee toun there now called Stanehoosemuir." Sitting back in her throne, Wee Maw smiles with glee when seeing the illuminated faces of the children hanging on her every word. She has another wee sip of the craitur then continues with the legend... "Now, as yie know, a Roman King was called Cesar, but our king is called, Artur Àrd Rígh, which means the Great Bear. Our Kings were titled by the same name as this wonderful beast, hence the name Artur. So weans, WHAT ARE OUR KINGS CALLED?"

"*ARTUR*," came the reply from the enthralled audience.

"Just makin' sure yiez are still listening," says Wee Maw as she laughs then picks up her large flagon and swallows from it copiously. Malcolm appears a little concerned.

"That's no' honey milk she's drinking, that's pure honey *craitur*?"

"Awe, Feck," whispers Alain shaking his head in resignation.

After many moments of silence, other than the sound of Wee Maw swallowing her precious *craitur*, she looks at everyone. "My that bainne mheala (Honey milk) has a very agreeable twang to it this night."

Alain and Malcolm look at each other and hope.

"Now where was I?" enquires Wee Maw. "Och aye, now I remember. These Roman fellas had a name for our five Kings, apparently they called them the *Artur* Pen Dragii, meaning the War Bears of the Dragon tribes..."

Gentle Andrew enquires once more, "Is that why the Wallace family have a blue dragon on our coat of arms father?"

Malcolm looks at his son then glances at Wee Maw with trepidation.

"Sorry Granny." says gentle Andrew.

"It is." replied Wee Maw. She smiles graciously at the delicate Andrew. Again there is no 'look' for him on his birthday.

Wee Maw resumes the story. "When the *Artur*'s and *Aicé*s were but weans themselves, they were taught about the mythical dragons who lived in the great rivers of Scotland, like the Avalon, Solway, Dee, Forth and Clyde, and how these dragons became their tribes totemic symbols. All of the *Aicé*s descendants' now carry a dragon symbol on their armour, shields and Flags to this very day, including that there English King who flies the Black dragon wie' bad intention."

The room fills with an approving hum of understanding as Wee Maw goes on. "Now the five Chiefs each had a different coloured dragon flag representing them, and that's what the Romans first saw when they faced our ancient armies. The Romans didn't mind fightin' the men, but they sure feared fightin' our women... and what did these fine Roman fellas call our bonnie women chiefs?"

"*AICÉ* PENN DRAGII..." is the tumultuous response.

Wee Maw grins as she takes another long drink of 'milk'. Having satisfied her thirst, she picks up the narrative. "Each *Aicé* Penn Dragii was bonded or wedded with an *Artur*, and weans, these proud women were renowned warriors in their own right. The *Aicé* Penn Dragii or sometimes called the *Aicé* Bahn-Sìhd, the warrior Queens of the *fae*... were blessed with supernatural skills of magic. And so respected were they, that only the *Aicé* and her Bahn-Ceitherne (Bannkern-Young warrior Women) were allowed to train the sons and the daughters of the Chiefs from each of the tribes of Scotland and Ireland. Now, as it was in those days, only the *Aicé*s could practice their young wards in the arts of the black smithy, poet, musician and songster. Equally important, the young warriors were also taught how to use the healing properties of the greatest cathedral of Magda Mòr… Mother nature. The warrior *Aicé*s taught their wards the importance of music and poetry as a way of recording history for future generations, until one day, each ward would grow to be a warrior-poet. For if you don't know where you come from, then how can you know where you are going? And remember this too weans, we're all simply the present echoes of our ancestors past. Anyways, all through their training, the young warriors were taught in the arts of war, and there was no' the stupidity of today where only the men are allowed to fight, what a waste of talent that is…"

She pauses to shout, "More *Craitur* if yie please *tá*,"

Her flagon refilled, she swallows more of her precious nectar, then continues. "Now weans, the *Aicé*s all had titled names passed through the generations as a mark of position. Down in the realm of Galloway in the heart of the Wolf and Wildcat country, she was known as the Devorguilla. In the eastern lands of auld Loth, the Gwydoddan. (Gidodann). In the Northwest, the Scáthach, (Skatha) in the southwest, her sister, the Aofin, (AE-Finn) and from here, your great granny many times past… the Morríaghan." (Moree-ahann-Morgyn).

"These *Aicé*s were renowned, loved and respected by our own people, but feared more than hell by our enemies. Even more feared than our *Arturs*' for these *Aicé*s trained all the finest warriors of Ireland and Scotland, from Cúchulainn to Ossian of Coehd (Awe-see-an of Coe) Colm Nuadha, Aengaba of the Norde and Conn Cétchathach of a hundred battles."

Suddenly, Wee Maw motions her hands like a fairy godmother, rippling her fingers gently with the glowing fire behind her, the motion cast a wondrous spell in the imagination of her eager audience. "Then there were the mystic mortal warriors that the enemies of the *Arturs* and *Aicés* feared most of all, known as the Companions of the Deities. In peace, they were much loved healers, but in war, they of all our people were the most feared by our enemies."

"Who were they, Granny?" enquires gentle Andrew, absorbed by the story.

Wee Maw replies, "The *Garda Céile Aicé*... Guardians of the *Aicé*."

All the children sigh, "Ooh..."

"Many have heard of the Druids of old, but few have ever heard of the *Cruinnè* Breitheamh Rígh or *Garda Céile Aicé*. The ancient Judges and Faith Guardians of the *Aicé*."

Wee Maw stoops for another nip of *craitur* then continues. "The *Garda Céile Aicé* are supreme warriors born from the loins of the Tuatha Dé *Cruinnè-cè*. Some say they're immortals who willingly give up their eternal existence for the perpetual life of Magda Mòr. Now listen to me carefully weans and take heed, the *Céile Aicé* still walk with us today, and they are watchin' yiez all... even now."

The elders all smile as the children look around the room while pulling their little brats tightly around their shoulders.

Their attention is brought back to focus when Wee Maw says, "Heed me well all o' you wee pixies... Listen carefully to the music in my voice and yie will hear the song o' the name Wallace."

The children are a totally mesmerized and enthralled audience.

"Now," says Wee Maw as she stretches her arms and stands her old aching bones up from the chair. "I must be going to the wee woman's hoose. Girls, will you attend to me this night? For I cannot be seeing very well in the dark, and I don't want to be havin' a wee accident."

Wee Maw and the "girls" wander toward the door, when suddenly, in the dim flickering candle and firelight, she startles everyone by quickly turning to glare at them all. She looks around ominously at the kinfolk who still hang on her every word. "And then…" she says, "When I come back, I'll tell you of a greatest battle of the *Céile Aicé*. Then you'll begin to understand why such a wee realm as ours can stand fast against giants, and them self same giants bein' so scared for their very souls that they run away home never to come back."

As Granny Wallace, the women and the girls leave, only the girls closest to Wee Maw can hear her chuckle to herself while everyone else takes the opportunity to relax.

Malcolm stands up and stretches his weary bones, for he had not slept since his long journey from Edinburgh with Alain. He reaches towards the ceiling and groans. "Dear Christ, my aching feckin back."

Gentle Andrew exclaims. "Oh Dá you just cursed in the hoose,"

Suddenly there's a blood-curdling scream from the back of the room. Startled, Malcolm and Alain quickly spin round to see the cause of such a commotion, but they see nothing untoward.

"What was that scream?" demands Malcolm, but he's met with silence. He enquires firmly, "Who screamed?" He looks around the dimly lit room when he notices William pointing at Wee John.

"I cannae tell a lie uncle," says William. "It was him…" Malcolm sees Wee John holding a hand over his eye, which is watering profusely. When Wee John notices everyone staring at him, he instantly points at William sitting innocently by his side.

"It wasn't me Dá," cries Wee John. "It was him, he did it… William stuck his big feckin finger right into me feckin eye. Dá, I think I'm blinded."

Gentle Andrew cries out once more. "Dá, Wee John has just cursed in the hoose too."

Malcolm calls out to his eldest son. "Malcolm óg, you're the eldest, keep your cousins in line before Wee Maw comes back, for yie know what your granny and your mother are like when they're no' happy."

William quips much to the amusement of everyone. "Worse than any Roman."

"Now settle down you weans, or yiez will be getting the back o' me hand of the side o' yer heads," growls Malcolm.

"What are you boys talking about?" enquires Wee Maw as she and the others return.

On her way back to her throne, she notices something about Wee John that she can't quite fathom. "And what's wrong with you Wee John?" enquires Wee Maw.

"Nothin' Granny."

Wee Maw notices tears streaming down his cheek. "Well why are you crying you stupid boy, get over here and sit down beside the bonnie Ròsinn… now!"

All the children snigger as Wee John gasps at Wee Maw's chastisement.

"Now where was I?" she enquires.

Gentle Andrew reminds her. "You were going to tell us about the Romans and the great battles of the *Céile Aicé* Granny."

"Good boy," replies Wee Maw. "Well then," says Wee Maw as she settles once more in her throne.

"These Roman folk were so busy sorting out the tribes o' the English, they didn't really bother us up here very much at all.

Not till word came from more blood-feed predictions from our *Duine lighiche* and *Bean míochnú* that those Romans had sorted out the tribes o' England and were heading up here to sort us out next. Ah but…" exclaims Wee Maw, "our auld folks knew different, for they were prepared. The Chiefs had already met at the Stane-hoose on the moor and planned what they'd do to the Romans when they came a' rolling over the Border marches. Then weans, there followed many battles the likes of which the world had never seen afore. So hard were they fought that a mighty Roman called Titus Fulvius Aelius Hadrianus Antoninus Augustus Pius… or plain Antoninus to you weans, built a great sod wall from Blackness in the east and all the way across Scotland to Dun Briton here in the west to gain a foothold in this the auld country."

Wee Maw calls out, "*Craitur* if yie please?" while expressing her unbridled desire with outstretched hands.

"Anyways," she says, "it all started to go wrong for the Romans when they got here. Aye, they stayed fine and peaceful for a wee while, but they soon started pickin' fights here, fightin' wee battles there, a bit like those two, William and Wee John. But those Romans just kept on a' nippin' and annoyin' everybody, till it all came to a head one day and the Romans wanted to fight the five tribes all together. Well weans, your ancestors were more than happy to oblige. And so it was, at a battle at the Alt Cluid Goram o' Dun Briton or Dunbarton as some call it, where our bonnie *Aicé* Morríaghan had her main fort, that's where the *Aicé*s armies fought the Romans and showed them what it was all about to get into a real fight. At the same time, away to the east, the *Artur*s and the *Cruinnè* men fought the Romans at a wee place the Romans called Mons Graupius (Groopius). But we call it Rossie Law. Now the *Cruinnè* didn't like it at all that the Romans had built this big wall with Glen blocker forts all along the length o' that great wall, and with it coming right up to our front doors too. Even to this day, we've never fathomed if it was to keep us in or keep them out? Well, our ancient folk bided their time to be fighting the big battle, and so it was that the Romans kept on adding bits on to this great wall, and with us standing on each side of it, their plan appeared to our ancestors that it wasn't really a very good idea at all..." Suddenly Wee Maw begins coughing, then she pauses for a moment as though in a state of shock.

Alain and Malcolm look at each other, slightly concerned.

Gentle Andrew enquires, "What happened next granny?"

Wee Maw shakes her head as though coming out of a trance, then continues... "Aye Andrew... Well, our kinfolk just kept attacking the Romans from both sides of the wall thank you very much. But instead of getting the hint and leaving, the Romans sent for more soldiers and the war with the five tribes only got worse, mainly for the Romans I might add. Finally the Chiefs decided that the time was right and took up the offer to fight the Romans at Rossie Law away up in Moray country, near to where the biggest army of the Romans were camped under the command of another Roman general called Gnaeus Julius Agricola. This Agricola fella wanted to make a name for himself where the Romans came from, so he prepared a final battle with the five tribes. The Romans called us Caledonians, Picts, Attacotti, Novantae, Britons and many other strange names. But we just called ourselves *Cruinnè* for Scotland is the home of the female deity of the *Cruinnè-cè* race of peoples... and who is that then weans?" Wee Maw puts her hand to her ear to catch the reply.

They all shout collectively... "Tuatha DÉ Cruinne-cè..."

Wee Maw smiles. "That's who we were weans, and under

the skin, that's who we still are… faithful to the tri-goddess, mother earth, Mother Nature and all the Wee Maws on earth… And don't yiez ever be forgetting it."

Everyone laughs then they all shout back. "NAW WEE MAW."

Wee Maw frowns then continues. "And the Irish are the home of the masculine deities, AND WHO ARE THEY?" Once more cupping her ear.

Excitedly, Wee John calls out all on his own, "Tuatha DÉ Cruinne-cè."

Slowly and deliberately, Wee Maw gives Wee John 'the look' making him feel the flushing of his cheeks with embarrassment.

After a moments silence, everyone calls out as one, "Tuatha DÉ Cruinne-cè."

Again everyone laughs, including Wee John. Wee Maw pauses to refill her cup with more of the *craitur*. "Well our bonnie leader o' the *Cruinnè* up at Rossie Law was a heroic wee Chief called, *Artur* Calg ua' Co'Cosdh (Kal-g'ow cocos) which in the auld tongue means, 'The forest bear of the silver blade.' Now Calg ua' Co'Cosdh came from the old Kingdom of Angus, the land of Angels, and he brought with him an army that was said to number ten thousand or more of the finest *Cruinnè* warriors of all the five tribes. But auld Agricola thought he would win, as he had thirty thousand men and four legions in reserve. Meanwhile, at the fort of Dun Brithon just down the road…" Wee Maw suddenly stops for another drink. William whispers to Wee John, "Ah think Wee Maw is getting drunk for I've no' heard this version o' the story before?" Wee John replies, "Me neither, this one is the best yet." Wee Maw struggles on with her stirring legend… "Near to Dun Briton, our ancient clan seat and capital of the kingdom of Strath Chluaidh (Strathclyde) the Romans had another force of ten thousand men gathered and all ready to attack us. What the Romans didn't know was that Scáthach, Devorguilla, Gwydoddan and Aofin had come to meet Morríaghan with their own wee armies at the ready. Now the *Aicé*s had a combined force of six thousand warriors. Each *Aicé* had two male and two female guardian bodyguards, sworn to give their lives willingly for their *Aicé*. Each Guardian in turn had two young women and two young men called Ceitherne (Kern) and so on and so forth, where the matriarchal and patriarchal qualities combined to ensure that those in their state of youth would always find a place in the *Cruinnè* society, not only in peace, but also in war."

"Did the women fight too?" enquires gentle Andrew.

Malcolm replies, "Aye boy they did, with equal passion and as much courage as any man of legendary Sparta."

Wee Maw coughs abruptly. Malcolm whispers. "Sorry, granny."

She glares at Malcolm, then her eyes soften. "As I was saying weans, the *Aicé*s Guardians had painted on their shields and flags, either the image of the Blue Dragon, or a naked faceless Goddess, the *Aicé*. When the *Céile Aicé* guardians formed around the *Aicé* they became the body or 'Wall of the Aicé' and each individual alternately held a highly polished bronze or silver shield, with the image of the faceless Goddess or Dragon facing forward. The tips of each their shields touched the ground between the feet of each warrior, and the shield crest rode across the bridge of their nose. The guardians in turn alternated with male and female archers, stone and lime ball slingers, arrow, hot-spear and long-sword warriors all standing close behind them. That was the Wall of the *Aicé*, the finest of the *Cruinnè* warrior caste."

Wee Maw begins coughing again, but this time it's prolonged. She raises her skirts and wipes her mouth, then looks at everyone.

For a moment all are concerned for Wee Maw, as she appears very tired. She sups the dregs from her jug, as her enthusiasm returns to the telling of her legend, as is that of the avid listeners imagination. She sits a moment gazing at the fire; as though she is witnessing the scene before her. "Ah, but it was a lovely sight to behold. The armies of the *Aicé*, some six thousand strong, all brought together to fight a common enemy. The *Aicé*s deployed their forces east o' Dun Briton to face the Roman wall when news came to them that the young warrior sons and daughters of Erin's Chiefs were being led by two Irish *Aicé*s, Carmán and Scotia. The Erinnach *Aicé*s had brought with them their dreaded slingers and fletchers. They disembarked from Aofins' fleet and alighted the waiting chariots or doubled up horseback with Devorguilla and Gwydoddan's horse-warriors, then moved fast to get in behind the south side of the Roman wall. Legend has it..." says Wee Maw as she points at Auld Stephen who smiles back ever so politely. "Those fine Irish slingers could put a water-stone through the back of a man's skull at one hundred cloth-yards, and our *Cruinnè* Fletchers who used but a strip of leather to loose their arrows could pierce the back of the same man's head with a long-fletch arrow before that same man hit the ground." Wee Maw continues enthusiastically. "The *Aicé*s moved the *Cruinnè* armies through the thick early morn mist close to each side of the Roman wall, without being seen by any of the Roman sentries. Then many groups of thirty of our strongest toughest *Cruinnè* warriors ran silently up to the wall, turned with their backs to lean firmly against it with their shields facing out at a slight off-angle. Another twenty warriors ran up and jumped on the first group's shields, climbing up to stand on their shoulders. Then another lithe group of ten warriors would repeat the run, and climb up the human ladder. Then finally, another five of the fleetest warriors would climb to the top, forming a perfect human pyramid..."

This happened all along the great wall. When all was in place, the lower guardians tilted their shields fully outward to face the remaining fleet-foot warriors of the *Aicés*. These Fleetfoot began pace run and time themselves till they saw the early morning sun break through the mist and reflect the Goddess off the polished shields of the guardians. Suddenly the signal horns of war were blown and battle cries went up from thousands of young voices. It was then the fleetfoot ran like the wind."

Wee Maw licks her lips. "My, I'm getting thirsty, More *craitur* if yie please."

Supping more inspiration, she continues with her story. "Startled by the noise of the war-horns, the Roman sentries sharp eyes scanned for anything that moved, but no matter how hard they looked, they never saw the armies of the *Aicé*, even as the Fleetfoot were fast bearing down on the heavily armoured guardians. At another signal, the slingers and fletchers launched thousands of fiery missiles over the Roman wall and into the camps where the Roman soldiers rested and slept. Simultaneously, the fleetfoot sprang onto the shields of the guardians, quickly climbed the pyramid and leapt up onto the parapets of the wall with their short blades flashing like swords of light. Long darts and spearheads were hot in the hands of the courageous youngblood warriors, with their fast and furious quenching in fresh Roman blood. Aye, it was some sight right enough," says Wee Maw. "Scáthachs' *Cruinnè* armies fought like young demons. The warriors of the *Céile Aicé* and Ceitherne all but destroyed the Roman legions at the western end o' Antoninius wall."

Wee Maw pauses for yet another sup o the *craitur*. "And then," she says with a slight slur in her voice, "the true prize for the *Aicé*s lay before them; and that prize me bonnie weans, was the severed heads off all the Romans. For these warrior women and their young Ceitherne liked nothing better than head-hunting to adorn the walls, houses and trees around their Duns."

Yawning, Wee Maw shakes her head. There is another audible gasp of horror from all the children. Wee Maw tries not to laugh as she studies all the faces around the room. "And for the special big heads," she says, "the *Aicé*s would have them steamed, limed and then adorned with the finest pearls, Gold, silver and jewellery, for it was known the skulls of the leaders o' their enemies made fine Grailach Ceann mòr (Grayloch kyown more - mystical drinking bowls made of skulls) and their skins made really soft garments, shield covers, horse-saddles, sword belts and the likes. And wouldn't it be such a lovely surprise for their men-folk to see when they return home, that their women and bahn Ceitherne remain as equals to them in both courage and valour."

A murmur of happy defiance fills the room as Wee Maw continues "Meanwhile, up at Rossie Law in the East o' the realm, the *Cruinnè* army led by Calg ua' Co'Cosdh, appears to retreat after inflicting heavy casualties on the Romans, but also at great cost to the *Cruinnè* too. Calg au' Co'Cosdh led his warriors back into the black forests of high Caledon where the Roman legions gave chase, but they Romans were running into a well-planned trap. The *Cruinnè* were now fighting in their home ground and knew the Romans couldn't employ their tactics or fantastical war machines that had won them most of the known world. Eventually the Roman's losses became too much so the Romans fell into a forced retreat. The army of the *Aicé* dealt the Roman legions a terrible blow at Alt Cluid Goram, and without their generals and leaders, many of the surviving Romans came over and settled with us. Folk like their fierce archers and horsewomen from Persia joined with us, they were part of a legion called a maniple and had wondrous names for themselves, like the Wings of Sagittarius, or gait of the Wolf..."

Then there was a particular maniple of women cavalry who left the Romans and joined with our *Aicé*s. They were called the Sámi-Skolotti, and if I mind right, these dark skinned lassies were blue-marked on their faces and on the muscles of the body just as our own people were, with their long jet-black hair, almond eyes and reputedly very bonnie they were too. Legend has it they left the Roman legions and joined with us in our war till the remaining Romans eventually treated for peace, which the *Aicé*s granted. Morríaghan ordered her divine Ceitherne daughters to meet with the Romans at the gates of the Antoninius wall, but she sent the feared *Garda Céile Aicé* instead, not greatly noted for their negotiating skills I might add. Once they attended a parley, they promptly slaughtered all the Roman peace negotiators. Aye weans, for that is the way of the *Garda Céile Aicé*."

Wee Maw pauses then grins. "The *Garda Céile Aicé* did not tolerate anyone who would threaten *THEIR Aicé*… More medicinal *craitur* if yie please."

After a long slow drink, Wee Maw continues. "So, the Romans in the east retreated from the Caledon fastness, but the Cruinnè kept up skirmishing tactics, never giving the Roman legions any peace till the Romans had no any choice but to flee across the border marches and back to their forts in England. But Morríaghan and her sister Aicés were relentless in pursuit. Each time the Romans approached the wall to negotiate, they were attacked and killed. Both Calg ua' Co'Cosdh, Scáthach and Morríaghan never ever slackened their pace. Day after day, night and day they attacked the Romans, till all of the Roman fellas eventually gave up and retreated to safety behind another big wall they called the Vallum Aelium (Hadrian's Wall) where the border marcher lands now are." Wee Maw yawns once more. "Weans, I'm getting very tired, It's been a long day and me self-inflicted medication is havin' a serious affect."

Suddenly she calls out. "Quick Uliann, fetch your granny's special churn, from away over in that corner... quickly."

Ulianns' face drops. "Awe naw granny, no' now, no' the churn."

"Quickly," exclaims Wee Maw with urgency. Malcolm puts his head in his hands. Alain and Mharaidh appear confused, and slightly bewildered as Uliann quickly rushes and fetches back the churn to her granny where she quickly places the churn on the floor, over which Wee Maw squats.

Sitting on the bucket, Wee Maw calls out loudly. "You men and you weans, git and turn around and face the doors, and don't you be a'listenin'."

Everyone stands up and faces the doors.

Gentle Andrew naively enquires. "What's she doing?"

William replies with a chortle..."Ah, I think she's pishin' in the bucket."

"She's what?" exclaims gentle Andrew.

Wee John sniggers. "I think she's just pissed on the brat where you were sittin'."

William, Malcolm and others who overhear the discourse, shake in silent laughter, especially at the look of shock on gentle Andrew's face.

Everyone tries not to laugh out loud at his distress, as well as hearing Wee Maw's noisy functions.

Wee Maw growls. "Yiez are listnin' ah know yiez are a' listenin'."

Everyone except Andrew, are almost peeing themselves trying not to laugh. Alain replies as he wipes tears from his face. "It's all right Maw, we can't hear a thing."

A mortified gentle Andrew whispers. "But I can hear her Uncle Alain, and I can hear *EVERYTHING*."

Alain sniggers upon hearing Andrew's emphasis. He says, "Me too Andrew, I'm sorry son, but I lied to yie.

"WHAT…" exclaims gentle Andrew.

With a sigh of relief and having finished her ablutions, Wee Maw stands up and straightens her long skirts. "Yiez can all turn around now."

As the men and boys turn, they see all the women looking very sheepish, with red flushed faces of embarrassment. All except Wee Maw, who is now back in her throne supping from her comfort jug of *craitur*.

Uliann, now holding the bucket, enquires, "What shall I do with the churn, granny?"

There's a moment's silence before Wee Maw replies. "What churn?"

Uliann begins blushing bright red and looks to the roof rafters, she doesn't know where else too look.

Margret says, "Here, Uliann, I'll take it."

She takes the overflowing churn from Uliann, rushes outside, empties it and comes straight back.

Gentle Andrew, who has regained his composure, calls out, "So where does the name Wallace come from, granny?"

Wee Maw replies. "The Guardians of the *Aicé* me boy, the *Céile Aicé*, Wall of the *Aicé* son?"

Gentle Andrew still does not grasp the answer.

Wee Maw sees this in his expression. "Right Andrew, here's another example especially for you me darlin' boy. When the Romans first came here and wanted to build their wall, we just let them get on with it, no problems there. It wasn't till they wanted to enslave us; that's when all the trouble really began. So our auld kinfolks carried the image of our Aicé and put it against their wall every time they fought back, eventually the bodyguard of the Aicé became known as the Wall-Aicé."

Gentle Andrew stammers. "But…"

Wee Maw continues, "I know, I know son." says Wee Maw "How did the guardian's actions relate to the name of our family of the Wallace. Well its like this Andrew, the guardians came from many different clans, families, tribes, call it what you will, but after we had driven the Romans back and away behind what is now called Hadrian's wall, and we still don't know why they built that wall, I've never known of an army yet that built a great defensive wall and then stand in front of it…? Anyways, the *Cruinnè* became so fanatical about never letting up their onslaught on the Romans; the *Garda Céile Aicé* would carry the image of the *Aicé* to Hadrians' wall emblazoned on their shields. By this time veteran Romans saw them coming, they knew what was about to happen, does that help you to understand a wee bitty better now me boy? Am I painting a picture in your bonnie wee head?"

Gentle Andrew nods and smiles knowingly as Wee Maw continues… "So, ma bonnie weans, the Roman army went back to hide behind that wall they had built by a César called Hadrian, apparently to keep us out of somewhere we didn't want to go anyway. But it must have suited both the Romans and us too, for then we had a long time of peace between us. After a while many guardians of the Wall *Aicé* wedded, and as I described earlier, it was those men and women who formed the personal guard around the *Aicé*. And so it came to pass that the sons and daughters of the Guardians became known as the Wallace, just like many other names from Scotland's past where the description of the folks duty became the family name."

Putting his hand in the air Gentle Andrew exclaims. "Like the name Stewart from the King's steward Granny or Wardrop, keeper o' the King's clothes? Or even Hunter, someone who hunts the Royal Lands."

Wee Maw smiles, "That's it ma boy, though there was one Roman everyone here especially liked, including the *Cruinnè* and he was a legendary war leader, but that was likely only because his mother was the *Cruinnè Aicé* Morríaghan. Legend has it this big fella was a Britonic Breitheamh Warrior known as Coroticus Aurilialis... Guardian to Ceretic *Ard Rígh*. I'm no' saying we are directly descended from him, but rumour has it... and the sound o' the name his a wee bitty familiar too." Wee Maw pauses. "That's another story."

Wee John chimes. "That's not what the old books in the priory say Granny,"

Wee Maw scowls. "Sometimes history doesn't need to be noble and learned Wee John. Sometimes these educated people have their heads so far up their own chutes it stops them seeing the obvious."

Everyone laughs, except gentle Andrew, who whispers to Wee John. "What's a chute cousin John?"

Wee John looks at gentle Andrew and shakes his head innocently, he explains in a whisper, "Arsehole!"

Leaning his head back, gentle Andrew looks at Wee John with an expression of absolute disbelief, then he bursts into tears.

Everyone looks round to see what's wrong, wondering why gentle Andrew is weeping. Wee Maw notices the tears and kindly beckons for him to come to her. He leans his head on her shoulder sobbing. She says, "There, there, me bonnie boy," as she pats his back and gently strokes his hair, comforting the upset child, Wee Maw enquires, "What's the matter with you, Andrew? Was the story too scary for yie?"

Gentle Andrew explains, "Naw granny, it was no' that. It is Wee John, he cursed at me, granny, he called me an arsehole."

"LITTLE JOHN WALLACE..." growls Wee Maw while delivering him a very serious 'look'. "I'll deal with you later."

"But..." splutters Wee John.

Wee Maw glances at Ròsinn, who understands.

"SEAN..." commands Ròsinn, giving him the first real broadside of her new found 'look', William whispers to Wee John amidst his angst. "You're fucked now brother... twice over."

Wee John mumbles, "Awe feck..." Wee Maw continues her story as gentle Andrew coories into the warmth of her bosom.

"So weans, always remember this. Some of these people who write history will scoff at this Legend. But it is just that, a legend. Sometimes things are that simple. The important thing to remember is the golden thread o' truth in the story. Many things you have heard this night you may not understand now, but they will grow inside you and you'll understand it more as you grow older... and wiser. We Wallace never ever came from one family bloodline, but we come from the finest warriors of old Strathclyde, from a time when men and women had pride and faith in the Breitheamh Rígh and the Tuatha De Cruinnè-cè warriors, and you young men of the Wallace, always remember the folk from whence you came. You must always protect the women of your blood, your mothers, sisters, wives, daughters, even us grannies... for we are your Aicés. Especially you Wee John, as you will be a father yourself soon, I expect."

Wee John grins at the thought of trying, and is promptly elbowed in the ribs by a blushing Ròsinn.

"I'm tired..." says Wee Maw, "but before I retire, you weans remember this. If yiez think the legend fits snugly in your wee heads, then there's an auld expression to comfort you when you think the entire world is against you... *'Many are chosen, few are Pict.'*"

Everyone grins, appreciating Wee Maw's analogy.

"Come girls," says Wee Maw. "The boys can be getting the morning scran prepared for us while we retire."

As Wee Maw retires to her chamber, Margret says, "Right, boys, you heard your Granny." Mharaidh moves to carry a sleeping Caoilfhinn up the stairs then she stops, looks back and winks at Alain. He understands that particular 'Look'.

He says in a flurry, "BOYS, you heard your mother..." All the boys and men moan and groan, but they get on with their chores.

Alain walks over to Mharaidh. "Ma darlin', I'll be up soon after me and the boys have cleaned up the place."

Mharaidh and Alain kiss passionately. She smiles as Alain holds her hand, he gazes at such evident pleasure now glowing in Mharaidhs' face from both of them experiencing this very fine and special day. A day they could not have foreseen nor dared wish for has finally arrived at the Ach ne Feàrna Fortalice.

The Fisher Wives

Long after everyone has retired, Malcolm, Alain, Auld Stephen and William, sit supping a nip o' Wee Maw's honey-dew *craitur* in front the great peat and log fire.

The midnight hour passes as they all sit close to the radiant warmth, relaxing after a long tiring day, but William's head is full of questions after Wee Maw's telling of the family Legend. He enquires, "Uncle?"

"Aye," replied Malcolm. "What is it you're asking me?"

"The story of the *Aicé*s, is it really true?"

Smiling at Alain and Auld Stephen, Malcolm thinks a moment. "Aye, well, most of it is true as far as family legend recalls it."

"Aye, I know that," confirms William. "But is it true the way Wee Maw tells it? An auld priest once told me up in Paisley that it was a fella called Aeongis, a descendant from the hero-king Caratacus who defeated the Romans at Alt Cluid Goram. And I read that it was the tribes of the Pictii Pretani, Selgovae and the Novantae o' Galloway who gathered on the Ochil Marlynn plains o' Camelon that attacked the Romans way out on the west end of the Antoninus Wall, no' the army o' women and weans led by our *Aicé*?"

"Jaezuz!" exclaims Auld Stephen upon hearing William's statement; Malcolm splutters out his *craitur*.

"Feck," cries Malcolm "eh well, you had better be asking your father about that William."

Alain laughs quietly to himself.

William thinks a moment then enquires. "Dá...?"

Alain replies amused, but dreading the same question. "Aye, William, what is it son?"

"The legend, it sounds a wee bit stretched this time by Granny. Every time I've heard her tell it, she always misses a bit or adds a bit, but this time she said the *Cruinnè* used shields with a naked woman with no face features adorning them? Then she said there was a Roman wall made out of sod stretching all the way across the centre of Scotland? And that's where we get our name... a big sod bank and naked woman with no face features?"

Glancing at Malcolm, Alain nods, confirming he'll continue with an answer... of sorts. "William me boy, surely you must have noticed that Wee Maw loves her special medicine?"

"Aye Dá, she sure does." William replies with a chuckle.

"Well, yie know too that legends are loosely based on true stories passed down from each generation, give or take a wee bit o' imaginative stretch to be filling in the blanks."

Malcolm and Auld Stephen laugh out loud hearing Alain's description as the self-appointed learned one, and it's not really the answer they expected from him. Auld Stephen leans in close to Malcolm and whispers. "This should be good."

"Could be better entertainment than Wee Maw's legend."

William continues with a flummoxed pitch in his voice. "Dá, when I was being educated by the priests in Dunipace, Dundee and Paisley, they had me reading many books in the Latin and all about Roman history. And in all the books I ever read, they said the Romans won the battle of Mons Graupius. Never have I ever read, heard nor seen any mention of a battle at Alt Cluid Goram on the Clyde."

"Son, I'll tell you this, academic history is what happens when actual facts are manipulated then retold by liars to serve the purpose o' their feckin paymasters.The Romans were maybe one of the biggest empires that have ever been on this old earth and they've defeated most, including many other great rival empires. The Romans even conquered the power-ful tribes of ancient England and that's a challenge on its own for the best of any army. You name it William; the Romans defeated it. But also Roman cruelty to their own people knew no bounds for any failure, and they didn't suffer defeat easily."

"Aye," quips Auld Stephen. "They defeated everyone except us fine Irish and you fellas over here."

Alain pauses for a drink of Wee Maw's *craitur.* "Now William, imagine yourself as that Roman general called Agricola and being in charge of the finest military legions and war equipment ever seen. Then you get the shit kicked right out of yie by a horde o' painted people on the side of a wind swept hill somewhere in Scotland, and them there same natives being so naked as well?"

Auld Stephen whispers to Malcolm. "Alain definitely has the educational touch about him."

Giving Malcolm and Stephen his version of the 'Look' Alain continues. "And as for Alt Cluid Goram, losing that battle gets even worse for any Roman general to try and explain away why the Romans in the west were all but slaughtered by our *Aicé*s and their youngsters. Yie have to remember son, that the Romans were a brutal patriarchal society whereas we are matriarchal, which is a society that's a wee bit more relaxed about everything. Now think about it. How would you attempt to explain to a big hairy-arsed Cesar that you failed in your empire buildin' task and lost the last of his auxiliary legions on this island in a futile battle against wee blue naked women and youngsters? And on the same day, you lose the bulk of your northern army to naked men and boys in another battle just along the Roman road."

William enquires, "Is that what they call propaganda Dá?"

Alain smiles. "It is son, aye. For as it's not that all things in history books are lies, it's just that not all things are true. You have to remember that greedy ambitious Kings' and religious empires can only swell their numbers if they impress feeble-minded masses with false rhetoric and a biased account of history. That's so those same famishin' bastards can strike fear into hearts o' those same masses by appearing knowl-edgeable and undefeatable. For sure, it's most certain they wont impress anyone if they tell the whole truth about their failures and defeats, that's if they mention them at all."

William asks, "Then how can we trust anything we read in books?"

Alain shakes his head, almost in despair. "Yie can't son, it's that feckin simple. Yie trust in your own instinct."

William thinks on his father's answer, then replies with slight uncertainty mumbling, "Right…"

Alain reaches for another wee nip of granny's special *crai-tur*, for he could feel he was getting through to his son. "Ach William, what I mean is, I just want you to be especially considering that everything in a history book or a religious codex, no matter how well it's presented, is nothing other than unqualified hearsay."

Alain looks into the glowing fire, ever more pleased with himself and thoroughly enjoying this new experience of conversing with his son, so warming his heart and soul this night. "William I want you to imagine you're still that Roman General, and you've just had your Roman arse well blootered (Destroyed) by the *Cruinnè*. Now you tell me, would you go back to Rome and tell Cesar the facts and likely get nailed to a pair o' planks for being a failure? Or do yie think that it would be better or at least consider, the best way to convey your disaster might be to embellish the truth and make what just happened sound a wee bitty better? And saving your skin for the sake o' a few wee white lies that no-one could ever disprove anyway."

Laughing out loud, William replies, "Naw Dá, I don't think I would want tae be telling Cesar the truth in that scenario. At least, not without trying to make it sound better."

Alain continues, "And if you're that Cesar who rules an empire with brutal force, would you let such a disaster be freely known about what really happened, and likely risk an empire wide rebellion as a result? Especially if the rest of your fragmented empire found out and thought you weak. Or would you write into your history books that you lost your army because you weren't smart enough?"

William thinks for a moment, then he replies, "Aye Dá, I would tell the truth, for is it not better to let the truth be known, good or bad?"

Alain laughs hearing the integrity of William's reply.

"Ach son, if only you were in charge of everything and folk like you, maybe then the world would be a much better place. But sadly I have to tell you, that for folk in power, the word truth is a perspective and conclusion enforced by the power of its employer." Leaning forward in his chair, Alain puts a fatherly hand on William's shoulder. "Listen to me son, and listen well, history is written by the victor and usually it's based only on a half-truth, which throws yie off when yer debating points of legitimacy with an academic eejit. Worse still, is when someone native from a realm the would-be victor has subdued or would wish to subdue rewrites history.

Those bastards write a biased version of that realm's history, and particularly destructive it is when it's someone trusted from within that community, being so duplicitous, takes gold to mislead their own kith and kin. Aye William, the greedy feckrs, that's when their 'truth' becomes a deadly destructive poison that sets a community divided against itself for all time."

Malcolm and Auld Stephen sit back comfortably in their chairs, enjoying this time old discourse between a father and son. "So, Dá," enquires William, "why did the people here no' tell the Roman scribes what really happened?

Alain guffaws. "The *Céile Aicé* and armies o' the Tuatha Dé *Cruinnè-cè* son, they were from the oral and art faith tradition, they didn't send reports to Rome, why would they? What benefit would that serve them even if they wanted too? And who else was going to tell Cesar that the naked armies of the *Cruinnè* had pushed their biggest toughest army back more than a hundred miles, not just once, but many times. Yie had better believe that auld Gnaeus Julius Agricola said he won, because he wouldn't want to be losing his Roman feckin head by saying he lost would he?"

William is interested and amused as Alain continues. "Of course he lied, that's what religious despots and the feckn nobility do, the dirty lyin' bastards." Alain pauses. "And that's lies pure n' simple son, or this fancy word nobles and Bishops use for lying that they call politics."

Everyone agrees heartily when hearing Alain's descriptive, explanations. Reflecting on these rarest of moments with William now in his life, Alain glances into the glowing fire, then in a sombre voice he says, "I'll tell you this son, you have your own thoughts, experience and questions about church hypocrisy. I see that you feel a great unease when reading a codex that insists you must believe it's the written word of God unequivocally *'This is how things happened, believe it or your damned.'* And William, you say it disturbs you what you've witnessed and seen with your own eyes things carried out in the name of God by his followers, when these feckrs conveniently forget the female face of God on earth, our bonnie *Aicé*, the feckrs."

Taking a large drink of *craitur*, Alain's facial expressions easily demonstrate his own struggle with unanswered questions. "William, one day I'll give yie some of the many reasons I want feck all to do with this modern religion and its so-called authority from Rome as it's taught. Fuck, what is the truth?"

"Feck Dá. It would seem as though lies when told often enough and supported by a duplicitous authority, eventually becomes the truth."

Alain laughs and takes another sup, celebrating his new-found theological partner. "Aye, William yer right, and devious religious authority and nobles have acquired great skills in that regard over time, making any lie they wish to manipulate based on a half-truth into an indisputable fact... dangerous bastards son. Yet when their disciplines and logic are challenged by any degree of intellect, they look down their pointy feckn noses and then say 'It is God's will' aye right, it's all a load feckin horse shit."

Stirred by Alain's logic, Malcolm quips, "Aye William, those religious bastards espouse their fanatical doctrine nonsense when an intellectual answer by reply is lost on them. When their wee ruse goes wrong, they say, God bless you my son, as they run for cover or beat yie wie a big feckn stick. That bible o' theirs is full of the Lord God's commands to kill entire nations o' men, women and weans, rape virgins and enslave all that survive in his name. What kind of God is that to follow when we have mother earth in Magda mòr who feeds and nurtures our well being, and without us killing anyone."

"Feck me," sighs Auld Stephen with good humour. "The three o' yie fellas reciting monologues now."

Ignoring Auld Stephen's remark, William thinks on Alain's words. "Dá, I understand what you're saying and the way you put it makes sense to me, but what about the noble oration of Calgacus and the declaration of Tacitus? And what about the Romans bringing us civilisation where we had none before?"

"Feck, we're back in Rome again?" says Stephen. Both he and Malcolm are greatly amused as they witness the historical debate continue.

Alain replies without looking away from the fire, "William, do yie honestly think that this fella, Calgacus as yie call him, actually stood on a hill somewhere in Scotland, delivered a speech to his army, then scribed a declaration then sent it to Rome by carrier pigeon... or even sent Tacitus a copy? Or do you think Calgacus invited a wee Roman scribe to sit and write shite down to impress everybody back in Rome about the noble savage to save face?"

Pausing to consider Alain's comments for a moment, Malcolm enquires, "Don't yie mean Calg ua' Co'Cosdh? Was Calgacus no' some poor wee pot makin' fella the Romans picked up near Edinburgh, then took him to Rome as a noble prisoner to feed hungry lions?"

Alain ignores his brother and turns to his son. "Anyways William, might yie consider that Agricola paid his scribe to write his version down after he lost the battle, maybe he wrote the noble savage speech himself simply to avoid being nailed to a wooden feckin cross when he returned to Rome?"

Alain can see the serious and thoughtful consideration in

William's expression. Then he continues, "When Agricola lost most of his army with no gains to show for his losses, economically it was a disaster, militarily it was a disaster, so the best he could come up with and likely the only honest thing Agricola could say, and that was that he fought a ferocious but noble enemy, after that little bit of truth that's when the lies begin. The Roman generals state there was nothing in Scotland of value, so they consolidated a defensive wall on the border with England to keep us out of Roman Briton? Horse pish son, but it did leave us with our own lands of the *Cruinnè* which is all we wanted to keep in the first place."

William laughs; then he thinks about what has been said, first from his Wee Maw, and now from his father. Seeing the joyous bewilderment in his son's face, Alain says, "William, whoever writes history, owns history, and they're se' feckn dogmatic in saying this is the way it was, don't question it. You tell me if Tacitus or Wee Maw tells a story closer to your heart's satisfaction when I say these next two words, are yie ready?"

William replies, "Aye father, I'm ready,".

Alain, Malcolm and Auld Stephen wait a moment; then they reply simultaneously, "HADRIANS' WALL!"

William ponders aloud with a blank expression, "Why build a wall right across the country and stand behind it if you've defeated everyone, THAT doesn't make sense?" He contemplates as to why the Romans had written they'd defeated everyone in Scotland, then retreated behind a wall where now sits the disputed territories on the border lands with England.

"Dá?" Enquires William, "The Roman accounts don't make any sense to me, but everything granny said makes much better sense."

"Then who would you believe, William? A classic academic scribe who needs a paid job writing for a lying scared Roman general, or your auld granny?"

A grinning William states proudly, "It's got to be me Granny." Extremely satisfied with his conclusion, William states, "Ha, our Wee Maw, she's amazing, just pure amazing!"

Malcolm and Auld Stephen smile as Alain continues, "She should be William, for she's a direct descendant of the *Aicé* Morríaghan *Bahn Rígh* who's supposed husband was that fella Ambrosius Aurilialis."

William stops laughing and appears absolutely incredulous upon hearing his father's last comment. "Naw Dá, really? Are yie jestin' me?"

Alain, while gazing solemnly into the fire flames, replies. "True enough William, believe me as your Uncle Malcolm and I believed our fathers, when we asked the same questions."

Leaning in close to William, Malcolm points at Alain. "William, see your Dá there?"

"Aye," replies a curious William.

"It took him far longer and he asked many more questions than you before his Groat dropped!" Everyone laughs as Malcolm yawns and stretches his tired muscles. "Listen fella's, I am so feckn tired, I think I'll be going to me crib now, for it's been a some long time since I slept in a warm chamber."

"Aye, me and all," agrees Alain. "Wie us travelling through the night from Edinburgh and then the wedding day too, it's been a day to remember for sure."

Now fired up by his bloodline discovery, William speaks with excitement. "Another question for both o' yiez before yiez go..."

Alain groans. "What now?"

William says, "A priest in Paisley told me n' Wee John that the Wallace are descended from some feckin Norman called Aelius Giallis or some name like that."

Alain sighs as he puts his hand on William's shoulder. "Son, me and your uncle here have heard we were descended from so many different types o' feckn folk, though we never heard it from any of the other Guardian families."

Malcolm yawns again, then he says, "Aye William, we've heard we're Norman-English or sometimes we're from France or sometimes even Irish, which is no bad thing in respect of our *Cruinnè* cousins, with your approval of course Stephen?"

Auld Stephen nods back, waving his hand in grandiose approval as Malcolm continues, "In fact, the last time I heard that story, some auld priest told me we were the original Welsh from the Henn Ogledd of Strathclyde, though we wouldn't use that term."

"Aye, I heard that too," says William. "The auld priest in Paisley told me the name Wallace meant we were foreigners or slaves and we're no' really Scots at all." William speaks of this as though delivering a falsehood, to which he desperately needs an answer to settle his angst at this challenge to his bloodline.

"Was the priest English, Norman, French or one of our own son?" asks Alain.

William replies, "English, Dá, though he sez he's a proud and true Anglo Saxon."

Sipping his *craitur*, Auld Stephen laughs. "Is there really such a creature as a proud Anglo Saxon? I for one have never met any of those rarest of fellas yet, nor do I know of anyone who has?"

Alain explains. "William, you speak the Gaelic, don't you?"

William replies, "Aye Dá, that I do."

"And what do the Gaels call Scotland and what does it mean in our own Language."

William replies, shrugging his shoulders and feeling confident he is extremely knowledgeable. "Alba (Alapa) the land o' Mountains."

"And if you were Welsh, what would yie call your country in the Welsh language."

"*Cymru*, the land of friends."

Alain smiles as he puts down his *craitur*. "Do you see what I am saying now son? The actual word 'Welsh' is no' a native word to us Scots, it's a Saxon or Norman word, not Scots, Doric, Erse, Lallans or Gaelic."

"William me boy," says Auld Stephen. "You've nothing to fear over your blood-lineage, for you're surely *Cruinnè* and Scots from the tip o that big feckin head of yours to the soles o' your big feckin feet. And you mind this now too, if someone calls you Welsh again, they must either be English, Norman or foreign to Scots blood. Are you getting that into yer head now?"

Replying with a sense of relief in his voice, William proudly states, "I'm certainly no' a slave to a feckin Anglo Saxon, nor any arsehole of a Norman."

"Arseholoffa Norman?" exclaims Auld Stephen. "Is that not that Norman Conker fella they call big bastard Willie?" He raises his jug. "Was he not the leader o' the Normans who invaded England in ten sixty something? Ha, and you foin fellas thought I didn't know about history." A proud Stephen winks and nods as he pours more honeydew *craitur* into his goblet.

Malcolm and Alain try not to laugh as William frowns at old Stephen. Then Alain says. "Remember what Wee Maw said William, our bloodline is from the *Garda Céile Aicé*. Some Normans' who moved here, have adopted native names or they married their daughters and sons to local chiefs. Folks like the Norman Fitz Allan, who are now the stewards to King Alexander, they changed their name to Stewart after their work as the King's stewards."

Pausing for another drink, Alain continues. "The Stewarts, are fine folks, very fine indeed. They're part Norman, who came here a couple of generations ago to fight for old *Artur Uilliam mac Eanric* (King William the Lion), and once the Normans settled here, many dropped their Norman names and adopted local names like our own."

William nods in understanding. "Aye Dá, then what about the Céile Dé and *Céile Aicé*?"

Auld Stephen looks over. "Feck me, the boy doesn't ever stop."

William ignores Auld Stephen and continues undaunted. "I read once that the Céile Dé came from one of Jesus' disciples when he went to Ireland and met wie a Breitheamh of the Dáln Araidi *Cruinnè* called Oengus of Kell de' (Angus Culjay) an Irishman who turned the scriptures into music? Not anything like the ancient cult that granny was talking about."

Auld Stephen now getting steadily wearier with the drink, looks at William. "That's it, me boys, blame the feckin Irish."

Alain grins. "William, as much as the Christians are fine folk generally, their leadership has an awful tendency to take from what already exists then call it their own. We were, and some still are, *Garda Céile Aicé* o' the *Tuatha De Cruinne-cè*, some are Christian religious, others are still simply *Cruinnè* religious, but all as one despite the different ways of individual faith practice. Our faith is to worship whatever way pleases yie in your own Obhainn (Skin\hide Longhouse-Shelter) but when we all meet at gatherings for the calling, we're all *Cruinnè Céile Aicé* as one, using our given skills to protect our mothers, sisters, wives daughters and to follow our Queen, the *Aicé...*"

Considering what he has just said to William, Alain laughs to himself, for he has unwittingly agreed with Bishop Wishart in a conversation he had with him in Edinburgh. Alain notices Malcolm and Stephen becoming tense and conveying to him to be cautious in his communication with William on the subject, for he, like Auld Stephen and Malcolm, are *Garda Céile Aicé* and Breitheamh Rígh.

Malcolm says, "William, we have to be very careful nowadays, for current religious intolerance means to be practicing the auld faith Christian hierarchy could never control, is extremely dangerous. Our faith can still have complete families or even entire communities murdered by the Holy inquisition,"

Alain says. "Aye William, the elders o' Dé *Cruinnè-cè* are acutely sensitive to the recent Albigensian Crusade blessed by Pope Innocent against the Cathars."

"What do yie mean Dá?"

"The Cathars adherence to their particular faith resulted in the extermination of the entire Cathar population of the Languedoc a mere fifty years ago, simply because of their beliefs."

Auld Stephen nods. "Aye, and that's within living memory and could easy happen to all of us. The vigour o' the Catholic Church has many examples of murderous intolerance o' killing and destroying any community who doesn't follow 'The Catholic doctrine."

William hasn't noticed the tension as he asks, "Granny brought me up to understand the ways of the *Garda Céile Aicé* Dá. She sez I'm all that and more. She also said we're similar to the Welsh Druids of old who have three classes of faith practitioners, the poet orators, the musician Bards and the healers, with the Irish and Scots havin' a fourth addition to our ancient faith, with our Breitheamh Laws to guide us, the warrior Guardians. But why is to be *Garda Céile Aicé* and *Cruinnè-cè* seen as a mortal sin by the Church? All it means to me is to use my gifts for the happiness of the females of our people and to nurture mother earth, Magda mòr. Why is there such a problem with the old faith that would have the Catholic Church want to torture and murder folk like me? Wee Maw said, to find love in the sanctity of the heart is a warm place to be, for yie'll never find that same warmth in a sanctity o' a church."

"And how do you feel about the ways of the *Garda Céile Aicé* now, son?"

William replies instantly. "I'm *Céile Aicé* Dá, through blood and belief in all granny has taught me."

Auld Stephen says. "Well you had better be keeping it to yourself, boy, for the Christians will hound and hunt yie down and destroy yie if they find that out."

"Why though?" William asks with passion.

"Why are Christians so a' feared of folk who are plain and simply happy and not searching for a faith we already have? We all gaze up at the same heavens, sun and moon that look down upon us. Why or what does it matter what faith we use to appreciate that?"

Alain shrugs his shoulders. "I don't know and can't answer that son. I don't think any of us could answer that question who are content with creation as it is and not seeking to hurt or kill others in this life over some faith in the hope that we'll be happier in the next life, I'm already happy."

Listening intently, Malcolm says, "William, it's best to keep it to yourself like Auld Stephen says. The forces of the Catholic church for whatever reason are too great to let them think of you as an enemy."

Alain after a brief thought says, "I do wonder what's going on with the Church sometimes? It's strange times within the church in Scotland. I don't know why Alexander has no' looked into what's happening of a' late, for I believe that many of the monks, Friars and Abbots that English Bishop Bek fella is moving into positions of power in Scotland is for no good reason, exceptin' that known only to him."

There's an audible murmur of agreement from Malcolm and Auld Stephen. Alain says, "I've spoken with true Tam and many of the mountain *Céile Aicé* and we all believe these new English clerics who are coming into the church are destroying or taking away our records and histories then replacing them with misleading information."

Malcolm says, "I cannot disagree with you there brother. Many of the Garda have noticed this religious zeal o' translating our history into some obscure Latin text or archaic Norman French. I fear these English priests are replacing our history, not recording it. There's something ominous coming for our people, ah can just feel it in ma bones. Our historical lineage and ancient history will be questioned and required to be brought to the fore as proof for our very survival, but it'll not be our history held in our holy places for future generations, it'll be the history Bishop Bek and his cronies have been putting there in place of our own. I see that good Alexander is too much taken with Yolande to notice and he'll have none of it when the subject is broached."

"What I cannae understand is why Wishart and leadin' church magnates do nothing about it? Bishop Wishart is ferocious about the independence of the Scots church. Ahm perplexed that he of all people, is not aware of what we and many others have noticed," Alain observes.

"Aye," says Malcolm. "Even our great theologians, Duns Scotus and his Uncle Elias the Guardian of Dumfries say naught about it, no' even young Baldred Bisset sez anything."

Malcolm sighs. "If those fellas are not doing anything, what the feck can we do?"

"It sounds like what you were sayin' earlier, Dá, yie know, about a realm being destroyed from within." William remarks innocently.

Malcolm and Auld Stephen hasn't really heard William, but Alain heard his words, and they strike him with a thunderbolt of realisation. But he can also feel his eyes forcibly closing and his mind drifting. Possibly it's just the whisky scrambling his thoughts, "Maybe we've all had too much of Wee Maw's fine *craitur* and it's doing the talking for us. Fellas, I really need to be sleeping soon or I'll find myself arse up and face down in the fire."

Malcolm laughs then he stands up. "Aye William, your question about your name? You be heeding these words son, for many who are no' Wallace, for some feckin reason, will desire with a passion to tell you who you are with such a measure of disagreeable conviction and venom in their voice and a maniacal belief in their own truth. There's that bad word truth again.

"William, son, these feckn people will insist on telling you what you are and what you're not. These feckrs cannot believe our glorious history exists, as the same experience does not appear to them in their own sad bland lineage, so somehow they become experts in ours. These feckn leeches covet our name, William, and make it their mission in life not to allow us Wallace's to be having our own opinion on our history, legends or birthright. Sometimes, it's best just to let these dinkies rant. It is simply good enough to know yourself who you are and where yer from son."

"Aha, there it is now," laughs Auld Stephen. "I knew it was only a matter of time before that old Wallace superiority complex came to the fore."

Laughing with his friend, Malcolm reaches for a last hearty drink of the *craitur*.

William looks at his father and their eyes meet, both acknowledging at a glance that it's best not to say anything till Malcolm has finished his point. It appears that under his calm exterior, this subject of birthright is a sore point for him too.

Malcolm resumes. "There are many folk with similar sounding names as us William, but they're no' of our blood, they say that if some part of our history is not in their history, then it cannot be true of what we say is in ours. So heed me William, those zealous self-righteous academics are fine as much as they may be necessary, but when it comes to knowing who yie are and where yie come from, who would you trust more than any other?"

"Ah, trust ma granny," replies a grinning William.

His father says, "Tonight, son, you were asked what story you wanted to hear? You had many options, but you and gentle Andrew asked about your blood. Granny told you where your name came from and who you come from. Then a wee while earlier you mentioned a priest told you that your name was not Scots and you cursed him without thinking, especially when you felt your name and birthright had been questioned by this cleric. Do you see what's going on when your birthright is questioned, how it makes you feel in your heart?"

William is taken aback by this outburst of personal feelings shared, and seeing his father and Malcolm still greatly indulging in grannies 'medicine'. He had noticed them cursing often to make their point, and it had worked.

Malcolm puts his hand on William's shoulder and speaks with a kindness in his voice. "That's it me boy, I'm feck'd and I'm tired, I cannot take any more questions, ahm near sleep-walking. William, you're a grand young man, but me, your father and Auld Stephen who's now sleepin' over there, we must be going to our cribs."

Alain says, "Aye, there'll be plenty of time for more of your questions in the morn, son."

"Uncle Malcolm, now is the time to be telling you how grateful I am that you had us taught by the Cluniac's o' Paisley Dunipace and Crossraguel. But I will tell yiez all that things I have seen, the lies I've heard and often witnessed the abuse of innocents by priests, monks and others of the cloth, and all in the name of God, it's no' something I can thole much longer."

Alain realises hearing William's frustrations are like listening to his own complaints when he was a similar age. He says, "William, I know you have doubts, all young men do."

"Aye, William, even us old fellas still have doubts, but feck the monks and feck the academics who have no heart for folklore or our legends. You just trust your instincts, trust in your family and closest friends, but most of all..." says Malcolm.

William looks at his father. Moments pass, then he realises his father, Malcolm, and Auld Stephen, wait for his answer... "Trust in Granny?"

"NOW yie are getting it, me boy," replies Malcolm as he slaps William on the back. Then he continues, "Oh, and another thing, William, before we retire, I want you and Malcolm óg (Young Malcolm) to go to the fish landings in the morn and bring fresh catch back for Wee Maw. I want it gutted, cleaned, salted, delivered and in the pickle or smoke houses first thing. And don't be messing with the fisher girls at the market, and you keep clear of the apprentice nuns too. Oh, and be taking young Stephen with yiez."

"Uncle, I'll be up first light and get that done. And Dá, I've another thing to be saying."

"Awe fer fuck's sake," mutters Auld Stephen as he clings to the end of a door.

"What is it son, for I'm starting to see double and I really need ma sleep?"

William blurts out, "I've got tae ask you now that I've got this far. See when granny mentioned a Cymric Cleric called Geoffrey o' Monmouth? I've read his book, as has near everyone in the priories. It's a good book to be reading called the Historia Regum Britanniae, but Geoffrey names only one man the Arthur, and that's what the English call one particular King, not the name for all our Kings as we do, why is that?"

The three elders are now exasperated by all these questions, but before they can reply, William says, "I also read a poem in another codex called the Black Book of Carmarthen, where King Arthur and his army fought two battles in defence of Dun Eidyn (Edinburgh) as defenders against the Saxons. If *Artur* was a Cymran king, what's he doing fightin' in Scotland against Saxons?"

"Son," says Alain, "it's common knowledge that Strathclyde is the original Henn Ogledd, old *Cymru*, that'll be why."

"I'll tell yie this too, Dá, I don't understand why it appears to be our history the Normans are claiming as their own for England. I see them rewriting our history, justifying changes then calling our history a myth, or worse. They call our history lies then laugh at me like I'm a fool when I question their meddling?"

An extremely tired Malcolm replies, "For fecks sake William, have yie swallowed a feckin religious library this night or is it your over-nippin' o' Wee Maw's *Craitur*?"

Auld Stephen, listening quietly to the Wallace story, staggers back from the door to take his seat by the fire. He mutters, "Holy feck, this boy is something else."

Although Alain is happy to hear all these questions, he's extremely tired and feeling fatigue setting into his bones. He says, "Naw William, that's like what Wee Maw said, it's another story, and too much to be telling yie the now son."

"Another thing for yiez, then," insists William.

Though sympathetic toward his son, Alain is almost falling asleep. "Feck me, William, what now?"

Malcolm pleads, "Naw please, don't ask another feckin question. Even us auld fellas can be too old for this much talking. I thought you were a hunter and lover o' the hills o' freedom, away from folk and idle chatter. Is that no' one of the reasons why you're leaving the church, to be gettin' away from folk who ask too many questions? You seem to have more questions than a Bishop catchin' a naked priest in a nunnery. I 'm going to ma crib before yie talk us to all to death."

Auld Stephen mutters quietly. "Be no questions if they caught a feckin Bishop with a wee boy though."

William pleads, "Please, Dá, just one more thing, and it's for you too, uncle."

Malcolm looks at William and sees a different expression in his face. His nephew says, "I would be thanking your Wee Maw and Margret for what you've done for me and Wee John, and I don't know how we could ever repay you. I might be young compared to all o' you, especially Auld Stephen over there, but I must be heard to say that I've never underestimated what you took on with me and Wee John."

Alain looks at his son, astonished at what he's just said for his words are beyond his years. But there's something in William's tone and presence that demonstrates he understands and means every word. He walks over and stands beside William. "I agree with William's sentiments, Malcolm. It would seem we both owe you more than we could ever repay."

Waving his hand to stop more talk, Malcolm says, "Brother, you, William, Wee John, would you have done no less for me had the situation been reversed? We're Clan and sons of the Garda Bahn Rìoghail. We're *Céile Aicé*.

A tired and drunk Auld Stephen speaks out. "Well, I cannot take any more of this fascinating Wallace chatter, sentimental though it is. Maybe we should sit down again some time and I'll be telling you all the legends of the brave warriors of ua H'Alpine and how we taught your women to fight for your men folks back in the day."

Malcolm sighs. "Aye Stephen, perhaps you're right. I think I'll be joining my bonnie lass in the crib now, for I've nothing left in me to keep me awake this night."

Everyone agrees that it's time to retire and warmly bid each other goodnight. As William and Alain are about to leave, William grins at his father. "We truly are alike Dá, aren't we? I've the same traits as you don't I?

Studying his son's face, Alain feels proud. Putting his hand on William's shoulder, he says, "It would seem we're more alike than we could ever have known or imagined William. And that becomes evident the more we are in each other's company. Many of the things I've heard you question this night, I've questioned myself." He pauses then says, "Yie know son, I couldn't suffer the same injustice and malicious hypocrisy that I too witnessed within the church o' my youth. That's why my life is in the mountains and forest of the Wolf and Wildcats, away from all the inane chatter of civilisation, we can talk more on this the morrow if you'd like?"

"Dá, I'd like to be with you in the mountains and wolf and wildcat's and no' just to exist hereabouts trying to make a life out of a being a toonie (Town person)."

"William, me boy, you're a son of ma loins right enough." Inwardly Alain is taken aback upon hearing William's wishes. He thinks on how he had expressed his own desires earlier to Malcolm and Margret, in that his dearest wish would be for William and Wee John to come back to their home in the lands of Glen Afton.

"Son..." Alain says proudly, "I could think of nothing better, I swear. If you really want to come to Glen Afton and hunt the Wolf and Wildcats and the Ettrick forest with me, we could make arrangements with Wee Maw and the family on the morn. And if you'd like it to be so, then you and Wee John could come down to Glen Afton as soon as you're ready."

William replies enthusiastically, "Feck Dá, I'm ready right now. I want to leave with you and Mharaidh for the lands o' Black Craig on the morrow."

Alain pulls his son close in loving embrace, fighting hard not to show William his true tearful emotions. "William, we'll talk more on this in the morn, son."

***

Early next morning, the three young men have saddled their horses and meander toward the Ynchinnan landings to fetch the sea-catch vittals required for the family. They're also to collect a house share and deliver it to Paisley priory where the boys received much of their education, and good beatings on many occasions.

Malcolm óg says, "Lets go see John Blair on the way back from Ynchinnan."

William yawns wishing the conversation of the previous night had been a little shorter. "Aye, that's if we can find him. Ho Stephen, wait till you meet this fella Blair, he has such a sense of humour, especially for a wee Cluniac monk. He's a very clever wee bloke and a handy fella to know."

Stephen enquires, "What do yie mean?"

"Well, he used to do all our written exams for us and he was the monks favourite, so he'd get us out of the most serious o' troubles. Sometimes even taking the blame for us. Now that wee fella definitely will make a good priest, for he's always writing things down like it really happened, no' like the feckin Romans."

Malcolm óg quips, "Aye and remember, MacLamroch and Gray too."

"That's right," agrees William. "I near forgot about those two, we were some raucous bunch together Stephen. Feck, I don't know why we weren't flung out o' the church years before now."

As they ride-on, Stephen is puzzled, "What feckin Romans?"

Malcolm óg is equally confused. "Are there Romans down at the fish landings?"

William snaps, "What the feck are you two talking about? I was talking about John Blair, MacLamroch and Gray, saying that Blair could tell you what we were all doing six years, six months and six sand minutes ago."

Stephen and Malcolm óg look at William with bewilderment on their faces. Stephen enquires, "Aye, that's fine we heard that, but what about these Romans?"

William replies, "Ah, the Romans, I'll tell yiez all about the Romans sometime."

They all laugh and chatter as they walk their horses down toward the Ynchinnan landings. Malcolm óg with a big knowing grin, nudges Stephen and nods in the direction of William riding a little ahead of them. He calls out, "William, will you be tellin' Stephen all about the fisher wives?"

Stephen enquires, "The Fisher Wives? Now who are they and what are they bein' all about?"

William replies, "Feckin amazin' lassies. Thanks for reminding me about the bonnie fisher lassies Malcolm óg. Well Stephen, when we were young, we were always sent down to the landings at Ynchinnan to get the fish to scale and gut them. Some were for the priory and some for the hoose, that's where we discovered a lovely little thing called fornication."

"Forni-what?" enquires Stephen curiously.

William replies with a knowledgeable tone of voice while nodding his head with an expression of experience. "Aye, fornication it was. For a long time, we thought our names *were wee bastards*. But that came from a time when we were young and running past the bothies o' the fishermen and the fisher wives would shout out to us, *'Come here, ya wee bastards.'* We thought they called us that because we stayed with our Uncle Malcolm after our Maw had died, but we found out later that's what they called all the young-blood back then."

"Same in Ireland," says Stephen with a similarly serious knowing look on his face, competing with the knowledge of women conversation. "Ceptin' with us boys o' the black lough, it was them there same old nuns. They would shout out to us, *'Come away here, ya toiny* (Tiny) *durty little evil fecker's.'*

The three friends laugh while giving each other knowing smiles of female experiences they never really had.

"Anyways," continues William, "the fisher wives used to shout us over to be going into their wee bothies then they would take off all our clothes, then they took off all their clothes and said things to us like, *'Now ya wee bastards, we are goannae show yie this thing called Roman wrestling.'*"

"Ah," sighs Stephen. "Is that those self same Romans you were talking about earlier?"

William enquires gruffly. "What?" For a moment he ponders over Stephen observation, causing him to think of how much the Romans really had influenced Scotland's history? Then he continues feigning annoyance. "Right, so the auld fisher wives…"

Malcolm óg interrupts, "Are the fisher wives Roman?"

William growls in annoyance as Stephen and Malcolm laugh. "Feck off and listen to my feckn story, and maybe yiez'll find out…"

Suddenly Malcolm óg cheerily cuts into William's oration. "Aye Stephen, when we were all naked, the fisher wives would do things with us that felt really nice in a strange sort of way."

William looks in disgust at Malcolm óg for stealing his thunder.

Stephen enquires, "And that was Roman wrestling?"

"Naw, it wasn't," replies William quickly. "Well that's what the biddies called it, but we know now that it was fornication. We didn't know that's what it was called then, but I can honestly say we weren't bothered. Feck it was good."

Stephen quips, "It sounds like these Roman fellas had a good time here in auld Scotland."

"I like Roman wrestling," Malcolm óg states innocently.

Stephen enquires with hope in his voice. "D'yie still see the fisher wives now?"

"We could do," replied William. "But we would need to be quick about it."

Malcolm óg scoffs. "No change for you then William."

"Why should we be quick?" enquires Stephen. "Is it fear o' the husbands to be coming back and catching yiez like a shrimp in a net?"

"Ha," laughs Malcolm óg. "Sometimes it felt like that."

"Your shrimp maybe, but I need a salmon net for mine." William says with good-humoured derision.

"Feck off," laughs Malcolm óg. He playfully pushes William and near shoves him off his saddle.

"Naw Stephen," sighs William. "The husbands didn't mind at all. Strange thing was, they used to say that when they got back from a long day out at the fishin', they were fine about us pleasuring their wives."

"They said what?" exclaims a bewildered Stephen.

"Aye," replies William with a grin. "They were no' short in telling us that their women were happy and not picking fights and how it made life so much easier for them. They said they could spend more time at the inns at night if we had been there in the morn."

"It's true Stephen," confirms Malcolm óg. "They said to us, that if we had been with their wives in the morning, then they got fed well and had a peaceful life at night. Though I'm still no sure what they meant by that?"

The three friends appear bemused then philosophically ponder awhile, but they can't fathom what the fishermen had really meant. Malcolm óg makes a suggestion. "Maybe we could ask Wee John now that he's married."

Malcolm notices Stephen's facial expression change dramatically. He utters, "Hmmm, maybe not then…"

He quickly changes the subject. "If we get down to the landings fast and we meet with a few o' the fisher women, maybe we could get lucky, what do yiez think?"

William considers Malcolm óg's wise suggestion, then replies, "Naw, we have to get back with the fish for the priory and Wee Maw's break fast gathering. We'd only have a wee while if we're to be se' lucky."

"Awe, lets go," pleads Malcolm óg. "It won't take us long."

Stephen comments, "A wee while is better than no while at all."

Seeing the forlorn expressions on both his companions' faces turning to big hopeful grins, William laughs then replies with gusto. "Feck it, lets go."

Stephen calls out joyously at the top of his voice. "And here's hopin' we are to be se' bleedin lucky."

Laughing, William says, "You haven't seen them yet Stephen, especially yours."

"Listen here now," says Stephen. "It sure must be better than the gutting o' the fish."

The cheery companions spur their horses and gallop all the way down to the Ynchinnan fishing landings. It's not long before they pass the first Bothie where they observe a disturbance at the front door. Suddenly, a semi-naked young priest comes running out of the Bothie with his cassock flying behind him, thrown at his head from a big bare-chested woman storming out the door behind him. William exclaims. "John Blair, what are you doin' here? I thought you were up at the Dundee set to become a priest or a Chaplain…?"

Blair replies as he hastily dresses. "Ach I was, or I mean I am, but I'm stuck here in Paisley priory for the while."

Suddenly, a booming woman's voice calls to them from the door of the Bothie, "Haw you, ya wee bastards, do yiez fancy helping me and ma pals here with some heavy liftin'?"

A large buxom fisher lady, naked from the waist up, points at Blair. "That wee priest is no worth a feck." She spits on the ground disdainfully then walks back into her abode.

"Ah told yie, Stephen," boasts William. Pleased with himself at such perfect timing to confirm his story. The three young men look at each other and laugh when the big ample bosomed semi-naked woman, appears at the door again and beckons them to come to her Bothie.

As they dismount, William calls back. "Aye, right yie are wifey, here we come."

The three friends rush towards the door of the Bothie. William calls out without looking back. "Be seeing yie later Blair." He stops at the door and shouts over to his friend. "Haw, Blair, will yie…?"

"I know," replied Blair. "I'll tether your horses and get the fish for yiez… Nothing changes with you Wallace's then."

A few hours pass in the little Bothie beside the Ynchinnan, and for William, Malcolm óg and Stephen it's been a memorable morning. They eventually leave the little Bothie and meet with Blair, who's sitting writing in his little book.

Blair says with a smile, "I didn't think it would take yiez that long."

"What do you mean by that?" enquires William. "Nothing," replied Blair.

"It's just that there is three o' uze and only one o' me. I'd been in there for near on two hours before the biddy said I was useless?"

"Aha," replied William with a grin. "But you were with the auld Maw. We had to entertain her three daughters while your auld biddy went to Paisley market."

"Haw Blair," says Malcolm óg. "Meet Stephen ua, he's Rosinn's brother, yie know, the lass Wee John married yesterday."

Blair offers his hand in friendship, which is eagerly taken by Stephen. "Good tae meet yie little fella."

With a satisfied grin, Blair replies. "Likewise."

William says, "We'd better get the fish vittals up to the Abbey and Wee Maw, or life will no be worth living if we're late."

Blair says, "I'll take the vittals to the monks, I've got a barrow load o' fish for the Templar's' up at the Ladyacre's preceptory at Greenend too."

"The house o' Northbar? Feck Blair, the floor o' that place is paved wie human skulls."

Blair laughs, "Well the Templars like to think they are above everybody else don't they. Anyways, ah'v got all o' their Friday fish, so at least I can say to the auld monks in Paisley I've been busy."

William replies, "*Tá mo chara.*" (Thanks my friend.)

Blair continues. "And I'll try and get up to *Ach na Feàrna* soon."

"Any time."

"I'll need tae be making it very soon though, for I'm away to study the priesthood in Dundee with Andrew Grey and MacLamroch, then ahm off to France for some more studying."

William grins at his friend."What, studying women or religion?"

Blair smirks. "Both... and in that order. I've heard that the French sisters and apprentice nuns are something else to behold with their dark dusky beauty."

"You're something to behold, Blair," says Stephen laughing. "And here's me been thinkin' it was only Irish priests who liked the cloth to be lying in and lying upon. You Scots make lying down with women and lying to a fella's face a feckin art form to be aspiring too."

Malcolm óg curtly retorts, "Well, it was you Irish that introduced us to Christianity, so we had good teachers then. Or bad luck depending on yer point o' view."

Stephen counters, "Why I'll be thanking you boys for admitting the Irish brought you primitives the opportunity for a good education and advancement."

The three friends all have a good laugh; then William turnss to Blair. "Will you say to Grey and MacLamroch that we were asking after them an' that we hope to see them soon?"

Blair replies, "Aye, that I will. They'll be sorry they missed you and mind say *Co'nas* (Galloway-Gaelic how are you) to Wee John from me. Feck, he must be over two clothyards in height by now? And tell him that I'm still paying for his burnin' down the Abbots hen-coupe. I have no' forgotten that he still owes me, its in my book."

"Ha, we've no' forgotten either Blair." says William. "Thanks for getting us out o' that one though. I'll make sure to tell Wee John, and mind you to be comin' up to the *Ach na Feàrna* afore yie go to Dundee or France."

"I will do. Oh, ah nearly forgot, ma auld father was always asking after you fellas. He said he misses all your antics at the nag wrangling', he says it kept him feeling young."

"Auld Bryce?" cries William. "Feck, mind and say to him that we'll soon be down about the shire n' barony to see ma uncle Ranald. We'll be wrangling more of Bryce's horses if he is of a mind. I fair like your auld fella Blair, some humour that man."

"Aye," replies Blair, "I'll be telling him you were asking after him. He'll be looking forward to seeing you Wallace boys, and you too Stephen I reckon."

William says, "You take care."

"Aye, and you, too."

The four young men say farewell, leaving the fisher wives very happy as the three companions bid Blair farewell.

CRESSINGHAM'S REWARD

A lain wakes with a thumping headache. Slowly, he climbs out of his crib and tentatively wanders across to a small window, opens it and looks out over the river Clyde, breathing in the exhilarating morning air. He knows he's had a good night and smiles thinking of all that's happened, then he sees William, Stephen and Malcolm óg riding through the gates of *Ach na Feàrna*. He reflects on how close he had came to missing this opportunity to be reunited with his sons and resigned to be accepting his life as mother nature planned for him. But yesterday's fortuitous reunion with William and Wee John, has caused him to realise how lucky he is to reconcile with them, especially after the genuine love and affection they have shown him. Feeling a surge of elation course through his mind, he quickly gets dressed and makes his way to the kitchens to meet with his sons. Along the way he thinks about Wee Maw's morning vittals and isn't sure if he can face the mountain of varied oatmeal and barnyard scran she will make him eat. He laughs as it also occurs to him he might have to wash it down with more of her lethal honeycomb *craitur*, the thought makes him shudder. Arriving outside Wee Maw's kitchens, Alain hears noisy banter as though a small market is being played out nearby. When he enters the kitchens, he sees his kith and kin busily doing chores, eating and chatting. Alain assumed he would be first up that morning when he hears Malcolm calling out. "Last again Alain?"

Wee Maw grins at her wayward son. She says, "Leave the boy alone." She wrinkles her face into an enormous smile. "Would yie be liking a decent break fast, son?"

Alain replies, "Aye, ah would Maw, but just a wee drop *tá*." But he was thinking *Feck, I'm no' really hungry, but if I don't…*

Mharaidh is busily helping to get food to all the children when Alain walks over and kisses her lovingly on the cheek. She smiles as she lifts some bowls of hot oats from the table. Alain moves aside to let the busy Mharaidh past to continue with her chores. He smiles and says with a cheeky grin, "Mornin' ma darlin'."

Mharaidh smiles back with a twinkle in her eye, "*Madhainn mhath*. (Good morning.)"

Alain yawns, then he enquires, "Has anyone seen where the boys are this fine morn?"

Wee Maw replies, "I saw them a wee while ago, just back with the Ynchinnan vittals, and I could see they have a strange smug look on their faces, a bit like their father I'll be thinking."

Wee Maw winks at Mharaidh then continues. "Has anyone checked to see if the maids are still intact this mornin'?" Wee Maw poses the question more to herself than to anyone listening.

Alain asks again, "Does anyone know where the boys are now?"

"They're sitting outside at the water vats." Mharaidh replies.

Wee Maw, still smiling says, "Away outside and be joining them Alain, I'll fetch your scran when it's ready."

Alain walks out the back door, where he sees William, Wee John, Stephen and Auld Stephen sitting around an old water vat.

On seeing their father approach, John and William warmly greet him.

Alain sits down and enquires cheerily, "Mornin' boys, are yiez havin' a good day?"

William replies, "Are you jestin' us Dá?"

Stephen has a broad smirk on his face. "It's been somethin' else Fadder-in-law."

William points across the bench. "Will you be looking at the rosy cheeks on Wee John's face Dá? We were asking him about his wedding night, but he just keeps going red in the face and saying nuthin'."

Malcolm walks out the kitchen door drinking a flagon full of fresh morning milk. He stands beside Alain, content to listen while he talks with his boys.

"William, Wee John… I'd like to be asking you both something very important, and I need yiez to consider with a care what I ask, afore you decide on an answer."

William and Wee John look at each other curiously and shrug their shoulders in agreement.

Alain begins. "Wee John, now that you're married to bonnie Ròsinn, what's your plan? I take it the church is no longer going to be your calling?"

"No fear o' that, Dá" replied Wee John. "I'm going to Ireland with Ròsinn and her father and staying there awhile. I think it'll be better for Ròsinn being near her family and I reckon I'll do well as a hunter over there."

"And what about you, William?" his father asks. "Your Uncle Malcolm tells me the both o' yiez have an amazing aptitude for the learning, but your ability with the hunt flights is exceptional?"

"Aye, that's true, Dá. The priests used to belt us all week, but they stopped the belting on a Thursday to send us out to hunt for wild game to fill out their expanding cassocks. After that, they were good to us... for a wee while." Everyone laughs as William continues. "A funny thing though, whenever we got into trouble, the priests and monks as well as everyone else said how much we were so like you Dá, that we had brains, but never used them."

Malcolm chokes on his creamy milk hearing these words. He laughs so loudly and chokes at the same time he turns red in the face.

William pauses a moment realising what he's just said. "Feck. I'm sorry, Dá, I didn't mean..."

Alain watches Malcolm's pleasure at the reference, then a proud grin appears as he begins laughing too. "Well, I cannae argue with that compliment son. I can only say that if it's true, then we're surely all in the finest of company this springtime mornin'."

Malcolm thinks it is best to leave father and sons alone to talk. "C'mon, Malcolm óg, we'll go see if the girls need a hand in the kitchens before Wee Maw comes out with a broom and bends the shaft over our heads for no' helpin'." Malcolm óg stands up resigned to kitchen duties as Malcolm continues. "Alain needs to be talking with his sons awhile."

Alain appreciates his brother's diplomacy.

Malcolm goes on, "Brother, I'll be bringing your vittals out when they're ready."

Auld Stephen rises from his seat to follow everyone else. "I think it's the kitchens that I will be visiting too Stephen, c'mon son." Stephen stands up and joins his father. He says to William, "Don't forget me Wallace..."

As everyone departs, Alain speaks directly to his sons. "Boys, I'll ask yiez straight. I'd like for yiez to come down to Glen Afton and spend some time there with me, Mharaidh and your wee sister Caoilfhinn, for it's your home too." Alain pauses a moment before he continues nervously. "I wouldn't expect that you would want to stay longer than you were happy though, and Glen Afton is a lot more remote than you may be used to up here in Glasgow and Paisley. But I could no' think of anything finer than if yiez were to come home with your family."

Wee John responds immediately, "When?"

Alain looks at Wee John, surprised at the speed of his answer. He replies, "I would like it if you were to consider stopping in at Glen Afton with bonnie Rosinn, Stephen and her father on your way down to get the boats over the water."

Wee John is both pleased and excited. He says, "Dá, I'd love to see Glen Afton, for I have heard so much about it, I know Ròsinn would love to see it too, just give us a few days and we'll be there, for it's on the way to *Dun Sgiath* (Duns-key) where we alight the Birlinns for Ireland."

Alain notices William has remained silent, perhaps he's pushed a little too much in his willingness to be a father to his boys, but he can't stop himself from asking. "What are yie thinking William? I know in your heart you've long finished with the church. Do you still want to come with me down to the Glen Afton? If you both have a liking, I'll teach yiez all I know about the craft of the master hunter and all the wee tricks o' my trade?"

William takes a deep breath and sits back, giving no obvious answer by his expression, then he says, "Dá, I cannot be telling you how long I have dreamt about the Black Craig and the Wolf and Wildcats, almost all my life I think. I'd dearly love to be coming with you this day, if it's all right by Wee Maw, Malcolm, aunt Margret and Mharaidh."

Breathing a great sigh of relief, Alain says, "Feck me boys, that's it settled then. We'll discuss this with Wee Maw and see what she says. And with her approval, we can plan for a clan gathering in Glen Afton later in the year. Boys, it's been a long time coming this day."

William looks at his father. "Dá, now that this day is here. I'm away to be packing my vittals and get all I need to take with me." William slaps Wee John on the shoulder. "C'mon John, we'll get all our stuff ready."

The brothers jump up and run towards the house, when William stops abruptly and turns towards his father. "Dá, don't you be leaving without me."

At that moment, Malcolm comes back through the door with a platter of cooked mussels, leaven ale bread and a jug full o' Wee Maw's honey *craitur*. He speaks to Alain with a wry smile. "Wee Maw sent this out for you as a wee bitty fill-up before you break fast, in case you're hungry… and thirsty."

Alain sighs painfully. "Awe naw, Malcolm. No' Wee Maw's *craitur*. I just couldn't face it. What's the chance of some o' that fine cold creamy milk yie have in your other hand? You can't have forgotten that I'm no use to man nor beast when I get feckin drunk just after breaking fast."

Malcolm hands Alain the jug. "Am only jesting with yie brother. It's just a hot jug o' a belted coo's (cow) finest cream with a wee dab o' honey. But I do have a dram here and it's Wee Maw's orders, she doesn't want you to be catching water in the head when you are out here sitting in the cold."

Wee John, William and Stephen come rushing back to the table. Wee John says, "Uncle, we've something really important to be telling you."

Malcolm sits down at the table and passes out the beverages. "Right boys, what's se' urgent yie want to be telling me?"

Before they can tell Malcolm about their plans, William notices young Sandy, Malcolm's stable boy, waving frantically.

He says, "Look, Malcolm, I think Sandy is needin' you at the gatehouse." Malcolm looks up to see Sandy gesturing to come over to the gatehouse urgently. Both Malcolm and Alain rush over to find out what may be amiss with Sandy. Everyone else follows cautiously toward the gates, watching curiously as Sandy gestures towards something in the distance. The small group congregate at the gatehouse where William looks to see what Sandy is pointing at. In the distance he sees a large body of mounted armoured men riding fast towards *Ach na Feàrna*.

William is the first to ask, "Who is it Dá?"

Alain shakes his head as he peers into the distance. He says, "I can see by the pennants that the front and lead rider is the Lord James Stewart. And there's the pennants o' Colin Campbell of Argyle too and there's Robert Brus the Earl o' Carrick…"

"Aye," confirms Malcolm, "and there's the Sheriff of Ayr's banner."

William points out. "That's Uncle Ranald, is he there as well? And there's Sir Bryce Blair's flag; I see his colours flying beside the house of the Boyd's."

Malcolm is concerned. "Something mighty serious must be happening for them all to be heading here." He quickly gives Sandy an order. "Go rise all our kinfolks."

Sandy immediately sprints towards the main house as Alain scrutinises the body of the column. "I see Bishop Wishart's standard, Feck, there's Bishop David de Moray of Bothwell and Lord Moray of Avoch riding beside True Tam of Ercildoune, and there's the standard's of the Comyn and the Douglas. What the feck can be going on?"

Watching the column gain ever closer, Malcolm observes, "It's a rare thing to be seeing a Comyn and a Brus in the same company."

Alain ponders, then he laughs. "Wishart said that he and True Tam might come over for the wedding tryst, but there must be at least five or six hundred men or more in that troop following them, even Wee Maw couldn't feed that lot."

Meanwhile, William instinctively grabs a large Wallace pennant on a lance from inside the gatehouse then he carries it through the gates to watch the horsemen approach.

Malcolm says, "There's something badly amiss there Alain, for it looks like they are all rigged for a war."

Alain frowns. "You're right, it does look like something's wrong."

The scene unfolding before William holds him in awe, he has never witnessed such a gathering of powerful looking men and warriors at one time, with their polished armour and fine chainmail glinting in the sunlight. So many beautiful coloured tabards, flags, pennants and multi-coloured horse caparison, all fluttering in the breeze as they canter towards them. It appears to William as though these are men of legend riding to do battle, dressed in all their regal finery. It's not long before the front of the column reaches the gatehouse, where William can see in detail many of the riders wearing full battle armour, each individual with emblazoned coats-of-arms. Others wear the ancient battledress, *léine*, Gambeson and Haubergeon of the *Galloway Gallóglaigh*. He also notices his old tutor and mentor's Lecky mòr and Bishop Wishart. The arrival of this fabulous war-column appears as though all the magnates, clan Chiefs, Mormaers and Knights of Scotland are arriving here in front of William personally. All the younger men of *Ach na Feàrna* gaze in amazement at this colourfully fascinating but very sombre looking gathering of men who approach them.

The front of the train finally comes to a halt at the main gates, where the leading dignitaries and magnates all dismount, their faces grim and ashen coloured as they meet with Malcolm and Alain. Sir Ranald Crauford looks back and waves the rest of the column on towards Glasgow as the delegation all dismount and gather with Malcolm and Alain.

A grim looking Lord Stewart approaches Malcolm. He says, "There's been a terrible accident Malcolm. You must accompany us to be guarding the *Bahn Rígh* at *Ceann Orran* at once."

Malcolm is perplexed.

"Grievous news Wallace," says Wishart as he joins them. Malcolm enquires with urgency in his voice. "What's happened? What is it? what…"

Wishart solemnly interrupts. "It's our beloved Alexander…" Wishart's voice becomes slightly hoarse. "He's dead."

Malcolm and Alain are dumbstruck. A numbed silence engulfs all of those standing at the gates of *Ach na Feàrna*.

Alain mutters, "This is no' possible, naw, not our bonnie Alexander, he can't be dead."

John, the Black Comyn Chief says, "I'm afraid it is true."

Malcolm in despair says, "NAW… This is a bad jest, it cannot be right."

This news of Alexander's death is devastating for both Alain and Malcolm. They glance at each other in disbelief then look at Wishart. It's clear by the pallor of Wishart and grey ashen expression on all these men, that their beloved King Alexander really is dead.

Malcolm stammers, "Alexander dead. How? Why? Naw Wishart, I don't believe it."

Alain asks, "What happened? I mean, how can Alexander be dead? We were together only the other eve, he was no' ill nor failing. Naw, this can't be right."

Lord Moray replies, "It's true Alain, Alexander is dead. We don't know the detail as yet, but it would appear he had a riding accident when his horse stumbled and fell from the sea cliffs near *Dun Ceann Orran*."

"No," spits Alain. "This must be a mistake. Anyone who knows horses, especially Areion, knows that to ride near on forty miles then stumble and fall, it just doesn't happen. There must be another reason or it's malicious information. Alexander cannot be dead, I wont believe it."

Wishart says gently. "It's true, Alain. All we know is that his horse slipped or stumbled on the cliffs near *Dun Ceann Orran* during the storm and it appears both Alexander and the horse fell to their deaths. We've been informed that our King suffered a broken neck."

Alain snarls tersely. "Areion never was feint of foot. Alexander and his warhorse are too experienced to simply slip and fall, that just doesn't happen, and in particular from a wide drove road and small cliff edge. I know that road well. Naw, I'll not believe it, there is mischief afoot."

"Hush, Alain," says Malcolm.

"NO," barks Alain in a rage. "I know in my heart that what you say cannot be true."

Malcolm places a hand on Alain's chest then speaks. "Wishart, we cannot readily be accepting what you're saying to us, for it just isn't possible for Alexander to ride off a small cliff face. It doesn't make sense to those who know him."

John Baliol, the Lord of Galloway, speaks. "Wallace, you cannot feel any more bereft and at a loss than we do. And you may believe me when I say we too are in as much disbelief."

Uncommonly enraged, Malcolm punches his fist into his open hand. "I should never have left him."

"You had no choice," says Wishart. "None of us could have foreseen such a tragic accident. It was Alexander's own command that you were to leave him, for I heard him order you so myself."

His anger burning, Malcolm replies, "It doesn't matter Wishart, I should have stayed by his side, it's my duty."

Robert de Brus, Earl of Carrick speaks. "No Wallace, your duty is now to be by the side of Queen Yolande. It's Sir Richard De Lundie, his personal retainer who should have been by his side. But as Alexander dismissed Sir Richard as he did you, Lundie cannot be faulted, nor be caused to feel remorse."

Lord Moray states, "Malcolm, a Council of the Realm is to be called immediately at Scone (Skoon) Palace where six Guardians of Scotland will be appointed to maintain stability till the coronation of Alexander's heir and successor is inaugurated. The Guardianship North of the Firth of Forth will be entrusted to Bishop Fraser of Saint Andrews, Duncan the Earl of Fife and Alexander Comyn, Earl of Buchan. The south of the Forth is committed to Bishop Wishart here, John Comyn Lord of Badenoch and Sir James Stuart, the High Steward of Scotland. Their remit is to keep peace, good and public order till good Alexander's grand-daughter, the Maid of Norway be brought across the North Sea and she is proclaimed Queen."

Shaking his head forlorn, Wishart says, "Scotland will suffer a deep depression of mourning for our much loved King. Riders have already been dispatched to convey the tragic news of the death of the great Canmore to Alexander's Lords, Magnates and his loyal kinsmen in the far Highlands, Islands and beyond.

Alain observes, "The Guardians will require sharp wits to bring together all that's best of Alexander's reign and maintain the realm's good order till his granddaughter can be inaugurated,"

His brother agrees, "Aye, but mind that should Yolande provide a male heir, it will be Yolande and Margret who will rule till the Heir is crowned King or Queen on *An Liath Fàil*, (The stone of destiny.)"

The Bishop of Glasgow speaks solemnly. "It will be the duty of the *Garda Rìoghail* and *Garda Céile Aicé* to protect them all should the realm become fractious."

The impromptu council confer a while and discuss much in a sombre and grievous atmosphere, with Malcolm, Alain, the Galloway and Ayrshire Wallace's, detailing the little information the delegation know of King Alexander's tragic death and the mission they are now embarking upon. William, Malcolm óg, and Stephen listen intently until the Earls and Barons, who conferred with the elder Wallace brothers, bid farewell, mount their horses and continue eastward toward Glasgow.

Wishart, Leckie, True Tam, and Ranald remain behind to speak further with the elder Wallace brothers.

"Malcolm," says Wishart, "after you and Alain left the Maidens Castle the other eve, True Tam came to my quarters. But I couldn't make sense of his ramblings, for I simply thought him blind drunk, and he was."

Wishart glances at True Tam then continues. "In his stupor, he kept repeating a rhyme that didn't make sense then, and it barely makes sense now, but do please listen to what he has to say."

True Tam, dressed in an ancient assortment of piecemeal rusty black armour and looking extremely gaunt, with his great red-greyish wispy beard and long bushy hair greased back, appears very odd and dishevelled, as his tall sinewy body is much too thin for his heavy black armour.

He looks at Malcolm and Alain with mesmeric bulging eyes. "I will tell to you what comes to mind ma friends. The other eve, I had a overwhelming sense of fear. I saw signs upon the height of the storm. Long before Alexander left the Maidens Castle I felt a great urgency to reach out to him, but ah fell ill from some malevolence and could not be at the side of our beloved *Artur* to be warning him not to travel to *Ceann Orran*, especially through the eye of the storm."

Wishart intervenes. "I thought it was just drunken ramblings that night, but Tam here had a strong foreboding of the tragedy, even before Alexander left Edinburgh. When Tam finally arrived at my compartments he tried to tell me this, but of course Alexander was long gone; and it wasn't until the next morn that we heard the news about the death of Alexander that we truly understood that Tam here had been visited with the sight."

Anxious, Malcolm enquires, "What did yie see, Tam?"

True Tam, still appearing as though he is in some strange trance, utters, *"I saw the storm blaws winter's leaves from springtime tree's, the Carron flies north on wings of death with ease. From Sudrons hand upon the morrow, shall blaw the greatest wind, tae Scotland's sorrow. Then blood frae a son twice o'er, shall slake black blood once more. For t'is man no' Deil' our faither from to other world shall steal. Then our friend o' the Corvus brood, will avenge us all, with his men of wood."* True Tam suddenly falls silent.

Wishart says, "We know what True Tam's like and we cannot be ignoring his prophetic sight, for we're *Céile Aicé*. He knew this day our Alexander would be dead, yet his words of mesmerism implies it's no accident, but the facts say that it was."

Ranald steps forward then puts a hand gently on True Tam's shoulder. "Tam, you've always been our Loacoan of Troy. But what you say from your visions, it makes no' sense to us, though we're long since understanding not to ignore you."

Alain's mind races trying to rationalise True Tam's babble. "I don't understand this Tam, blood from a son twice over and men of wood will gain us freedom, from what?"

Malcolm states, "We must reason the meaning of Tam's words soon, and we must also find out what really happened to our *Artur* and all that anyone may know of this tragedy before we reach a judgement upon this terrible business."

Alain, on the edge of rage, "If it were not an accident..."

Wishart interrupts, "Wallace, you must still all wanton machinations and not speak the unthinkable, clear your mind of these thoughts." Wishart then softens his tone of voice, "Malcolm I am needing you to be clear-headed and make ready to leave as soon as possible and follow us to *Ceann Orran*. The *Céile Aicé* and *Garda Rígh* must be told to gather and be prepared for all eventualities. Let it be known there's to be a gathering of the entire *Céile Aicé* and *Garda Rígh* at the earliest time possible either at Muthill or Scone."

Malcolm replies, "Aye, it shall be done."

"Malcolm, our *Aicé* Yolande needs us now, and if True Tam is right about something amiss, we must be on our guard and ready to defend her at all costs and to protect Yolande's unborn child, with our lives if needs be."

Leckie mòr, who has been unusually silent, says, "Malcolm, you must leave with haste to be with Yolande. Donnachaid MacDhuibh (Duncan MacDuff) the Mormaer of Fife and the *Ceann Orran Garda Bahn Rígh* are by her side at this very moment. I'll see to it that the other leaders and chiefs of the *Céile Aicé* are informed and prepare for a council of the realm, for our future is most uncertain."

After a further brief conversation the Guardian delegation bid farewell to the Wallace brothers.

As the delegation mount their horses and canter off to catch up with the solemn vanguard. True Tam suddenly stops and looks with piercing eyes toward the gates where everyone is beginning to disperse. He looks directly at William.

Stephen whispers…"Jaezuz Wallace… what the feck? The auld buzzard, look, he's staring right at yee."

Wee Maw, standing beside William, speaks. "That's True Tam of Ercildoune boys, he's a spiritual man of the old faith. Some do say he's a seer and that neither man nor any woman of station may disregard his tongue for fear of the curse. But you must speak of him with a hearts kindness, for he is all of that himself."

Malcolm enquires. "Maw, you heard all that was said?"

Wee Maw wrings her hands in her apron then replies, "I did son, and my heart is greatly saddened by the news."

She looks up at Malcolm then reaches out and places a hand upon his chest. "So must you be leaving us then son?"

"Aye mother, my duty now is to be by the side of Yolande. Then I must assemble all of the realm's *Garda Rìoghail* at *Dun Ceann Orran* as soon as possible."

Everyone makes their way back into the heart of *Ach na Feàrna* to prepare for their individual duties in this time of crisis, all except William and Stephen, who are still watching, fascinated by the odd looking knight, True Tam. For a long time True Tam sits motionless, holding on tight to the reigns of his handsome Arabic cross stallion. He looks curiously at William, making no obvious movements to follow the Magnates column.

"What the feck," exclaims Stephen. "Look at that old feckin warlock Wallace, he's still staring at you."

William is frozen by the intense gaze of True Tam, but he also feels there is no malice.

"Fuck, he is pointing at you now… Oi, don't feckn like this Wallace, I tink he is puttin' the hex on yie me boy."

Eventually True Tam pulls his horse around and begins to canter east away from *Ach na Feàrna* towards Glasgow.

Watching True Tam canter off into the distance, William is captivated by the strange character who occasionally glances back at him, as if he had something to tell him, but he does not yet know what it is. Finally True Tam gallops off into the distance and out of the sight of the spooked young men.

Malcolm and Alain return to the wedding guests and families gathered near the main house.

The two Wallace brothers are ashen faced and appear with fortitudes grim. "William, Stephen, come over here..." commands Malcolm. "Gather all and tell them to congregate at the centre water-well, for I must convey to everyone this terrible news."

Before long, all the folk in the Balloch of *Ach na Feàrna* congregate at the water-well, where the elders of Clan Wallace are already gathered. The atmosphere is now far from that of the joyous wedding celebrations the previous day. Malcolm climbs the stairs to the platform of the cross-bridge walkway to address the gathering. Grey faced and still obviously in shock, tears can be seen in his eyes.

"My friends, family, and all our kith and kin gathered here this day. I must tell you such grave news." Malcolm pauses, clearing his throat, then continues with broken voice. "It is with heavy heart that I must confirm to you all, that Good King Alexander has been killed in a riding accident on his way to *Dun Ceann Orran*, apparently caused in his haste to be with Yolande *ban Rígh*."

There is an audible gasp from everyone, though all had an idea of what had been said at the gates of *Ach na Feàrna*. The facts delivered simply and so concisely by Malcolm only confirms their worst fears. Malcolm continues, "I have been tasked to be by Yolande's side and command the *Garda Rìoghail*, therefore, I must leave you and make haste for *Dun Ceann Orran* today."

Malcolm raises his hands to regain everyone's attention. "Please go back to the *Fèis*, I know there is no heart warmth for our grief and the loss of our bonnie King, but for the sake of bonnie Ròsinn and Wee John, we must temper our sadness with thoughts of this young couples first day of wedded union, and for us to bless their future with smiles of good fortune on their fey day."

He retires from the cross-bridge to join Alain and members of the Galloway Wallace family. The solemn gathering disperses slowly to their various individual crofts, obhain's and bothies around *Ach na Feàrna*, much in a daze, for no one can truly take in or wish to believe what they have just heard.

"Alain", says Malcolm, "We need to talk…"

Alain makes his way over to his brother where Malcolm speaks quietly. "This is a bad business Alain. The atmosphere emanating from Wishart and the magnates hold a lot more than grief and mourning. I felt their unease about this story of Alexander falling from Areion is just not something that's acceptable and there is much more to discuss. But first I must meet with Lord Lennox and Patrick of Dunbar in Glasgow, then I'll make haste with them to *Dun Ceann Orran*."

"Do you really believe what they are saying about Alexander's death being an accident?"

Malcolm replies shaking his head, "No Alain, I don't. But no one can be certain of anything till Wishart and the Lords examine every piece of this bloody puzzle. We heard Wishart say it was a horse riding accident and that's all he knows at the moment. But I cannot believe it. I've never known a warhorse to fall and stumble such as in the way they are describing, and not a horse ridden by Alexander."

"Never, I still wont believe Areion could fall like a yearling of no experience." Alain pauses before continuing, "Do you want me to come to with you Malcolm?"

At that moment Bryan, Seoras and Dáibh from the Galloway Wallace Clan approach and overhear Alain's offer to travel with Malcolm.

"Aye, Malcolm," says Bryan. "We don't have our armour, but me and ma brothers and all yer cousins, we'll ride with yie too if yie think it best."

"No, but I thank you. There's no' much you all could be doing right now, and the likely tensions that will unfold abroad in the realm will surely bring unrest. I think it best if you're all prepared for any eventuality in your own homesteads. But be ready to ride out should I give yiez the call."

Still agonising over Alexander's supposed accident, Alain says, "Malcolm, it's so feckin hard to accept this story about the King having a riding accident. There was hardly a better hablar (horse soldier) in the realm than him. And the great Areion has hooves the size o' grand shields and a heart as sound to match. Naw, something just isn't right. I'll never believe it was an accident."

Nodding his head by way of agreement, Malcolm then turns to Bryan and Dáibh. "Wishart said we must all be on our guard till the next coronation, which will be that of Alexander's grand-daughter Margret, or Alexander's unborn."

Alain is concerned. "But the Maid is only about five years old and away across the great sea in Norway. How long will take to get her across to Scotland? Unless Yolande is to rule as regent and possibly her heir when she gives birth to their child, that will sure no' be easy."

"Ach Alain, Matilda of England ruled in the place of an infant. If Yolande doesn't take the regency for any reason and wee Margret o' Norway doesn't accept the crown, it will be Yolande's first born to be our sovereign, then it is Devorguilla of Galloway who is next in line."

Spitting on the ground and looking across the great Clyde River to the hills and mountains beyond, Alain responds, "This is going to be a time we have never known before brother. Does anyone know with any certainty what will transpire I wonder?"

Malcolm says, "I don't know what will happen now. I feel there'll be mighty serious problems to face soon. Some o' the Chiefs and Magnates I know will not accept a child as their sovereign, be it male or female."

Alain agrees vehemently. "Fuck, you're right, no one could have thought or imagined Scotland without Alexander's firm rule. He was a great King, a great man, and a friend to us all. I just hope the Guardians manage this black time that's come upon us."

Dáibh says, "Listen, Malcolm, I'll be gathering our kinfolks together and making our way to Galloway as soon as we are ready to travel. We'll muster a standing army of *Gallóbhet* (Male and Female *Gallóglaigh*-Galloglass) and have them in readiness should you require us. Just keep us informed. But for now, we shall bid you both farewell, so you all be taking care."

He embraces Malcolm and Alain, then leaves to gather his people for the long journey southwest to the wild remote lands of Galloway.

Turning to his brother, Malcolm says, "I'd better be getting my royal mark on with much haste for this journey, Alain. Will you get the boys readying my horses and tack them while I see to Margret? I'll take some o' the *Ach na Feàrna* guard with me, if you could also let them know to prepare."

"Aye, Malcolm, that I will."

The mood is very dark amongst the gathering and a long hour passes before Sir Malcolm returns from the main house. It's been a number of years since anyone has seen Sir Malcolm in his finest garb of the *Garda ban Rígh* and wearing his impressive flashings as *Taoiseach s' Garda Ban Rìoghail nan Alba* (Chieftain of the royal bodyguard to the Queen of Scotland). He appears almost larger than life and a true martial warrior of distinction, wearing his finest beaten polished plate armour, chainmail avental, haubergeon, chausses and sabatons. All the dragonhead link catchments and armour pieces are emblazoned with inlaid gold knotwork at hinge and breast. Malcolm's helm bears the symbol of the blue winged Dragon crouching upon the apex, symbolising the house of Wallace. Exquisitely crafted, the blue-bodied Gold veined Dragon with scales of turquoise blue running the length of its body, has skin wings extended as if gliding toward its prey. The two claws reach past the temples of Malcolm's helmet, grasping at the lower jaw guards, are complemented with a long forked blue horsehair tail flowing down and over the curved lower back rim of Malcolm's helm to his middle back. The boys look on in wonderment at this display of the Armorial bearing that demonstrates so vividly, the ancestral symbolism of the Wallace blood.

Pointing, William exclaims, "Would you be looking at the grace of your father there now Malcolm óg? I've never seen the likes before in all the time we've been here."

Malcolm óg replies. "Your father has the same armour, too."

William exclaims. "Feck, I wouldn't mind wearing that outfit going down the Paisley village taverns for a stramash (brawl)."

Malcolm óg says, "Look at Janus, his warhorse."

"Janus? Jaezuz, Wallace, what kinda name is that for a horse?" asks Stephen.

William replies, "It's a Greek word for the god of chaos. Our

Artur Alexander presented the horse to Uncle Malcolm not long after the battle of Largs. The King named all his Arab cross war-horses after Classical gods."

The proud jet-black stallion Janus, is cloaked in full armorial caparison for this solemn occasion. The colourful coat-of-arms of the Garda Ban Rígh detail, is in a blue and white-diced border around a wheaten background, with the golden turquoise blue dragon of the Wallace emblazoned on the caparison rear-flanks and breast quarters. Sir Malcolm and his personal guard look magnificent astride their great warhorses as they leave to follow the eastern road and the Magnates column.

William, Malcolm óg, Stephen and Wee John watch Sir Malcolm and his bodyguard ride into the distance, with an inner feeling of respect and admiration, shared by all who witness them leave. But there is also a sense of great foreboding and apprehension in the air.

Late in the afternoon, Alain, Mharaidh, Wee Maw, Margret and Auld Stephen talk in the kitchens, while William and Wee John walk to the sweet ground of their mother with Stephen.

Wee John says, "Feck, it was only a few moments ago the world seemed a such different place."

"Ah know," agrees William. "Can you feel the air around us now? I've never felt anything like this before, it's so feckn... odd. And with you now a married man Wee John and us really meeting our Dá for the first time with us all getting on se' well together too, then this all happens?"

"What d'yie think will happen without the *Artur Àrd Rígh*?" William sighs. "I don't know."

"Well, I hope it will not be the doin's o' auld Erinn." says Stephen.

"Feck, you too?" shouts William.

"What are yie sayin' there Wallace?" says a puzzled Stephen.

"Ach Stephen, when you called Ireland Erinn, it reminded me o' something my Dá was saying about the Welsh." William waves his hands. "I'm sorry Stephen, what were yie saying there afore I cut yie off?"

Stephen continues, "Aye, I have never known a time with a King of all Erinn, and this notable absence has caused endless fighting over there between the chiefs o' this and the chiefs o' that. Then you've got the feckin Normans in the *Duhblynn Pale* shutting all us of us Irish out. Then yie be havin' the Normans o' the North where they're becoming even more Irish than some o' the bleedin' Irish themselves and there's Irish becoming Norman. Jaezuz it's a right feckin mess over there now that I bleedin' think about it all."

"Whoa there…" says William. "What the feck, Stephen, how do you keep up with that mince? That's some fine mixin' o' madness you're talking there."

"Aye, to be sure it is," sighs Stephen. "And it's getting worse. The Normans are bringing their feckin laws and courts to Erinn and treating us native folks worse than sick livestock. And them there same Normans with the backing of the church are colluding to kill off all the Cruathnie Breitheamh they can find."

Wee John intervenes, "Wait a minute fellas, what d'yie mean Normans? I thought they died out a couple o' hundred years ago."

"Aye well," says William, "they call themselves English now, which is feckin strange. Maybe it's because the Normans consider themselves the original people of England, driven out by invading Saxons, Jutes and Angles a while back. When they returned to England calling themselves bleedin' Normans they fair hammered the shit outa' the Saxons for shoving them out of the country in the first place. Now the feckin Normans call themselves after the Angles who pushed them out to begin with, saying they are now English. But some o' us call them for what they are, feckin Normans."

"Feck, I only asked, I didn't want a history lesson," replies Wee John.

William growls as he thumps a giant fist full force knuckle-point into the thigh of Wee Johns leg "Well, I just feckin gave yie one, so shut it ya illiterate midden."

Wee John screams aloud as he falls to the ground. "Arrgh, ya bastard, yie've killed ma leg yie big feckin feckr."

William sneers, "Stop yer moaning, ya big arse."

Wee John holds his hand high, imploring. "Ah cannae feel a thing. Jaezuz what have yie done William? Help me up for feck's sake."

As William stoops to lift his brother, Wee John Suddenly raises himself from the ground at speed and punches William on the muscle of his arm, knocking him against Stephen and Malcolm óg. Wee John dives onto his brother and a fearsome young buck wrestling fight breaks out between them.

Stephen looks to Malcolm óg. "What the feck do we do? "

Malcolm óg shrugs his shoulders. "I don't know, just jump in and grab the first one yie can."

Stephen and Malcolm óg joyfully fling themselves into the fray with the two Wallace brothers. Wee Maw, Alain and Auld Stephen walk out of the main house to see the fracas; they stop to watch the boys fighting.

Auld Stephen smiles proudly. "My now, it's nice to be seeing the boys enjoying themselves on such a solemn occasion as this."

Exasperated, Wee Maw says. "May it always be in such good humour that they fight like that."

Auld Stephen says. "I pray that it will always be so. It's well known that your Alexander brought so much peace and prosperity to Scotland and also a fair share of trade to Erinn too I may add."

Alain smiles as the boys tumble about in front of them, glad of some light relief.

Auld Stephen continues, "I just hope Scotland doesn't end up with the troubles we are seeing over in old Erinn, for life there is a hard place in hell without a righteous King."

"Where?" asks Alain. "Scotland or Ireland?"

"Both I reckon." replied Auld Stephen, "we're two small nations joined at the hip, and our own families by blood now too I'm happy to be saying, me Brother."

"Feck, you're right, brother."

Wee Maw says, "Thank Magda for that, yiez had me near crying' in ma porridge with your miserable faces and sad stories. And here's me listening to yiez like a hungry orphan waiting on a morsel o' food."

Alain and Auld Stephen laugh as Wee Maw continues. "With bonnie Ròsinn and Wee John hitched, that's a fair match made in heaven I'll be thinking. She'll keep that big ox John in check and he'll be good for her too Stephen, for he's definitely from the finest stock."

"Would yie want that I should be staying here with you till Malcolm comes back from *Ceann Orran*?" asks Alain.

"Naw, son, you get going when yiez are ready. The sooner yiez get away and safely down to Glen Afton the better. It's as Malcolm said, everyone should be looking to securing their own homesteads in this time of uncertainty."

"Are yie sure, Maw?"

"Aye, I'm sure, son, we've no need to be worrying here, but the rest of the country could go to ruin if the Guardians don't get a grip right quick."

Auld Stephen agrees. "Bheitris (Beatrix) is right Alain."

"Bheitris…" says Alain sitting back in his chair in mock astonishment.

Wee Maw appears to flush then she squints her sharp steely blue eyes at Auld Stephen and with gritted teeth and a glare intended to turn Auld Stephen to stone. She says, "Margret, Bheitris, Morríaghan Wallace if yie be proper."

Alain beams. "I've no' ever heard you being called Bheitris before Maw?"

Auld Stephen laughs. "Sure I'm sorry about that, is it improper to be calling yie Bheitris?"

"ALAIN…" growls Wee Maw. "You be going for the bonnie Mharaidh and get ready to leave. And I want yiez taking anything extra you need if young William is going with yie, for that boy can fair eat."

Wee Maw has spoken, ensuring on the pain of her wrath that the Bheitris conversation is at an end. She continues with a wry smile. "Me and dear Auld Stephen ua H'Alpine here will be sorting out the necessary vittals for Wee John and Rosinn's trip to the bonnie emerald Isle."

She coyly smiles at Auld Stephen then places her wee hand high on his thigh, causing him to blush, and speechless in front of Alain. Wee Maw thinks with a grin, *'That shut Auld Stephen up, calling me Bheitris indeed.'*

Noon turns to eventide, with everyone making an effort for the joy of the wedded couple, but most are still quietly sombre at the news of Alexander's demise. Things are returning slowly to relative normality in the kitchens of *Ach na Feàrna* when Malcolm óg comes in from the doocots (Pigeon lofts) bringing Wee Maw a message.

She calls out, "Ulliann, will yie tell everyone to come here the now, I've some news from your father." Alain, William and Stephen approach Auld Stephen and Wee Maw.

William says, "That's us about ready to leave Wee Maw."

"WHAT did you just call me, master William Wallace?" She gives him the dreaded 'look' then winks at Auld Stephen.

In his excitement, William hasn't thought, he mumbles, "Eh, well um, GRANNY, we've got the horses ready and hope we'll be leaving in the hour if we want to reach the Glen Afton for first light."

Wee Maw says, "Just you wait the now, I've a couple o' messages *fae* the doocots here from Malcolm to be telling to yiez all."

The families' of the Wallace and H'Alpine's gather round the grand feasting table in the kitchen, while Wee Maw unravels the messages taken from the doo's of Malcolm. There's an expectant silence as she sits and squints at the small notes... "I cannae be reading these," says Wee Maw. She sighs, "Ach, Malcolm always does scrieve se' small. Uliann come here, will you be reading out aloud your father's messages for everyone?"

Uliann takes the notes from Wee Maw and begins to read out the messages. "Father scrieves he'll be taking Yolande to the citadel of Snowdonia and he expects to be back home by the end of the month. He also said that there's to be a council of the *Garda Ban Rígh* in Paisley by the end of the month too. He requests that Uncle Alain is to be there."

Uliann pauses, then she says, "That's everything in the messages, Granny..."

Everyone sits quietly for a moment, the messages reminding them that a grievous air is descending upon Scotland, and all are sincerely hoping that normality will return soon.

Wee Maw breaks the silence. "Well, Alain, you must be excited to be gettin' goin' to the Glen Afton are you no'?"

"Aye, that I am," replied Alain "But I must be asking this favour o' young Stephen's father first."

Auld Stephen raises an eyebrow. "Aye, and what is it you'll be asking of me then Alain Wallace? Is it about me young spring lamb wanting to be staying wit yiez awhile?"

"It is, aye," replied Alain. "And he'll be most welcome if he's wanting to be coming with us to the Glen Afton to learn the skills o' the *Artur's* hunter. Do you think he would like that?"

Auld Stephen looks at his son with obvious pride. "I would be honoured for me young fella to be learning from a master archer and hunter such as yourself Alain. I mind o' watching you and your father's *Gallóglaigh* bowyers fight at the battle o' Largs many years ago, and could only wish we had your particular skills back in auld Erinn right now. Maybe there would be no' se' many Normans left there now I'll be thinking." Suddenly Auld Stephen turns to Wee Maw. "Oh, I am so sorry, Bheitris, I wasn't thinkin' abroad, for my happiness is indulgent with young Stephen to be staying here awhile wit yiez."

"Ach, no harm, no matter Stephen," replies Wee Maw. "Father is long time passed to the other world and he'll be so proud o' his family as he watches over us all for the way all our weans have turned out." Curiously a twinkle shines in Wee Maw's eyes. "And I'll be thinking too, that young Katriona has caught the eye of young master Stephen over there hidin', if I'm no' mistaken."

Stephen goes uncharacteristically red; he looks like he's been caught by his private parts in a gut snare. Both he and Katriona had thought none had noticed the budding romance between them.

William whispers to Alain while Wee Maw and Auld Stephen talk together… "What's Auld Stephen's apology all about, Dá?"

Alain replies, "They're talking about ma father William, your grandfather and namesake. He was *Ceannard* of the

Wolf and Wildcat *Gallóglaigh* at the Battle of Largs, he died while protecting our good king Alexander."

William's eagerness to find out more is interrupted by Wee Maw, "Well Alain me boy, will you be staying a wee while longer for some fine vittals before yiez leave or d'yiez want me to be packing them for the overnight journey?"

"Can yie be packing it for us, Maw? I'll be checking the horses then we should be about ready to leave."

"Right son, away now and do your chores, then come back when you're all prepared and we'll have some fine vittals ready to be taking with you."

Wee Maw is about to tend to the fireside irons when she stops and calls out. "Wait William, if you bring the pack horse to the big house stores, we have plenty spare vittals there and you can fill the bow-wagon with everything a' plenty that yie can never find in that wilderness o' Glen Afton yie'll fine fellas dwell in."

Auld Stephen and Alain grin at each other, knowing an extra horse loaded with Wee Maw's vittals would be enough to feed a small army.

As Wee Maw makes her way to the larders, she calls out to them without looking back. "And I've some fresh boiled duck eggs yiez can be eatin' on the way down to Glen Afton."

Alain looks at Auld Stephen. "I don't know what you're smiling at H'Alpine, wait till you see what she has planned for you to be feasting upon when you make the trip back to Erinn."

Auld Stephen laughs, then says, "We'll be leaving here in a couple of days and Alain if its all right by you, we would like to come a' calling in to see yiez at Glen Afton and we could bring the vittal overload down for yie."

As they leave the kitchens to walk to the stables, Auld Stephen looks to the heavens. "Would yie be looking at that thunderous black sky Alain, it's sure getting so very late in the day to be leavin. Should you no' be waiting till the morn to be getting a fresh start on the day?"

Studying the overcast night sky, Alain nods his head in agreement. "Aye Stephen, I think you're likely right, it looks like heavy rains will coming soon too. I think I'll go back in and say to Wee Maw that we'll leave by the morn's first light. And we can be sharing some more auld stories around the fire tonight again if yie wish?"

Auld Stephen calls out to Alain, who is now walking toward the kitchen doors. "So long as that walking history book William doesn't drink se' much o' Wee Maw's *craitur*."

Alain laughs as he enters the kitchens where he sees Katriona and Wee Maw fixing vittals for the trip to Glen Afton. "Maw, I reckon it's getting too late to be going back to the Craig this night, and we've everything ready for the journey 'ceptin your vittals. We can load them in the morn and be leaving fresh and early with a clear day ahead of us."

Wee Maw looks at her son. "That makes more sense me boy."

"I should be telling Mharaidh right quick for she's already advised me that was the sensible thing to do."

"Aye, she's a fine lass yie have there, son,"

"Aye, she's so like you Maw, so I'd better let her know that we're no' going back this night, if she's packed everything away, life will no' be worth living."

Giving Alain the dreaded 'look', the matriarch says, "Exactly what d'yie mean by that? She must be a very fine young woman, right enough then to be keeping you in your place, Alain me boy."

Alain sheepishly replies, "Eh, aye... that's what I meant Maw."

Wee Maw is pleased with herself as Alain disappears through the doors to find Mharaidh.

Later that night, when most have retired to their cribs, Alain and William are sitting round the large peat fire talking of all that has taken place over the last few days.

"Dá," says William.

"Aye?" replies Alain while happily watching the mesmerising dance of the little fire flames.

"Who was that skinny fella in black ill fitting armour at the gates when some o' the Guardians army was here?"

"That would be Sir Thomas of Ercildoune. Some folks call him True Tam, others call him Thomas the Rhymer."

"He really is a knight?"

"Aye, he is. Why do you ask?"

"When you all had finished talking, he was walking towards his horse, but he kept staring at me. It was feckin scary, well no' scary, but strange. Ach, I cannae explain what ah felt. But it wasn't just that, it was when he mounted his horse, he pointed at me and began talking awhile to somebody that just wasn't there. Then he turned his horse and rode away after the others, but he kept turning round and looking directly back at me, feck ah didn't like that."

"True Tam is a sooth-sayer or a gifted Seer. He has the gift of the second sight William. Thankfully for him though, he has powerful friends like Wishart and yer Uncle Malcolm, otherwise, many in the church would have him sunk into a barrel of soft pitch then command that long horseshoe nails be hammered into the barrel and then for the barrel to be sealed, rolled down a hill and boiled in a vat, with him in it. After that, they would like the barrel flung into the sea."

"Fucks sake!" exclaims William. "That's a bit harsh. Why would folk do that to him Dá?"

Thinking there is no easy way to describe True Tam, Alain says, "Ach William, folk are fickle and I don't really know the answer to that. Some say the reason is that they think he works for the devil and they want his soul to be trapped in the barrel, but none will do it for fear that if it doesn't work, he'll come back and take their souls to hell."

"That's no' natural, Dá."

Alain shakes his head. "Naw, its no', son. Your uncle and I have known True Tam for many years. Aye he is strange, but he's a good man. Another of his gifts is the power to heal. If it wasn't for True Tam on more than one occasion, myself and your Uncle Malcolm would no' be here this day."

"Really?"

Stoking the evening fire with a poker iron, Alain continues. "True Tam has the gift to predict future events and the ability to see things we cannot, that's long been proven. But he sometimes gets into an awful state over it. You can't tell if he's drunk, mad or in a divine flux. He usually writes things down when he is in that state, in verse like a poem, carol or song. That's why folk call him Thomas the Rythmer."

"It was strange how I felt when he stared at me though."

"Trust me William, never judge a man by his cloth, you mind to always have a welcoming heart for those less fortunate than you, or for others regardless of different beliefs or faith. True Tam is all of that and more. He's cursed and he's blessed by these gifts. For in helping others, the cost to his own well-being is great. William, there are many types of folk in this world and if none would harm you then wish no harm on them. If their nature is driven pure, then defend them, for as you grow older, you'll develop your own special gifts. There will be those who will love you for those gifts but there will be others who will despise you, for they would covet those same gifts you own so freely. Your strengths, your inner sense of honour in doing what is right, let that be your guide if you ever feel lost."

The younger man nods and thinks long and hard on his father's words.

***

Next morning, on the East coast, Bishop Wishart and True Tam are walking their horses where Alexander's horse supposedly slipped and fell from the cliffs. Wishart strokes his beard. "There's definitely something amiss Tam, but there's nothing here to see. There's nothing to confound what we've been told, but everything here unsettles my senses."

"I feel it too," says his companion. "Something is not right."

"I fear too many folk have walked and ridden this old road now, and what do we search for anyway?"

True Tam glances at Wishart, as their eyes meet Tam enquires curiously. "That boy standing at the gates of *Ach na Feàrna*, holding the blue dragon o' the Wallace? Is he Alain's son?"

"Which one? The big lad with the long blond hair holdin' the Wallace pennant?"

"Aye," replies True Tam. "That boy, who is he?"

"Aye that's Alain's son. His name is William, he's a good young man, why do you ask?"

True Tam looks across the great Germanic sea, then back at Wishart. "There's something about him. I must tell you this Wishart, some day that boy will be a man and that's when he'll deliver to you an answer to a question you have yet to ask."

"What do you mean?" enquires the curious Bishop.

True Tam replies in a semi-trance. *"There are flocks of swirling flights from the south and blue. Yet when his blood is earth and reach is great, with hearts of oak and Yew, shall this realm will gain freedom."*

True Tam comes out of his trance. "Hear me, Wishart, and hear me well. Young William Wallace holds a key to Scotland's future, you mark my words. Be aware of him, nurture him, most of all, you must listen to him."

"I hear you," says Wishart. He thinks ominously. *'I do hear you.'*

***

Sailing for almost four days, the ship carrying de Courtney finally reaches Tilbury docks near London. Taking young de Percy with him upon disembarking, de Courtney leaves strict instructions with the Royal dock guards, under pain of death, that none of the crew nor any soldiers on board are to communicate with anyone ashore, nor is anyone to leave the ship. There can be no risk taken that word of their exploit be spread. De Courtney conveys that it is imperative that all remain on board till he returns with anticipated reward and honour for their endeavours. The English sailors and soldiers aboard are all loyal men and hardened veterans, they know only too well the severity of penalty for disobeying their master, for they have witnessed and dealt out his harsh measure many times before. They also know the reward for their unquestioned obedience would be great.

De Courtney and de Percy ride a fast pace towards London, not stopping till they approach the doors of King Edward's apartments at the Tower of London, where they dismount. They are met immediately by sir Hugh de Cressingham, a large stout Norman-Englishman; his status peculiar to those of noble Norman extract being identified on first glance by a bowl-cut style of haircut, short and shaved up the back of his obese neck to just above his ears, with a waxen fringe cut completely circular around the top of his head. His pale pock-marked face appears exaggerated and bloated.

This man is a most devoted servant to Edward Longshanks as a leading member of the King's inner council and Edward's personal royal treasurer. Cressingham barks out a command "Well... what news do you bring me de Courtney?"

De Courtney answers, "It is with heavy heart that I must tell you this my lord, King Alexander of Scotland has met his death in a terrible accident."

De Courtney pauses to gain a reaction from Cressingham, who is apparently unmoved by this news. he says, "I am waiting to hear of how the Scotch King met his death."

De Courtney commences his delivery of the detail. Then he concludes, "My Lord, apparently Alexander was in such haste to be with his Queen, yet despite all advice, he ventured through the night of storms to be with her, and that his horse did slip and fall from the cliffs near Kinghorn. It is true all that I tell to you, that King Alexander broke his neck and died of his injuries."

"Most unfortunate," says Cressingham. "And what of the pirates you captured on our seaboard, have they been dealt with yet?"

De Percy is bewildered by Cressinghams comment, but he says nothing as de Courtney replies. "They are under Guard and still aboard the ship birthed near Tilbury docks, the ship is moored offshore my Lord."

"Then you must return and reward them with much haste," commands Cressingham.

"My Lord," acknowledges de Courtney.

"Burn the ship, too," orders Cressingham as an afterthought. "Do not leave even a a ship's rat alive, should you not wish the same reward."

"My Lord."

"By your return, you shall assume the position as my personal spy-master of all England, young de Percy is to be your squire, do I make myself clear?"

"My Lord." The knight nods his assent.

Cressingham's piercing eyes chill his subordinates with a menace transcending any threat their ruthless King could issue.

De Courtney suddenly realises Cressingham waits impatiently for a response. "I assure you, my Lord, your wishes will be carried out to the letter."

Later that day, de Courtney and a large detachment of heavily armed tower guards take over the harbour master's house and orders that his men of exploit aboard the ship, are to be led into the dock house one by one to receive Cressinghams reward."Bring them to me," commands de Courtney.

Each man, boy and every soul on board, including the assassins, enter the harbour-master dock house one by one. Immediately upon entry, they are brutally subdued,, bound by ropes and unable to move. Their captors quickly force them into a kneeling position, their heads are pulled forcibly back and a sharp blade pressed against their throat, with no warning the head of the victim is quickly pushed forward and the blade is pulled violently backwards toward the spinal column, cutting cleanly through the carotid arteries and jugular veins, causing each victim a relatively swift and silent death from extreme blood-loss.

As each individual is dispatched, the still warm bodies of Cressinghams "Pirates" are taken outside and flung in a grotesque pile at the rear of the building. When all the mercenaries and entire ship's compliment has been dispatched, the bodies are hung on the pier walls for the gathering public who witness the developing spectacle. The corpses are then publicly defiled as they hang from short gibbets above the Thames. Each body in turn has the eyes, tongue and ears cut out and the bodies are completely relieved of their manhood, coarsely disembowelled and their gut strung out around their necks for public amusement.

De Courtney announces to the gathered crowd "By order of our liege lord King Edward, this is to be the punishment of any pirates caught in lord Edward Plantagenet's seaboard who would dare attack English trade vessels."

The gathering crowds at the docks of Tilbury observing the gruesome spectacle begin and cheer hurrah de Courtney as a hero of the English seaboard. Marmaduke de Percy observes the spectacle in fascination and awe, and not a little fear.

GLEN AFTON

omunnach Castle, the western residence of *Blackbeard*, Lord Cospatrick Dunbar, stands on the confluence between the Afton and Nith rivers a few miles north of the infamous Wolf and Wildcat Forest. This vast primeval woodland covers four fifths of the old Galloway kingdom landmass. The northern frontier borders of this great woodland is defined by the rolling fringe peaks of Carrick, a great natural rift rising from the forest floor to form a natural terrain barrier that dominates the boundaries between the ancient Kingdoms of Strathclyde and Galloway. A few miles south of Comunnach Castle, the dense Wolf and Wildcat Forest screens a secretive entrance to a solitary Glen in the boundary rift, created by the beautiful river Afton. This is the northern gateway and ancient frontier access into the notorious untamed lands of Galloway, and home to Alain Wallace, the King's tenant hunter of the Black Craig.

Deep within Glen of Afton, Lady Mharaidh Wallace impatiently waits on the steps of the King's hunting lodge, Taigh nam Darrach Rìoghail (The Royal house in the field of Oak) known locally as 'Wallace Castle' a large wooden fortalice, stockade, corrals and Keep (Tower) surrounded by *Obhainn baile beags* (little hamlets of willow longhouses) and oak forest. Mharaidh's heart can scarce contain her joy as she eagerly awaits the imminent return of Alain, William and his young friend Stephen of Ireland. It has seemed only moments since William and Stephen's whirlwind arrival in the glen was quickly followed by their speedy dep*arture* to join the fall hunt.

Almost four months have passed since Alain, William and Stephen had departed Glen Afton to cull the deer and wild boar in the Wolf and Wildcat Forests, now they're coming home. The three companions gallop at a fast pace, returning from their last season hunter camp on the eastern edge of the Wolf and Wildcat Forest. As they pass the lower lands of Cumno and the formidable Comunnach Castle. They see in the distance the tip of the great hill of *s' Taigh am' Rìgh mòr* (Stiy-am-ree mor - the great hill of the King's house/fortress) the sentinel ridge of *Craig Branneoch* and another impressive skyline landmark, the Black Craig hill that guards and shelters the beautiful Glen of Afton.

The hunters thunder their horses through Cumno pass into the rift fastness and past the sporadic Obhainn's of the glen Afton community. Eventually, they bring their horses to a halt where the three-point boundary of the ancient kingdoms of Galloway, Lanarch and the King's Kyle of Carrick in Ayrshire conjoin. 'Wallace Castle.'

Lady Mharaidh hurriedly rushes down the steps to greet the returning hunters. As Alain dismounts, he's welcomed with the affectionate warmth of a loving heart. Alain and Mharaidh embrace passionately while William and Stephen hold the reigns of their breathless sweating horses. Waiting patiently for Alain to end his embrace with Mharaidh, the young men look at each other, grinning boyishly upon seeing the intimate lovers' passion displayed before them.

Mharaidh welcomes William and Stephen. "My Alain, would you be looking at these fine strapping young *Ceitherne* (Kern) of yours."

A proud Alain replies, "Aye, it has been the best hunt of my life with these two budding master huntsmen by my side."

The young men smile as Mharaidh walks over to embrace both as kin. After such an emotional warm welcome for her husband and her two adopted sons, Mharaidh places her arm around Alain's waist and speaks to the two young friends. "Did you enjoy the time out on your first hunt with the Wolf and Wildcat hunters?"

"Aye, we sure did," reply the grinning pair.

Replying with gusto, Stephen says, "*Sma' sin*," (Smashin; Very Good).

William is jubilant, he says, "I've found out more about the hunt in the last few months Mharaidh, than I have learned in a lifetime trapping around Glasgow Shawlands and Shields forest."

Mharaidh is delighted to hear their enthusiastic reply. "Do you think that you will both be making your time in Glen Afton more than just a visit, or will you be going back to *Ach na Feàrna*?"

Hearing Mharaidh's question causes Alain to feel anxious at what William may say by reply, but William simply shrugs his shoulders and with a broad smile. "I've come home."

Handing the reigns of his horse to Stephen, William steps forward with an outstretched open hand offered to his father. "If you'll have me Dá?"

Alain clasps his son firmly by the hand then he pulls him close to embrace. Both have lived for this moment.

Mharaidh says with great excitement in her voice, "Oh, William, its fair grand you're going to be living here in Glen Afton at long last. And to be seeing you and Alain both here together, we've so much to be talking about, and we've a surprise prepared for you William, and you too Stephen."

At that moment, Katriona comes out of Wallace Castle and stands behind Mharaidh, where she immediately begins making seductive eyes at Stephen and plying her fingers in her long flowing auburn tresses while smiling coyly at him. Stephen cheeks flush red once more as she flutters her sparkling hazel eyes.

Katriona is in her late teens, of athletic stature and buxom in her low cut Cottee. Tactically pulled tight with lace-hemmed broillich màlan (Breastbags brassiere) clearly emphasising her pronounced heaving bosom to her bo'. She continues to happily tease Stephen until the look on his face changes from boyish lechery to panic when a loud voice booms out behind Katriona.

Auld Jean, Katriona's ample mother, grand-mater of the household and ever-suffering wife of Wee Graham, Alain's erstwhile manservant, glares directly into Stephen's eyes.

"And who might this be, this fine young man who dares to stand before me with the mucky wild tresses of the wild Galloway Gallóglaigh. Aye, he who would dare to ogle at my bonnie Katriona with bloodshot eyes that would best a ruttin' stag?"

Stephen swallows hard as he observes this large intimidating woman with her fist menacingly clutching a wooden flour baton and brutally slapping one end of it forcefully into a cupped hand.

William laughs at Stephens' dilemma. "This is Stephen of Connaught from Ireland, ma'am. He's the son of Stephen the elder, ua H'Alpine chief of the same name Clan and country."

"A MacAlpine indeed," snarls Jean. "And what brings such a fine looking youngblood Irishman as yourself to Scotland?"

Stephen nervously replies, "Well, Ma'am, it's me little sister Ròsinn that's just after been and gone an' marrying Wee John

Wallace a few months ago. And this is such a foin country, I decided to stay awhile."

"Aye," growls Auld Jean. "Yie reckon?" With motherly menace, Auld Jean continues the interrogation. "Well, that was a few months ago young H'Alpine of Connaught. So what's holding you from going back to that fine country of old Erinn?"

Everyone but Stephen is hard-pressed not to laugh, and all are acutely aware that he had better produce an answer that pleases Auld Jean, the over-protective mother of bonnie Katriona. Stephen gets a bit flustered and very hot underneath his leather hunt jack, he stammers quickly without a pause. "I'm here with me boy William to be learning the craft of the hunt like I could learn from no other, in that we be getting' from his fadder good Alain Wallace himself...Ma'am."

A cynical Auld Jean continues to interrogate the petrified Stephen. "Are yie sure?" Tucking a fist tightly into her ample waist, Auld Jean steps forward a pace while holding the flour baton menacingly within striking distance of Stephen unprotected head.

"Eh, um..." is all that comes out of Stephens' mouth. He glances at a blushing Katriona, who despite her Mother's overly protective presence, continues to tease Stephen behind her mothers back.

"Well, I'm waitin'," demands Auld Jean.

Katriona decides it prudent to quietly disappear back through the kitchen door, leaving Stephen to his fate. He just grins nervously as Auld Jean continues to scowl at him. "Hmmm, I thought as much. Right then, me fine handsome hunters."

She smiles without any hint of menace, "Your hot vittals will be ready soon If you would like to make your way in to the big house. And you boys, remember to be washin' and scrubbin' yourselves before the eatin'."

Abruptly, Auld Jean turns and makes her way back to 'her' domain. Alain and Mharaidh chortle at what they know has only been motherly interrogation, and also a formal warning to Stephen should he pursue any wanton thoughts in regard her beautiful Katriona, and get caught.

Alain says, "Boys, take the horses to the stables then brush and wash them down, feed them then set them out to graze. And mind and clean yourselves up for supper."

Mharaidh says, "William, I want you to be calling me Mharaidh, as we're family now, and you too, Stephen. I want you both to be feeling at home, for this is your home. No matter where you find yourselves in this world, when you need to be somewhere that is safe and far away from all the trouble and tribulations, always remember Glen Afton is a wee piece of Scotland you must always call your own."

"Aye, Ma'am," reply both William and Stephen.

Mharaidh notices Wee Graham loitering near the keep cellar doors, she calls out, "Wee Graham, can you come over here a moment please?"

A little scrawny wiry framed man, looking very ancient in appearance with his long thick curly unkempt tresses of grey-black hair hanging halfway down his back, immediately jumps up from behind a small haystack, as though a lightning bolt has struck him recently. Looking over to Mharaidh with wide, bloodshot, puppy dog eyes, Wee Graham wipes his straggly goatee beard with his shaking boney fingers. "Aye, Ma'am." before quickly bundling a jug of whisky below the haystack. He rushes over to Mharaidh at the brisk pace of an old soldier on muster, with his long curly grey-black hair bouncing about his head like an mangy French hunting poodle.

"William, Stephen ..." says Mharaidh, "I would like to introduce you to Wee Graham, Katriona's father and Alain's personal bodyguard. He'll show you to your new crib. All of your personal chattel that was in the Keep, has been moved to your new abode, and the surprise we have for you both is that we've made a very fine stout *Obhainn*."

William and Stephen are elated, then Stephen whispers, "What's a bleedin' *Obhainn*?"

"Now, boys," continues Mharaidh. "I want you to go with Wee Graham. He'll take you to your *Obhainn*. Once you've settled in, come up to the Keep for your supper."

Lady Mharaidh leaves with Alain and returns to Wallace Castle while Wee Graham leads the boys to the stables.

As they follow Wee Graham to their *Obhainn*, Stephen asks, "That tiny little feckr, he's you're father's bodyguard?"

William replies, "I think that's what Mharaidh said."

"Guard against what?"

William thinks a moment then laughs. "Fleas ah reckon?"

Wee Graham suddenly stops, turns around then approaches them. He looks up into their young faces with his black piercing eyes. "You fellas better be away and get your horses fed n' brushed down first." He points toward a cluster of *Obhainns* with his shaking bony finger. "The stables are over at the Darroch crag. I'll be meeting yiez there when yiez have finished with the nags, then I'll show yiez yer *Obhainn*." Wee Graham spins on his heels and makes a hasty beeline toward his precious *craitur* hidden under the haystack.

Watching Wee Graham spindle away, the two friends shake their head bemused. Stephen asks again, "What is an *Obhainn*?"

"It's a kinda longhouse built with a base of two low stone walls with sod filler in between, then it has a willow or Hazel trellis frame arching for the sidewalls and roof. We use hide, deerskin or bracken for roofing shelter. Usually the inner walls are filled with hay plastered with mud and dung for winter warmth."

"What the Feck? Dung? Yie mean we'll be sleeping in a shithouse?"

William shoves Stephen playfully. "Fuck off."

The two friends chat and banter about the hunt, while leading the horses to the stables, but in particular they talk about the interesting parents of Katriona.

After washing down, feeding and setting the horses to graze, they walk towards the Darroch Balloch, a cluster of *Obhainns* sheltering amidst an oak glade that appears at first glance like a grouping of giant molehills.

A little while later they notice Wee Graham is waiting for them below a broad old oak tree. He wanders over clutching his precious *craitur* flagon and chewing on some ale bread. He says, "*Co'nas* boys, I would offer yie both a wee nip from my *craitur*, but time is short. C'mon, I've no' got time to be wastin'."

The three erstwhile companions saunter through the little *baile beag* till they come to an *Obhainn* near another large spreading oak, close to the Afton riverbank.

Wee Graham says, "We've made this fine *Obhainn* dry and winter-ready for your stayin'. It's all yours now boys, Lady Mharaidh, Jean and Katriona have laid out much for your comfort, too much if yie ask me, but should you both need anything else, I'll be introducing yiez to all the folks residin' here soon enough. And on the askin', all the folk hereabouts will provide for your needs, and if yiez want to build another Obhainn later on for either one of you, then we will fix that for yiez, too."

William says, "We appreciate your hospitality, Wee Graham."

The older man replies, "Ach, it's not a problem son. Now I must be getting the fine wines and drinks ready for the Lady's supper, so I'll be seeing yiez later." He turns and waves back at them as he makes his way back up the hill to find another jug of nectar.

William turns to Stephen and says, "Well Stephen, it could be you've just met your future mother and father in law this day."

"Steady on Wallace," cries Stephen. "Did yie see the feckin arm muscles on Auld Jean? I reckon she could o' picked up our horses and flung them into the stable corrals from the big house up there."

"I don't think it's her you need to worry about, its that wee fella staggering up the hill in search o' *craitur*, ma Dá said he's likely the most dangerous murdering wee feckr in all o' Scotland."

"What, that wee man?"

William lifts up his saddlebags and replies, "Aye, that wee man. Well that's what ma Dá said. I reckon you'd better be minding your ways wie bonnie Katriona there, or yer a dead man."

The two friends study the outside of their new home, amazed at the size and pleased the robust looking structure has already made a good impression on them. The building is almost forty feet long, eighteen feet wide and nearly ten feet tall at the curving apex. The walls and roofing are made almost entirely from willow and densely packed bracken thatch, covered with deerskin tile. It is secured with cross-tied netting, purposely weighted down with large water-boulders hanging around the base like a giant skirt of rock beads. A haze of smoke filters through the roof.

William says, "This is a fine lookin' *Obhainn*, and it looks to be a sturdy looking structure from the outside."

"Is this thing really for us?"

"Aye, I reckon it's so."

Stephen grimaces. "But this is a feckin dung hut?"

William bundles up all his kit then walks towards the small leather-hide entrance door of the *Obhainn*. "Aye Stephen, but its 'OUR' dung hut."

He throws back the thick leather skins of the door and stoops low to get his big frame through the small entrance.

Once inside, Stephen hears William cry out. "Holy feck!"

Outside, Stephen, waiting impatiently calls out. "What is it Wallace, are yie all right in there big fella?"

But there's no reply hailing from inside the *Obhainn*.

"That's it…" states Stephen. "I'm no' feckin going in there, I'll be sleeping with me bleedin' horse out here."

William calls to him from inside the grand home. "Get in here H'Alpine ya moanin' feckr, you've got to be seeing this."

Stephen picks up his kit and bows his head low, muttering to himself as he squeezes through the small door opening. He stands erect once inside the *Obhainn* beside William and looks around the darkly lit dwelling. As his eyes begins to familiarise in the low light, he exclaims, "Jaezuz… Would yie be looking at this now?"

***

Later that day, after they have all feasted on Auld Jean's fare, everyone is relaxing and talking for many hours in front of the grand fire, till finally, Alain says it is time for him to have his early evening sleep.

With a wink and impish grin, Alain glances at a blushing Mharaidh. "I'm no' as young as I used to be boys, so you two be getting on with your vittals, me and Mharaidh here will be taking some time together."

William and Stephen grin then bid their leave to walk wearily to their *Obhainn*. Finally as they reach the front door of their new home, Stephen stretches his arms in the air and yawns. "Feck me boy, after months o' sleeping under bull-hide skins, I am so joyous to be resting me tired bones in a warm crib."

William, feeling fatigue catch up too, agrees. Once inside, they compose their cribs comfortably and lay down by a central hearth peat fire. They're both extremely tired from their long journey and a season sleeping under the stars.

Resting comfortably on his crib, Stephen looks around the inside of the longhouse then remarks. "These are some fine and dandy living places yiez have here in these here *Obhainn's*."

"I know," agrees William. "You'd think by the look of them that they would be dark wet and stinking inside, but it would make yie laugh wouldn't it? All those lords in their fancy castles freezing their tiny nuts off, and here's us living in a wee dung hut as cosy as yie like."

"B'jeazuz Wallace, would yie be lookin' at the very place of it now, would ya? I would hardly be calling this a dung hut. And would yie be looking at those fancy decorated rugs and all of that fine weaving they have hanging about the place for us. And look you at all that soft felt in the roofing." Stephen prods at the thick feather padded quilt beneath him. He says, "Wallace, me boy, that's chicklet down on our cribs too, I've not touched anything so soft since last in auld Erinn when I had a tryst with a bonnie serving wench in a Norman household, and then I burned the place down."

Amused, William enquires, "Yie don't like the Normans very much then?"

Stephen shakes his head thoughtfully. "They've not been o' a humour to be giving us much to be liking them for. They're a cruel race o' people with their laws and punishments. Sometimes they just punish us Irish for the sake of it with their torturin' and murderin' in the name of some feckin God. What really gets my feckin' goat is they've the support of the feckin church. No Irish man, woman or child is safe from that Divill's alliance."

Curious at the deep feeling of resentment accompanying his friend's comments, William enquires, "Then why do the Irish no' throw the Normans out of Ireland? They should be subordinate to you. Are they no' just guests in your auld country?"

"Guests???" laughs Stephen, "The reason the Irish won't fight as one I reckon, is because we have no King, just like you Scots now. So many of those Norman self seeking bastards just lusting after power."

"Surely if the Irish fought as one they would be too much of a force for the Normans to deal with, then yiez could drive them out? Or at least let them know they are to have a place and that place is not to be ruling over the Irish."

Stephen replies with concern, "Wallace, I don't like to be saying this to yie me new found friend, but that's what our fathers thought too. The wealth o' the Normans bought the servitude of many powerful Irish Chiefs, now they too be called nobles, and that will happen here. Once one dirty bastard of your own kind sups at the table of a Norman and accepts his siller in exchange for his allegiance, then unity between the clans and family is lost forever. That's the price we've paid with eternal blood-feuding as the purchase."

"Naw," says William "that couldn't happen here."

"Do yie know a funny thing Wallace? The Normans in England call themselves English, the Normans here are

Norman Scots yet the English in Erinn still call themselves feckn Norman. Aye, but they all have something in common, for all o' them are feckin ruthless bastards, and none ever to be trusted."

"It's not the same here though Stephen. The Normans that have settled here in Scotland are fine folks. We've never had any trouble from them?"

"Aye, that's when you fella's had a King," says Stephen. "The Normans are a strong military race of people and respond well under discipline. But you watch yourselves Wallace me boy. If no King or Queen strong enough leads your country, the Normans will fight amongst themselves and kill all you Scots off as battle fodder in the process, just like they are now doing in auld Erinn."

Poking slow burning peat fire, William ponders over Stephen's words. "Tell me more about your country's plight Stephen? Ahm findin' it interesting; yet hard to believe that you Irish are rolling on your backs like old mangy lung titted bitches, but believing it I am if yie say it to be so. Both my Dá and Uncle Malcolm said that when a H'Alpine speaks to yie in earnest, yie had better be listnin' or more the fool you are if yie don't."

Stephen sniggers, almost in embarrassment at the high esteem he hears that the Wallace have for the house of H'Alpine. "Wallace, me boy, it could weigh heavily that mantle on any man, these names we carry as a birthright. But I'll tell yie this, there are many good fightin' Irish who are not rollin' on their backs, and we never will."

The two young friends talk and blether into the night as the darkness settles over Glen Afton. The exertions of the last few months hunt takes its toll, the young friends soon fall into a deep sleep in their 'dung hut'.

***

William and Stephen are awake early next morning and already exploring the perimeters of Glen Afton, when finally they climb to the summit of the Corrie Crag (Rock of the Raven) they see a stupendous vista. To the west, they see the mountains of the Arran isles and Kintyre peninsula. To the north, the peaks of Ben Lomond and mountains of the Lennox. Eastward stands the sentinel outcrop of Loudoun hill, gateway to Lanark and the Lothian. To the south, the beautiful wild rolling hills and small mountainous lands of Galloway.

Stephen says, "Sure now 'tis wonderful land yie have here," William agrees as they lay awhile resting peacefully and talking in the morning sun, when they notice two groups of riders galloping up the northwest drove road toward Wallace Castle. "I wonder who that is?" asks William.

"Sure now, let's be goin' down and finding out," says Stephen. "Anyways Wallace, am hungry and getting well used to the way you Scots be feastin' over here mornin, noon and night."

William enquires, "Is it no' the same in Erinn? Do the auld biddies no' just love over-feeding you too, specially when there are guests?"

"Sure they do," laughs Stephen. "WHEN there are guests." Stephen turns to look back down the glen and points. "Look Wallace, quick, there's the bonnie Katriona. I am sure she must be missing me foin' company. C'mon lets be going now, for I cannot live wit me'self easily by denying her this much unbridled happiness."

William looks at his friend with warm curiosity as Stephen jumps to his feet and starts bounding down the glen-side. "C'mon yie fat hairy Scottish bastard, I'll be showing yie how fleet of foot the boys o' Connaught and Monaghan can move."

Stephen quickly disappears over the side of the outcrop, running jumping and weaving through the rock fall like a surefooted mountain buck. Laughing heartily at Stephen's comments, William thinks to himself… *'I really like this mad feckin Irishman. I reckon me n' him will be a match for any good times life will be throwing at us. Especially now Wee John is no' going to be in my life as before.'* Grinning at his own thoughts, William quickly sprints after Stephen. Bounding down the Craig-side, William uses his body weight and strategically placing his brogan (Boots) perfectly on grass tufts and jag rocks where he knows the sole will purchase and grip. As he closes on Stephen, the two young men careen into the *baile beag* around Wallace Castle. Mischievously, William clips the heel of Stephen 's back foot, tripping him and sending him crashing over and into a mature hen's midden. Just then, William sees a little barrel of a man in front of him… *"Awe feck, its Leckie mòr…"*

Leckie sees William careening and almost on top of him on a collision course. He hunches and moves forward, driving his powerful shoulder into the William's stomach then throws him over his head and high into the air, landing him directly into the midden beside Stephen.

"Wallace, is that you?" growls Leckie while picking up the reigns of his horse. He glares at William sitting in the hen shit beside Stephen. "WALLACE, what the fuck are yie doin' running at me like a big stupit' young bull on heat?" snarls Leckie.

William can't muster a sensible reply.

Leckie snarls, "I'll speak tae you young feckrs later… yiez had better believe it." Leckie mòr mounts his horse then pulls on the reigns to join with the other riders who are laughing heartily at the scene before them.

Covered in hen shit and trying to block his nose from the stench, Stephen asks, "Feck Wallace, do yie know him?"

"Aye, I feckn know him," replies William. "That wee fella is the last man you ever want to be on the wrong side o'. Do yie know him too?"

Stephen frowns, "Aye, that I do. He comes to Erinn with Bishop Wishart two or three times a year where he trains all the young chieftains of Connaught in his peculiar style of the fight. I get his mean type o' trainin' wit me *Gallóglaigh* chieftain Rogan O'Flanagan, and a mean pair o' bastards they are the pair o' them. Do yie think that's maybe how our fathers might have met?"

"I don't know, but I reckon we'll be in even deeper shit later when Leckie gets his muckle (Very big) hands on us."

Stephen stands up and finds himself knee deep in hen shit. "Awe feck, we're in trouble now Wallace, never mind later. Jaezuz, have yie got the smell of that chicken shit up your big feckin nose yet?"

Trying to wipe himself down, William replies, "I thought the smell was coming from you because you saw Leckie mòr."

The two young men laugh and drag themselves out of the pungent smelling midden and make their way to the river where they wash.

Meanwhile, Leckie and his companions arrive at Wallace Castle. Alain greets them and indicates they go inside, when he notices something unusual, curiously he looks down toward the river Afton where William and Stephen are both naked, standing knee deep in the water washing themselves.

"Don't ask," says Leckie as he brusquely marches past Alain into the keep. Alain ponders a moment, shakes his head, then follows his friends into the keep, where Mharaidh welcomes each of the guests as they enter the feast hall.

"Mharaidh," exclaims a knight. "I do believe you grow more beautiful each time I see you."

Mharaidh blushes. "Why, Sir Ranald Crauford, you are forever a prince of chivalry."

She welcomes all her guests warmly and bids them to take a seat.

Alain begins the meeting. "My friends, I wish to thank you for your attendance and make introduction, Alexander Marshall of Galloway, Sir Richard Lundie, Lord Cospatrick of Dunbar, Leckie mòr, master hammerer to the late *Ard Rígh* these are my kinsmen Patrick Auchinleck of Greenrigg and Gilban and of course you all know my kinsman the Sheriff of Ayr and Carrick Sir Ranald Crauford."

Ranald enquires as he takes his seat, "Was that young William I saw a wee while ago Alain? Is he staying here now?"

"Aye, he's living here in Glen Afton and hunts the great Wolf and Wildcat Forest with me."

"That's wonderful news to be hearing Alain. He's a very clever young lad. Your Uncle James in Dunipace used to tutor him in history, Latin, French and the Gaelic, and I'll tell you this, none could slate his fascination and eagerness to read all the books in my library." Ranald pauses as he removes his gauntlets. "What good fortune brought you two back together?"

"We met only recently at Wee John's wedding and there came an opportunity for his moving to Glen Afton. I tell you Ranald, I'm more than happy the bonnie Glen has won him over to the life o' a freeman."

"I can understand his choice, I'm sure pleased for you both."

Alain confirms his happiness, "I'm certainly blessed by his choice Ranald."

Leckie speaks, "Ma friends, shall we…"

The small council settle to discuss the perilous situation abroad in Scotland, while down in the river Afton, William and Stephen are still naked and knee deep trying to scrub the smell of chicken shit away from their bodies.

They finish scrubbing then go back to their *Obhainn* for fresh clean *léine* and some vittals then return to the riverside to sit enjoying the views of the Glen. "It really is a fine place yer father has here," says Stephen gazing around the Glen.

"Aye, that it is, I'm only here moments in ma lifetime, but never has a place felt so much like home."

As they look around at the natural beauty of the secluded Glen Afton, Stephen says, "Now that's a grand feeling yie'll be having there Wallace, and I must be sharing it wit' ya, if ya don't mind. I'm liking this like me home me'self."

While they sun themselves on the riverbank, Stephen notices something in the distance. "For such a place to be hidden away in the wilderness, it's a lot of visitors yiez seem to be havin'."

"What d'yie mean?"

"Look over there…" replies Stephen pointing to the southern gateway to Glen Afton.

They both look on with interest as more people arrive. Before long, three people on a small trundle cart travel past them, but William doesn't recognise anyone, though the elderly knight of fine composure seems familiar. Then his eyes fall instantly on a beautiful young woman sitting beside the knight. She notices William staring at her, she blushes and giggles in response to his gaze. William watches them drive on towards Wallace Castle. Occasionally the young woman glances back at him as both he and Stephen walk slowly behind.

William nudges Stephen and points at the young lady, "She's beautiful Stephen, whoever she is… I think I'm in love… She's like a Persian princess from one o' Wee Maw's legends."

As the new guests arrive at the front of Wallace Castle, the doors open. Mharaidh and Alain walk out to greet the visitors. Mharaidh notices William and Stephen and sends Wee Graham to bring them to meet the guests. Before long, both duly arrive at the door of the hall as Mharaidh bids them to enter. "Would you like to be coming in for some vittals boys, as we'll be serving some fare for our guests?"

Stephen clears his throat. "If its all right with you Mharaidh, I'm going over to be looking at your horses, for I've never seen such fine greys before, and your lead hunter Thieran, he asked me if I'd like to ride the Afton marches wit' him."

Mharaidh, slightly distracted for a moment, gives instruction regarding her guests to Katriona.

Nudging Stephen, William whispers humorously, "Ya liar."

Stephen laughs. "Och, now Wallace me boy, an Irishman can lie and still be telling the truth when needs must."

William glances at his friend who grins inanely. The Irishman winks, then he whispers, "Wallace, you keep them busy eatin' will ya, and I'll be nipping round the back to see Katriona, my bonnie wee Scots rose."

Mharaidh returns to the two friends and enquires, "And you, William? Would you like to come in for some vittals or are you riding out too?"

William is gazing at the beautiful tall and slender maid standing behind Mharaidh. "Oh, I'd like some vittals, Mharaidh, and thank you for the asking."

"Then come in William and I'll make your introduction."

Mharaidh links arms with William and whispers, "William, you must be closing your mouth and start blinking, or the maid will think you're a tanner short of a groat."

William embarassed says, "Oh, sorry Mharaidh, am I being obvious?"

Mharaidh smiles. "Oh aye, you are."

"But she's so beautiful Mharaidh. I've never seen a woman like her before."

Mharaidh suddenly steps away from William as though something distasteful has repulsed her. "William, what is that awful smell?"

He gasps, "Awe naw, I'm sorry, Mharaidh, eh… I fell into the chicken midden."

"You what?" exclaims Mharaidh.

'Feck,' thinks William, *'It's too late now.'*

Mharaidh looks at William curiously then takes him, tentatively by the arm. As they enter the hall, all the visitors are chatting and deliberating.

Mharaidh is about to introduce William when a voice booms out, silencing everyone by the authority of such a commanding delivery. "Sir Hugh Braidfuite, Laird o' Lamington, his bonnie daughter, the heiress of Lamington, Maid Marion. And the honourable son of the aforesaid sir Hugh Braidfuite, squire Brian Braidfuite of the aforesaid Lamington."

Everyone remains silent, though the formality is not entirely unexpected. Alain's erstwhile manservant, bodyguard and master of ceremonies of sorts, Wee Graham, stands proud. Even though he is not much taller than the tallest child in the Glen, with his wiry frame as thin as a beanpole and old battle scars all over his face and body. For his size, Wee Graham has the courage and valour of ten men. In his prime, he was a feared ruthless and proven killer in war, and peacetime on occasion. To the unwary, his outward demeanour is that of a happy little character with a zeal for his very own version of hospitable communication around a good jug of whisky *craitur…* Alain groans, putting his hand on his forehead with resigned angst for his erstwhile bodyguard.

Mharaidh raises her hand in the air. "Wee Graham, I know yie used to be the King's gillie, but we're not in the royal court now."

Wee Graham replies cheerily. "Aye, m'lady Mharaidh, I know that fine and well, but thank yie for tellin' me anyway."

Wee Graham, a respected and experienced veteran of many battles with Norsemen, Dane's, and Saxonach, and of course the *craitur*, turns to exit as swiftly as he appeared.

Suddenly he stops at the door and turns back abruptly to face everyone like a little soldier standing to attention. "Sorry sir, just doin' ma duties as is proper and beholding o' me."

Alain calls out, "Graham, away and find Auld Tam. He's bound to have his head buried in the estates accounts this day. I feel he needs a wee break and he is to be away to the fishing for me. Tell him to get going and that we eat too much meat here anyway. And mind and also tell Tam it's urgent that we have a fresh catch to smoke and salt... and you're to help him. Have yie got that? Now away with yie."

Wee Graham straightens up as though he's still a braw fighting soldier in Alexander's proud army. "Aye, sir, that will be the right thing to be doing. Will I be taking him some fine wine or *craitur* to be drinkin' with his mid-day vittals?"

Exasperated, Alain replies, "Aye Graham, just make sure the both o' yie don't make it the catch o' the day."

"Aye, sur," replies Wee Graham as he happily marches out of the little wooden 'castle', knowing he is entrusted with a very important mission.

With another sigh, Alain explains to Sir Hugh. "He's a great fella Wee Graham, trusted and loyal to a fault."

Ranald laughs, "Aye ah can see that."

"I care for Wee Graham deeply as his adopted Chief. Though in truth, I think we both find rare friendship and much peace in each others company." Alain pauses when he sees William and beckons him over. "William I would like to introduce you to a dear friend? This is Sir Hugh Braidfuite of Lammington."

"*Co'nas.*" says William while he shakes Sir Hugh's hand.

Sir Hugh replies, "No need to be speaking the *Gallgael* twang young William. The mither tongue will be doing us all just fine." But the Maid captivates William's attention as Sir Hugh continues, "This is my daughter the maid Marion, and this is my son Brian."

William goes to speak, but nothing comes out. In a fluster, he turns his attention back to sir Hugh. "Sir Hugh, I have heard so much about you from my father. It's good to meet the man he has spoken so highly about."

Sir Hugh smiles at William's polite endeavour. "And you too, young William. I have heard much of your exploits from your father and from Leckie mòr too I might add."

William is distracted as he looks into the sparkling deep brown almond eyes of Marion. Her jet-black shining hair is tied and draping over her shoulders. He offers his hand but quickly pulls back as he feels his face flush. William bows his head in respect then he stammers. "Aye… aye… and it's so very nice to be meeting you Marion. Oh, and eh, you too Brian."

Alain saves his son. "Come, Sir Hugh, I'll show you to your seat."

William and Marion continue exchanging glances as she walks away.

"William," He vaguely hears a voice calling him away in the distance. William fails to respond "WILLIAM!" says the voice sternly.

"AYE… what th' feck is it?" snarls William tersely. The voice says, "It's good to be seeing you here." William looks round then exclaims with delight, "Ranald," William spins around as his uncle Ranald laughs and puts a friendly hand on his shoulder.

William shouts joyously… "Uncle Ranald… it's great to see you again…"

Ranald smiles. "How are you boy, we've missed you down about Crosshouse."

Taking his mind off the beautiful Marion a moment, William is pleased to see his favourite uncle, he replies, "Ach, I'm fine *tá* and I miss the long debates with you and Uncle James."

"Then perhaps we may share those times again now that you're back in the shire, and only but a few hours ride from Ayr town."

"I'd like that."

William is clearly pleased to be seeing one of his old mentors, he enquires, "And how is Uncle James keeping up in Dunipace?"

"He's fine, he often asks about you and why you've not been to see him in a while."

"Ach, so much has been happening these last few months. Coming to the Craig to stay with father, then the fall hunts. It's just that time runs out for some things to be as they once were."

Ranald looks fondly at his nephew. "You must make the time then William for we miss you." Seeing that William is distracted, he says, "That's If you can pull yourself away from your flirtatious thoughts with the young Maid over there."

William is relieved he doesn't have to explain about his feelings as Alain comes over at that moment. He says, "It's time we gather for the council."

Ranald replies, "Aye, you're right, Alain." Ranald turns to William. "Well it's been good to see you again William. You must come to Ayr and see me soon." Ranald leans forward and whispers. "I thought I'd better say William, but there's a bad aroma about you. Have you stood in shit or something?"

Mortified, William replies, "Aye, something like that uncle."

Amused, Ranald shakes his head then rejoins the small council gathering at the table. Alain calls out, "William, will you escort Maid Marion and lady Mharaidh down to the kail-yard's while we deliberate here for a few hours?"

William replies instantly. "Aye, that I will Dá, but I need to be changing my clothes first." Alain looks at William inquisitively. "What? Ach you'll be fine, you're only going to pick some herb, no' going to a hop."

Aware that his cloths are still airing of chicken shit, William awkwardly makes his way to the door. Marion begins to follow, thinking that she's never met nor seen such a handsome looking young man so well suited to her own desires. And he makes her laugh too. William appears to have a similar attraction, more entertainingly demonstrated in his clumsy humility and humorous demeanour towards her.

At that moment, as if breaking a magical love spell, Wee Graham walks back in through the main door. "Sir," he calls out. "Message delivered, one full bottle of wine, some fare and your instructions have been passed to Auld Tam. By return, he sends his thanks and gratitude and now we'll be going to the fishin'."

Exasperated by the constant distractions, Alain replies, "Fine Graham."

Suddenly the door opens behind Wee Graham and in walks Auld Tam. He looks at Alain with a hint of frustration apparent. "I'm going to the fishing Alain, but I need to get a jug of nectar, this one Wee Graham brought me is near empty."

Alain glares at Wee Graham, who is swaying to attention, complimented with a rosy glow under his battle scarred and ruddy complexion. Realising that Alain awaits an answer, Wee Graham blurts out innocently, "Leaky cork sur."

Alain shakes his head forlorn, "Graham, I've another important task perhaps more suited for you, and there's no river that you may fall into. William will be escorting Lady Mharaidh and the Maid Marion to the Kailyard's, I want you to chaperone, maybe you could tell them all about your stories in the wars with the Norsemen?"

William cringes, he mutters to himself. *"Awe naw, I'm really starting to like Wee Graham, but no' as a chaperone, not war stories, no' now, please..."*

Marion sees the consternation in William's face and playfully grasps Wee Graham by the arm. "I would love to hear about your adventures Little Graham."

"Eh," stutters Wee Graham. "Its no' little feckin Graham bonnie lass, its Wee Graham, there's a big difference yie know."

Marion replies, "All right Little Graham, Wee Graham it is." She smiles at William, teasing him with her sparkling eyes and affectionate contact with Wee Graham.

At that moment, Mharaidh walks through the door, inviting her entourage to follow. She says, "I'll collect some willow baskets and meet you at the Keep gates." William looks to the ceiling as Wee Graham escorts his delicate charge Marion past him and out the door behind Mharaidh.

"Hadn't you better follow them, William?" suggests Sir Hugh. "Or are you chaperoning Wee Graham?" Regaining his composure, William rushes towards the door to catch up with 'Little Graham' as the gathering prepares for a long day's deliberations.

Many topics urgently require their attention regarding the situation in Scotland. In particular and personal to Alain, is the surety of tenure for the Wallace of Black Craig and Glen Afton, as the land is the King's property, but now under the jurisdiction of Cospatrick the Earl of Dunbar, a particular noble that Alain does not favour.

Rushing out the Keep door, William calls out. "Wee Graham, Marion, wait, I'm coming with you."

Waiting outside to greet William with a large toothy grin is Wee Graham, standing to attention, with hair so long, wild and full of curls it appears as though it may weigh more than the rest of the little man all together.

He stands his ground, stoically looking up into the big red face of William, who is over six feet tall. Wee Graham simply stares at William with the tenacity of a small wiry terrier looking into the eyes of a wild bull. He coughs politely. "Now don't be getting so close to the bonnie lassie young Wallace, yie know how sensitive fathers can be. I don't want to be giving yie the Norseman's knock..."

Foolishly William asks, "Norseman's what?"

Wee Graham replies, "Lean forward and I'll whisper it to yie, for it's no' for the ears of one se' gentile as the Maid Marion."

Leaning toward Wee Graham, William thinks he's about to hear something interesting, suddenly Wee Graham deftly grabs him by the centre of his top lip, squeezing hard with his thumb and second knuckle, pulling William forward with speed and great ease, then he deftly grips him by the tip of his nose. William tries to resist, but the pain in his sinus is too great, he has no choice but to be pulled to the ground by Wee Graham. He sits on the ground dazed.

"I can't see for tears," bleats William pathetically. "My face is killing me. What the feck did you just do to me wee man?"

Smiling at Marion, Wee Graham states proudly, "And that me dear, is how we pulled Norsemen out of their Longships at night. Aye, we used tae swim out in the darkest o' nights to their ships and knock on the gunnels o' their big boats. When they leant over the side to see what the knocking was, we simply pulled them over the side by their hairy top lip and the rest o' the lads finished them off."

Looking through his bleary tear-filled eyes, William can see Marion smirking. *'Awe naw,'* he thinks. *'This is just going from bad to worse.'*

Marion enquires, "Are you crying William? Was it very sore?"

William replies emphatically, "Naw Marion, I just think I've got a wee spec o' dust in my eyes, and I like Wee Graham to feel good about his height, so I thought it best to humour him."

Wee Graham and Marion laugh, then she links her arm through his and they begin walking down the path, leaving William sitting on the ground nursing his painfully sore face.

Mharaidh comes out a side door with a handful of little herb baskets. As she walks past William, she looks at him curiously. "Why are you sitting on the ground William? Are you not coming with us?"

She walks onto the path and on down toward the Kailyard's. Frustrated, William shakes his head as he pulls himself together and follows meekly behind, trying to work out how he may find any time to be alone with Marion.

Meanwhile, Wee Graham, so fond of his legendary history, recognises Marion's name. "And you ma bonnie young Lassie from the Braidfuite hills," says Wee Graham, "I knew of yer folks, blessed be their departed souls. Did yie know these lands of Cumno were once the lands of Colm Nuadha of the Tuatha Dá Danann and that your ancestors were the hill-foot smithies who struck all the fabulous weapons and armour in the magical waters of *Maghfada*?" (Moffat)

Marion looks at Wee Graham with bemused curiosity. She asks, "You knew my mother and father?"

Wee Graham sighs. "Aye, well I knew of them darlin', but I know your family history better. Did yie know your ancestors made the swords of light for the Kings of Kyle? Those same giants who resided here on this very spot when they hunted the deer and wild boar on foot? Aye, your auld folks made armour and precious jewellery from the purest silver and freshwater pearls for the famed Colm Nuadha too. The greatest of the *Dá Danann* Kings of legend?"

"But…" exclaims Marion, "you mean…"

Before Marion can finish, Wee Graham continues, "Aye darlin, it was Colm Nuadha himself, a descendant from the loins of Goidal Glas and so fond of his adventures was he that the bonnie Nuadha left this dear place and departed for old Erinn to become a King there too. Ach, but it was there he lost an arm in battle. Aye, it was your ancestors who made him up a new arm, made from the purest of silver dug up from the deepest mine workings from the Clyde and the Boyne. After that, folks called Colm "Airgetlám" Silver Arm. Ah know lass, yie must be askin' yourself, how did he lift, pour and drink the *craitur* with only one arm?"

Marion hasn't heard much of the story as she and William are distracted and keep glancing at each other.

Wee Graham hadn't noticed her romantic distraction. He says, "Mind this wee bit o' advice darlin', you never forget who you are lass, or where yie come from, for then will yie know for sure where yer goin'."

Almost an hour passes before Wee Graham stops talking, and only to take one too many little nips from his flagon. He says in a slurred voice "Now, where was I?"

Marion points in the direction of Lady Mharaidh and William. "I think we're supposed to be over there Little Graham."

Shrugging his shoulders, Wee Graham mutters, "Woman, it's Wee Graham, I tell yie."

They meander over to where Mharaidh is picking herbs and placing them in little ornamental willow baskets, held ever so patiently by William. Wee Graham stops beside Mharaidh and stands to attention, arching so far back he's in danger of falling over. He blurts out, "William Wallace, son of..."

Wee Graham stops abruptly when Lady Mharaidh put up her hand up to silence him. "I'll be thanking you Wee Graham, but I remember who William is."

Wee Graham stands swaying to attention. He says, "Thank yie Ma'am."

Mharaidh enquires, "Is Wee Graham keeping you fine company then Marion?"

"Aye Mharaidh, he's been telling me tall tales," Marion replies, while sneaking glances at William, teasing him with little smiles and making eyes at him.

Mharaidh packs some more herbs into the baskets. "I'm glad Wee Graham is behaving himself. Now, shall we go to the kailyard's? Oh William, will you bring the baskets for us please?"

The odd little group walks toward the kailyard's with Lady Mharaidh in front. Marion links arms with Wee Graham as William walks behind with little willow baskets in each hand, with Wee Graham the battle scarred veteran, still talking of legends past, though Marion is still oblivious to Wee Graham's history lesson as she keeps smiling at the red faced young Ettin.

Mharaidh enquires, "Is this the first time you've been to Glen Afton Marion?"

In good humour, the young woman replies, "Aye, Ma'am, it is."

"I see you have a little twinkle in your eye."

"With Little Graham chaperoning me and telling me such amazing stories and the history of this land, it's a very beautiful and romantic place to be."

Wee Graham mutters to himself out of earshot of the two women. "Oh, I just pure hate that, it's Wee Graham, not little feckn Graham."

William grins seeing Wee Graham's discomfort.

"And what are you grinning at yie big feckin lump? You with such pretty little baskets in each hand."

"Nuthin'," replied William his grin widening. "Nuthin' at all little Graham, my sweet wee soft-tongue darlin'!"

Wee Graham growls, "Right, that's it…" He rolls up his large *léine* sleeves, throws back his long matted hair then sticks his fists in the air. "Now yer gonnae Fuc…"

"Wee Graham…" Mharaidh calls out, "Would you fetch us wine and refreshments? We'll sit awhile in the Darrach meadow on such a fine day as this."

Wee Graham's eyes instantly light up. He replies with unfettered enthusiasm. "Of course, ma'am, would yiez be liking a drop of the *craitur* too, in case yie should be getting the cold water cough about yie?"

"That would be nice Graham, but please, don't take too long."

Wee Graham turns to leave when Mharaidh calls out to him once more. "Just to be warning you against any leakage, Jean has marked all of the jugs and canter levels, so don't you be spilling any on the way back. And check for leaks too before you leave. I want to make sure that you actually do come back."

As the mid-day sun beats down, Mharaidh, Marion and William sit in the shade at a course wooden table underneath the blossoming foliage of a great oak, while Wee Graham marches off at a brisk pace to fulfil his duties.

"Now, William," enquires Mharaidh, "You must be telling us about what you studied when being tutored for the priesthood."

William smiles as he toys with the little baskets. Then he replies, "The teachings of the cloth has served me very well Mharaidh, and I've enjoyed the learning of our history and languages too for sure. I can converse freely in Scots, Gaelic, French, Latin, even in the English."

Both Marion and Mharaidh laugh at his last addition.

William blushes, unsure of what he's said that amuses them. He continues, "But I love the hunt, archery and swordsmanship studies more. My life and the crafts here are what I really wish to pursue, I don't feel that..." Suddenly William pauses.

"What is it, William?" enquires Mharaidh as she sees he has a problem with his train of thought.

"Ach Mharaidh, I don't want to be going back to the calling of the church. I wish to follow in the footsteps of my father here, or like Malcolm and become a Knight of Scotland's realm. The priesthood is no' for me. Although I do see many good things in the church, but I see more wrongs and misuse of power applied by many in the name of God."

Mharaidh replies thoughtfully, "I can see you have much to consider William, though the religious world does have much to offer a young man, I think that you fair take after your father. I too am aware of evils unspoken within the church, but there are many good clerics, including your elder brother, who may change things for the better. Perhaps this is a conversation we may continue at another time, if you require my thoughts and guidance on the subject."

"Aye," replied William, "I would like that."

William sits down with his back against the old oak tree, obviously lost in deep thought while Mharaidh and Marion converse.

Eventually, they notice Wee Graham approaching with his eyes glazed, and much to their amusement, he's not quite walking a straight course toward them. He finally arrives at the table with a little refreshment, very little refreshment, for there is not much left in any jug as Wee Graham has managed to 'lose' most of it.

Mharaidh turns to the younger woman, "And you, Marion, how fairs your thoughts for your future?"

"Well, Mharaidh, I too have been educated very well and can converse in the same languages as William. Ever since my mother and father's passing, I now see to the maintenance of the Bruin House of old Lanark, looking after the needs and wishes of the poor. I feel that is my true vocation. Though I have these last few years served as a lady in waiting to Queen Yolande."

"That's very commendable Marion."

"Ah the Bru'," sighs Wee Graham, "Feck, ah'v needed the salvation an' saviour o' the Bru' on many an occasion, I can tell yiez."

Mharaidh exclaims sternly, "Wee Graham... you're drunk."

Clinging to a large jug as though his life depended on it, Wee Graham replies with a slur in his voice. "It must have happened when I tested it to make sure it was fit and proper for yiez to be drinking M'lady."

Mharaidh states severely, "Graham, you are definitely drunk, as that's the only time you ever call me M'lady." Annoyed at herself she continues, "Why didn't I notice earlier, I must be so used to you staggering about the place drunk all the time."

Wee Graham hazily replies, "Aye, M'lady."

Mharaidh speaks to William in a commanding voice. "William, take Wee Graham to his Bothie. For I fear for the dignity of our conversation should he remain in our company, and be sure to secure him inside his Bothie, as he likes to escape in search of more sustenance when he's in this condition."

A much-relieved William replies, "Aye, that I will Mharaidh, and it'll be my pleasure."

He reaches down and picks up Wee Graham like a corn dolly then he throws him over his shoulder. Marion's eyes smile at William when Wee Graham suddenly squirms. William loses his grip on his struggling charge and drops Wee Graham onto the ground like heavy sack of wriggling eels.

Grinning nervously, William picks up a now groaning Wee Graham and throws him over his shoulder, securely this time. With Wee Graham hanging like an old bladder bag over his shoulder, William and Marion gaze at each other. William looks deep into Marion's beautiful dark almond eyes.

"WILLIAM," says Mharaidh forcefully, "Are you still with us?"

A surprised William replies, "Aye, Mharaidh."

She points toward William's shoulder. "Then much as I like Wee Graham, would you please cover his bare buttocks, as they appear to be smiling at Maid Marion."

Quickly pulling Wee Graham's plaid down over his bare buttocks, William blurts out, "Oh Mharaidh, sorry I…"

He hurriedly walks off with his charge toward the bothies when Mharaidh calls out, "Please look after Wee Graham, William, and stay with him till he wakes or till he's sober. And don't under any circumstance let him escape."

"Aye, Mharaidh, as yie wish," replies William while quietly cursing Wee Graham under his breath as he walks away, he whispers into Wee Graham's deaf ear. "Ya wee feckr Graham. I wanted tae stay beside Marion, for she's se' bonnie."

Wee Graham groans. "Stop moanin' and bumping me about ya big feckr, awe naw... am gonnae be sick..."

"Awe, naw," mutters William, "not now, please..."William rushes towards Wee Graham's Bothie.

Mharaidh laughs then she speaks with Marion. "I can see you both have warm hearts for each other?"

Marion fawns and smiles. "Who? Little Graham and I?"

They both laugh then clasp hands affectionately. Mharaidh says, "I can see we'll get on very well you and I. Though I'm not wrong in feeling that both your hearts beat stronger when you're together? And certainly I do mean William this time young lady."

Marion blushes. "I do like little Graham, but I fear he's already taken by another, and yes, I do feel an affection for William, though we have only just met."

Pleased upon hearing these words, Mharaidh says, "Then should you require my assistance in this fledgling hearts dominion with William, I will gladly give my experience over to you. William is a good young man and will be a fine husband and father, of that I am certain. And you my bonnie bluebell, I think you will be the measure of any man you choose as a husband."

Marion replies, "I thank you Mharaidh. I truly believe that you are best suited for guidance on this matter of the heart. And should I be requiring your advice and assistance in regards to Wallace men, then I will gladly listen."

They nod at each other knowingly, then they look in the direction of William and Wee Graham away in the distance.

Marion enquires; "Will Little Graham always be our Chaperon?" queries Marion.

"That depends on William's countenance towards you," replied Mharaidh. They both laugh and set about conversing freely when there are no men about to hear of women's romantic chatter.

On the way towards the Bothie, Wee Graham groans, "Wallace…"

William replies gruffly, "Aye, what is it?"

"Have yie met ma wifey, Auld Jean yet?"

"Aye, of course I have ya daft wee scunner…"

"Do yie know that I met her near on forty years ago? Man, I'm telling yie, she was a right ugly feckr then, but I told her only this mornin' that she hasn't changed a bit since the first day we met…"

William laughs as he kicks open the door of Wee Graham's Bothie and dumps him on a pile of furs and skins that resemble a crib. He throws a rug over Wee Graham who is already sleeping like a baby.

Leaving the Bothie, William pushes a heavy sandstone millwheel against the door and thinks, *'That should hold the wee feckr.'* He stands at the door awhile, making certain it's secure and there are no attempts to escape.

William turns and looks over at Marion thinking to himself, *'Feck, I really like her, I sure hope she likes me.'*

Forgetting Wee Graham, William meanders over to where Mharaidh and Marion are pulling herbs and stands beside Marion, as close as he would dare. As he moves closer, she quickly steps aside with a curious look on her face.

"Oh dear William… what is that terrible smell?"

William sniffs the air. "What smell?"

Appearing repulsed, Marion asks, "Have you stood in something bad?"

Suddenly, William remembers, *'Awe naw, I hope that's not chicken shit she can smell. Awe, feck naw… I hope she doesn't think it's me?'* Then he notices a smell like a baby's been sick. He looks behind him, then at the soles of his boots.

Marion puts a kerchief to her nose, pointing and waving her finger toward his back. "What is that?"

"Awe fuck," sighs William, "Wee Graham's been sick down ma back."

Marion laughs heartily at William's apparent dilemma. A flustered William enquires with utmost sincerity. "Is it baby sick or is it chicken shit you can smell?"

Marion stops laughing. "What did you just say Wallace?"

Meanwhile, Mharaidh who's still pulling herb a little distance away calls out. "Marion, your father's leaving soon, it's time for us to be going back to the keep."

Marion waves back, acknowledging that she's heard Mharaidh, then she looks at William. For a moment they stand transfixed, gazing into each other's eyes then they hear a voice in the distance call out. It's her younger brother Brian beckoning her return.

"Marion?" enquires William.

Marion replies, "Aye William, what is it?"

He asks cautiously, "Can I see you again?"

Suddenly he feels his heart pounding in his chest. He tries desperately not to show how much her next few words could mean. Marion simply smiles at him as she walks towards Mharaidh. She says, "I should be assisting Lady Mharaidh and taking the baskets back to the keep don't you think?"

William's heart sinks as he watches her walk away. Her scents linger and make him feel a hunger for her.

He feels the urge to run over to be with her when she stops, looks round, smiles and then calls out to him. "William." He replies anxiously.

"Aye?" Marion grins then continues, "I do hope you smell much better when next we meet.

For a brief moment William is unsure, he needs to know, he blurts out "When?"

Marion giggles. "Whenever..."

He can't believe his ears.

Marion smiles then turns and walks over to Mharaidh, where they collect the little herb baskets and stroll up the hill towards Wallace Castle. Before she enters through the keep doors, Marion turns and glances at William, smiles and waves to him. He raises his hand meekly and waves back as she enters the keep.

Feelings of euphoria, joy and elation surge through William as he looks up at the Keep doors, he's never felt this way before. His mind is racing. *'She didn't say no... Feck, and she said the next time we meet...'*

He looks up to the sky and shouts with joy. "Fuck me, thank you jaezuz, thank you... She didn't say no, she didn't say..."

Interrupting his moment, a familiar voice from behind him enquires, "Who didn't say no?"

William spins round, then much to his horror, he sees Wee Graham, who instantly recoils and jumps back a few paces, wiping at his face as if he is swatting cow flies away from his nose.

"Feck William, you should wash son, for yie smell like you've been sick or have yie been rolling about in chicken shit or somethin'?"

William is speechless as Wee Graham picks up the empty whisky and wine jugs then nonchalantly walks past him on his way towards the keep, and Wee Graham's second home—the *craitur* cellars.

Dunes o' Largs

Sitting on the banks of the river Afton, William thinks of his encounter with the Maid Marion and smiles to himself, these feelings and thoughts he's having are new to him, and he likes them. He whistles as he walks happily down toward the Afton flow to wash away Wee Graham's excess in the hope he will be rid of the awful smell. Approaching a deep pool in which he can bathe, he notices Auld Tam contentedly fishing and reading his accounts book on the riverbank.

Auld Tam is the record keeper of Glen Afton, a man of gentle demeanour, portly with his long shocking white hair tied back and his long white beard beaded and combed, bedecked with a sprinkling of amber beads, as is the want of a veteran Galloway *Gallóglaigh*. His appearance is more like a warlock from one of Wee Maw's scary stories.

Auld Tam looks up and welcomes William. "*Co'nas*, young Wallace, how are yie doing this fine day?"

William sits himself down beside Auld Tam. "I'm fine, *tá*,"

Tam immediately sniffs the air then leans back a little, perplexed.

William can't offer an explanation that will make much sense, but he tries to explain regardless. "Tam, before yie ask, I've just carted Wee Graham to his Bothie and he boaked down my back, before that, I fell into the chicken midden up at the big hoose."

Tam laughs heartily, slaps his thigh and exclaims, "Chicken shit? Feck's sake Wallace, hen shit this morning, Wee Graham and his liquid dinner too, and all this afore supper? Is there something you like about bad smells young Wallace?"

William explains, "I had to lock him up in his Bothie Tam, but he managed to get out again, feck knows how he did it, for I rolled a big millers wheel against his door and leather tied the wee windows shut on his Bothie from the outside. Mharaidh told me to stay nearby and make sure that he didn't escape but he's feckin gone already."

"Aye, that will be Wee Graham for yie, he'll be on the hunt for his stash o' *craitur*."

Smiling and looking into the deep pool, William replies, "I do like the wee fella, though."

"Aye, he is some man right enough. You have to understand the wee fella to appreciate him."

"What d'yie mean?"

Casting a line out into the deep pool, Auld Tam says, "He was always a rogue Wee Graham. When he went into Alexander's service, he quickly gained the respect of our bonnie *Àrd Rígh*, your father, grandfather and all of the *Garda Rìoghail*. That wee fella could fair fire a short bow second to none at close quarters, and for his size, he just plain destroyed anything and everything that came near him. I've even scars in ma own back ma'self where I got in his way at the battle of Largs."

The older man pauses for a moment and reflects on glories past. "Aye, that's where your grandfather Big Billy was killed bless his soul."

William sits up immediately, intensely interested in what Tam is saying. "Will you tell me what happened at Largs Tam?

I love to hear old war stories, but haven't really heard much about ma grandfather, Billy."

"Aye…" replies Tam. "Just let me lubricate ma vocals a wee bitty first son and ah'll set out ma lines, then I'll tell yie all about it."

Laying on the grassy riverbank, William settles down and waits for Auld Tam to swallow some *craitur*, set out his fishing lines and tell him all about the battle of Largs.

His peace is disturbed when Stephen unexpectedly returns from his ride out and tryst with Katriona.

William sits up. "How was the ride out on the horses?"

Stephen shakes his head as he takes off his brat. "Great wee ponies, them Garron greys o' your father's. Fine and fit for the purpose o' scaling these toiny mountain lands o' this fair country o' yours."

"So you really did ride out on the Garrons? So what about your tryst with Katriona, did yie no' get to meet her?"

"Ah sure now Wallace, wasn't she not after being busy in the kitchens all bleedin' day with the feedin' o' the visitors?"

"Aye, that's our luck Stephen. Auld Tam here is about tae tell me about the battle o' Largs."

"Excellent." Stephen gleefully he rubs his hands while he stomps a thick clump of grass flat then he sits down on the bank beside William."Me auld fella was there too,"

Then he looks at William with delight, "Ah now Wallace, how did you get on with the Maid Marion?"

"Great, I think?" William confidently chews a stock of corn grass. "I reckon I left a good impression."

"Ho, Wallace!" says Stephen with a look of disgust. "What the feck is that bleedin' smell?"

"Awe, Feck it," sighs William. He jumps to his feet, runs to the water's edge and throws off his *léine* for the second time that day then jumps naked into the Afton water, completely submerging himself. He washes brusquely then wades out of the river completely naked, just as Lady Mharaidh and Maid Marion stroll past.

"Awe naw," exclaims William in a panic. Hastily he wrenches a clump of rushes out of the bank to cover his manhood.

"WILLIAM!" exclaims Mharaidh as she and a giggling Marion immediately turn round and begin to walk back towards Wallace castle.

William calls out feebly, "I… I thought you had left."

But his pathetic plea falls on deaf ears as Mharaidh and Marion walk away, greatly amused.

"What the Feck is going on?" asks a puzzled Stephen.

William sighs, "Don't ask, it's too long a story." He clambers out of the river and sits down beside Stephen and begins drying himself with grass while cursing under his breath; then he wraps himself in the thick warm brat.

Stephen quips, "Wallace, that was sure a big bunch of reeds you pulled out there, was it not a bit o' an exaggeration in the quantity to be impressing Marion?"

William growls, "Feck off Stephen, though I'm thinking that Marion did enjoy my company this day. I reckon she just needed a wee look-see to confirm her deepest desires."

Auld Tam chortles, "Is that why she laughed when she glimpsed your mighty winkle Wallace?" Looking up at the sky thoughtfully, Auld Tam grins. "It's got a wee bit o' charm that… winkle Wallace."

Stephen and Tam laugh as William ignores the banter. Stephen asks, "What was that smell about yie anyway winkle, eh, William?"

"Ach, Wee Graham was sick down ma back when carried him to his Bothie awhile ago and…"

Auld Tam throws his books down. "Do you fellas want to hear ma feckin story of how Wee Graham, Big Billy and me won the battle o Largs, or are we gonnae discuss the size of your manhood young Wallace?"

Stephen splutters a laugh as William replies, "Naw, we're fine and finished Tam, you go ahead, for I've never heard an actual account of the battle o' Largs or what happened to ma grandpa."

"Right then," grins Auld Tam. Clearing his throat loudly; Auld Tam begins his story. "It was like this then lads, nearly thirty years ago, King Alexander, the Scots army, and also some of our fine amiable Irish cousins, the H'Alpine's, McUidhir's, McMaghnuis and O'Cuinn's boys from Connaught, all led proudly by Auld Stephen of Clan H'Alpine's I may add.

"We were all gathered near the shores o' Largs, waiting for the biggest Norse fleet ever to set sail from wherever. Aye boys, we knew the Norse were coming to invade mainland Scotland, for many o' the isle fisher folks had told us a' fore-hand o' the great Norse fleet gathering in the north and western isles. But waiting to welcome them wie itchin' hot spurs was King Alexander, the entire Scots army, me'self and yer Grandfather, 'Big Billy' as we called him then. That's when yer grandfather commanded the Wolf and Wildcat *Gallóglaigh*. Then there was Cailean Mòr Cambeul (Colin Campbell) Leckie Mòr, Wee Graham, yer father and your uncles. Well boys, I'll tell yiez this, that's the day we saved the King of Scotland."

William and Stephen look at each other smiling, thinking they definitely hadn't heard this yarn before.

Tam pauses and thinks of that glorious day. "Aye boys, I remember it well. I was standing there on the Machars o'

Largs with your fathers, when they was no' much older than you two boys are now. We were tasked with the Wolf and Wildcat *Gallóbhet* to muster with your Uncle Malcolm when he was but a young Guardian Ceannard, standing right in front of the king himself he was, for that's where the Galloway warriors had won right of place to stand in battle through merit and distinction since Roman times."

His pride obvious, Tam continues, "We were all in the tree-line above the dunes o' Largs where we watched the grandest fleet o' near on a thousand long-ships that ever did set sail to the four winds. And all those ships had mark o' the black raven on their sails, that's how we knew it was the fleet of King Håkon. Aye, the proud Norsemen had sailed from Norway, Denmark, Sweden n' Dublin to rally at the western isles, setting their minds on invading Scotland and making it their very own."

He pauses to take the customary swig from his flagon as storytellers do when spinning out a legend. "Aye boys, we watched the Norsemen sailing across from behind the *Cumaradh Mòr* (Great Cumbrae), then they lined up to beach their long-ships on the shores o' Largs. The Norsemen thought if they landed near the mouth of the River Clyde on the western gateway to Alexander's Kingdom, they would quickly sweep across central Scotland like they had done previously in the English kingdom o' Mercia many years afore. But they picked the wrong feckin realm this time, ah tell yiez." He chortles.

"Anyways, there was all o' us observing the thousands of fierce looking Norse warriors pouring off their ships and landing the cream of their fighting forces on the beaches."

William interrupts the monologue. "Did yiez no' fight them as they came off the boats?"

"Naw," replied Auld Tam with a sneer. "Too easy...

Alexander wanted to get as many as he could beached, for he was a master battle tactician. Our King knew that if he dealt the Norse invaders a mortal blow, it would be the last attempt the Norse would make for many generations.

"The left flank of Alexander's army was led by Lord Alexander Stewart of Dundonald, the right flank was led by Blackbeard Cospatrick o' Dunbar and the centre was led by Alexander himself, with the *Garda Rìoghail*, the *Gallóbhet* and the cream o' Scotland's' chivalric mounted knights at his back, all hidden out of sight in the trees behind the dunes. For a long time we just watched, and we waited.

"Now lads, here was the make-up o' Alexanders army, the *Gallóbhet*, they were commanded by Marchal ua Bruan of Galloway. Then on our left flank, that was commanded by Sir Hervy Cunningham and on the right flank, that was the border marchers, led by the Black Douglas and your kinsman William, Sir Robert Boyd. And then..." Tam has a quick swig, "Where was ah? ...Aye, just as the right amount o' Norsemen had landed; Alexander signalled Dundonald and Cailean Mòr, who was the Unicorn pursuivant for Alexander by the way. It was he himself who raised the very flag o' battle, followed by Scrymgeour raisin' Alexanders war flag, the mighty blood red n' gold rampant lion o' Scotland. When Cunningham's men raised the Saltire upon Alexander's signal, the Scots, with an almighty roar, poured over the dunes of Largs heading straight for the Norsemen as thousands of our bowyers, cross-bowmen and slingers sent whole swathes of arrows, quarrels and round-stones flying, like great flocks of starlings soaring skyward to fall upon the heads of those Norse invaders, at the same time as the missile storm hit the Norse ranks. Knights of Scotland's realm led by Stewart of Dundonald, streamed forward, accompanied fearlessly by his men-at-arms.

"Suddenly the Norse were caught in two distinct groups, the main force of *Hirðmenn* (Heerthmen Mercenaries) and *Lithsmenn* (Professional soldiers) were in front of their boats on the beach, but a smaller unit of *Hirðmenn* had made it up to a great mound on our right flank. The initial charge of the Scots led by Stewart had divided the Norsemen at the boats into two groups, the smaller group o' Norse on the mound were attacked and utterly destroyed by the Clan o' Mackays. By this time, Stewart and Cailean Mòr's ranks o' freemen and slingers threw what looked to be balls of mud into the faces of the front ranks of the main group of Norse warriors. But it was no' mud that they threw into the melee, naw boys, very quickly the invaders found that out when great clouds of lime began burning their eyes and throats. Soon it was blinding and choking them. Aye... their 'Byrnies' (Long tunics of mail armour) and big round shields didn't save them that day. When the lime clouds finally settled, the Scots force hammered into the Norse front ranks, then the fighting was ferocious and became merciless on both sides. We were hacking at them with sword, Spear, axe and mace, fighting headlong into the blinded ranks of the Norsemen. There was no time or thought for any mercies I can tell yie. We kept fightin' hard and pushing them back into their own friends who were trying to charge forward, and it caused absolute mayhem and carnage in their ranks."

The two young men are laid back with their eyes closed, totally lost in the imagination of the scenes Tam is describing. They can see everything vividly in their mind's eye.

Auld Tam continues, "The fighting strategy of the Scots was to charge straight for the head of an opposing army, then at the last minute, wee fighting units would branch off by degrees just before impact, hitting hard into the corners of the massed ranks o' the invaders. Other wee independent units would run to the back end and soft underbelly of the enemy, inflicting maximum chaos into the rear o' their disciplined ranks. So, from around both headlands the Scots light cavalry appeared, numbering more than a thousand, and they begin flanking the Norsemen, forcing the Norse warriors into a jug-neck, pushing and crushing them tightly together. Our heavy horse crushed the flank ranks while the light horse skewered any escaping Norsemen as we fought the main body at the front on foot, together we kept pushing at the Norse till we had forced them all into a tightly packed three-sided wedge to stop any more of them from disembarking from their ships. And I'll tell yie this boys, the fighting was savage, vicious and uncompromising. But through it all, I saw what our Alexander was waiting for, then we all saw it, King Håkons' royal Longship sailed in and beached, then a massive and proud lookin' warrior wearing a white wolverine brat with full-face gold helmet adorned with big black raven wings jumped onto the shore, followed by his bonnie *Húskarlar* (Bodyguard)."

He stops once more for another quick drink.

"We sure knew that it was Håkon all right, for this mighty looking warrior immediately led a push forward with all his giant *Húskarlar* flanking him, aye, we knew that this man was King Håkon himself, for he was the bravest o' the brave, for a Norseman."

He suddenly shouts aloud, "ALEXANDER!"

William and Stephen jump up startled.

"That's him, there's Håkon" cries Tam. "That was your grandfather Billy shouting to the King and that's who Alexander had been waiting for all this time, the King o' the Norsemen. The Scots had hemmed his warriors in against the long-ships, but inspired they started to break out. Feck, it was sheer chaos boys, with war horns blasting endlessly on both sides; screams o' dyin' men and horses, the clash o' metal and skirmishing all around the place. Norsemen began breaking in all directions with many cut off from the main group and trapped at the rear by their beached long-ships. Soon though, the front ranks of the Scots started pulling back from a powerful Norse fight-back led by Håkon himself. It appeared as if we Scots were in retreat. Alexander meanwhile, is observing all this from the top ridge of the dunes where the Scots infantry had first made their charge. But waiting behind him hidden out of sight o' the Norse, were the ancient *Garda Céile Aicé, Garda Rìoghail*, the Royal Guardians and Galloway *Gallóbhet*, men and women whose ancestral blood had defended the *Dragii Artur Ard Rígh* and the *Aicé ban Rígh* since the beginning of time… Like the immortal guard of Sparta's Leonidas, the Guardian army would soon push the Norse warriors back into the sea by the sheer determined force of this dynastic force. Soon, it would be time for the Norsemen to find out what real wrath, pain and slaughter would be like at the hands o' the Guardian army,it would no be long now." Auld Tam stops talking to drink more of his favourite *craitur.*

After a few moments silence, William opens his eyes and sits up."What's wrong Tam?"

Auld Tam pushes the stopper back into his jug of *craitur* and sighs. "Nuthin' son, I was just lubricating my throat. Anyway, boys, it was then that Alexander, accompanied by Big Billy and Marchal ua Bruan, rode fast along the blind side of the dunes to stop in front of the ranks of his *Gallóbhet* Immortals, and still totally unseen by Håkon or any of his Jarls. Alexander had prepared our army for this moment. Your

Uncle Malcolm took his place beside your grandfather, standing at the head of the *Gallóbhet* in front of the Guardian army. Aye, numbering near five thousand heavily armed Knights, Cavalry and Men-at-arms, the finest o' the *Gallóglaigh* and the feared warrior horsewomen of the *Gallóbhan*. They all raised hundreds of their clan and house war colours till they were flying full and proud from the brisk sea breeze in their faces. It was a sight I'll tell yie."Auld Tam shakes his head, then he continues… "NOW TAM, cried Alexander as he spurred his great warhorse into a action. He galloped over the tip o' the dunes and rode directly towards the beach. At the same time the front line of the fighting Scots were giving ground to the ferocious *Hirðmenn, Lithsmenn* and berserkers of King Håkon. The Scots appeared to be breaking into a full retreat and Håkon could sense victory was near, but suddenly, in the melee, he must have become aware that Alexander was no' anywhere to be seen." 'NO' screamed Håkon, for he realised it was a trap. But the ferocity of his berserkers and their mistaken sense that were winning the battle, had turned them into a ragin' bloodlust frenzy. They were out of control all around King Håkon. His warriors in thinking they had broken our fighting spirit, began pushing forward to break free of the stramash. Meanwhile, as a storm began to blow up a gale, the Norse armies that were still on board the offshore long-ships were crammed together and their ships started colliding with other ships at the beachhead."

Another wee obligatory drink for Tam, then, "The skippers o' the Longships upon seeing the flanking Scots pull back, ordered their men to row fast to get onto the beach where they began disembarking more warriors. Just one more push forward against our brave Scots defenders and it was obvious the Norse thought they could break out and escape from the nonstop slingshot, quarrel and arrow-storm onslaught to gain a victory over the Scots. Aye right, it was then that Alexander saw Håkon and his *Húskarlar* were franticly trying to stall the outpouring of Berserkers, *Lendemenn* and *Hirðmenn* from the long-ships. In sheer desperation, the masses of the Norse were trying to break landward. Aye, Håkon was being pushed forward by the weight of his own men. He had no choice now but to fight his way forward, even though he knew it was the wrong thing to do. Alexander knew his trap was now being sprung, and at a pre-arranged signal, the Scots front ranks totally gave way, much to the horror of Håkon. As the Scots lines opened up, Håkon finally saw King Alexander at about three hundred cloth yards away thundering down the beach at full speed on his mighty warhorse directly toward him, and followed by his entire Guardian army."

"Feck, Tam, it sounds amazin'," exclaims William.

Tam smiles as he swallows another dram. "Aye son, it was amazing all right. The sands trembled and shook with the pounding of Alexander's heavy horse cavalry and the entire warrior caste storming down the beach. Anyway, when auld Håkon saw that Alexander was leading thousands of his hardened Guardians fresh into the battle, and he could also see that Alexander was aiming his main force directly toward him. This Norse fella's worst fears were now being realised, for he also knew this incoming force was the elite of Scotland's fighting army, and I swear to yie boys, I actually witnessed Håkon prepare himself for a quick entry into Valhalla." Another swift pull on the *craitur* for Tam, then he cries, "Feck…"

"Now then," says Tam, "Håkons *Húskarlar* also saw that Alexander and his immortal guard were hurtling down the beachhead towards their King, and fair play to the bonnie

Húskarlar, as heroes to a man, they immediately threw themselves in front of Håkon to try and break Alexander's frontal
attack just as the Scots heavy horse slammed into them, but it
cost them there Norse boys dear for their courage. Aye, it was
a grand panic that immediately set into the Norse invaders.
Håkon could see more Scots cavalry crashing into the flanks
of the panicking Norsemen with a renewed vigour, tram-
pling and slaughtering those brave Norse warriors with their
heavy warhorses. It was then Alexander signalled the dunes,
suddenly, hundreds of dog soldiers appeared and ran their
Mastiff, Greyhound, Wolf and Deerhound war-dogs straight
toward the lower flanks of Norse at the waters edge where
they were all hemmed in. The dog soldiers' suddenly halted
just yards from the Norsemen, with the ferocious dogs of war
straining on their chains, howling, snarling and going crazy
to be unleashed. All o' the dogs had vicious lookin' hooks and
spikes in their broad collars, with barbed hooks attached to
their flanks and chest-plates, solely meant to rip deep into
human flesh to stop anyone from trying to throw the attacking dog off them. Some dogs were dragging long lines behind
them with big barbed fishhooks to snag legs and make the war
dogs even more feckin insane. The poor Norse were feckin
petrified, but their worst nightmare was just about to arrive
right on top o' them…"

"What was that?" asks William.

Tam replies, "The *Gallóbhan*… fuck me boys, those women
are savage, let me just say, if any o' those Norse fellas who
survived the initial attack o' our women, sang in awfy high
pitched voices when they got back home."

Stephen asks, "Did the Norse no' surrender?"

Tam laughs, "Naw, no time. Alexander gave the signal to
release the war-dogs into the mass of bloody wounded and

dying Norsemen. Feck boys, even though the Norse had set their hearts on enslaving us, for a moment ma heart sank as I watched those war-dogs from hell and the bonnie *Gallóbhan* tear the Norsemen apart. It was a savage, sickening affair. I'll tell yiez this, if yie ever need to strike fear into an enemy, send in the dogs of war, and the *Gallóbhan*."

William and Stephen are totally engrossed as Tam tells the story, as he recalls it.

"The bonnie *Gallóbhan* finished off the Norse at the boats then they rode along the beach and got in amongst another bunch o' cut-off Norsemen and tore them apart too with their short bows, javelins, grapplin' hooks and ring spears. What feckin' carnage the bonnie lassies caused, feck the vengeance o' the *Gallóbhan* has no thought for givin' out any mercy." Auld Tam has another drink of his inspirational nectar… when Stephen enquires, "Did the Norse no' have women fighting with them?" Tam sighs, "Aye there were some, their renowned Shield Maidens tried to put up a fight, but our *Gallóbhan* made short work o' them. But while the *Gallóbhan* were killin' the wee Norse lassies, it gave the surviving Norsemen trying to get back onto their ships time to escape. They clambered over the slain bodies of their friends while fleeing from the slaughter behind them. They would have done anything to get away from the rabid dogs, arrow-storm and the King's warhorses crushing them underfoot. Largs was a mighty big mistake that day for Håkon.

"To try and save the day, Håkons fleet commander sent his remaining long-ships around the bottleneck to outflank the Scots, and they almost succeeded had it not been for the fleet of Alexander's royal Birlinns, commanded by Morrison mòr and the wee fleet of the Jura Birlinns commanded by Sibhdaidh Ewan MacDougal o' Aros Dounarwyse. The Scots

Birlinns are similar to the Norse long-ships to the layman, but to the trained eye, the King's Birlinns are leaner, lighter, much faster and more manoeuvrable than the Norse boats. Aye, they were proudly known as the Greyhounds of the sea right enough. They Birlinns o' Morrison and MacDougal were manned by expert sea-warriors, tacking full wind in their distinct blue and maroon sails. They outflanked the Norse ships and rammed into them in an effort to be blocking any escape. The battle was now at its zenith when the skies fully broke and a most fearsome storm blew all the ships offshore, including many ships from those that had been stuck at the beachhead. Both Norse and Scots alike suffered natures wrath that day."

Pausing, Auld Tam thinks for a moment, then says, "More luck so the Norsemen or we would o' fixed them for good, I'll tell yie that for sure. Aye, the storm came as a severe disadvantage to us as it freed the packed body of Håkons fleet, which until that moment had been stuck on or near the beach. With this ill-wind, pounding rain and sea squalls, Håkons moment to escape was upon him."

It was William's turn to ask a question. "So what happened to my grandfather Tam?"

"Well son, it was like this yie see, Alexander was fighting like a feckin demon, slaying all Norse who came within reach of his great sword, and he was getting so close to Håkon he could spit in his face. That was when a Norseman flung a war hammer and felled the King's horse, throwing Alexander at the feet of Håkon's *Húskarlar*. Well, your grandfather Big Billy, me'self, Wee Graham and your father too Stephen, with Scrymgeour, Cailean mòr, Robert Boyd, Bryce Blair and Leckie mòr quickly surrounded the King, when I saw three o' those Norse axe-men make to cleave our Alexander.

"Now with me being a hot spear expert, I skewered the first one through the face as your grandfather Billy dispatched another two with his great two-handed claymore. Wee Graham was in the thick of it too with his short bow, sticking it to them with his arrows faster than the eye could see, and your auld man Stephen, feck, he was takin' heads asunder and cleavin' men near in half with his great Spart-axe…"

Stephen says, "Jaezuz Tam. Ah didn't know…"

Auld Tam resumes, "…Aye well, yie do now. Anyway, I fought beside them, fast and furious till I felt ma hot-spear vibrate and sing its song o' blood to ma rhythm. Then I heard Bryce call out to me above the noise of battle. I spun round as Alexander tried to get to his feet and ah speared over his shoulder skewering another *Húskarl* right in the face, then ah stuck another by rammin' ma spearhead straight through his foot, pulled the spear out fast and lunged forward with such force I embedded ma hot-spear deep into the same man's chest, where it got feckin stuck didn't it, and I couldn't feckin retrieve it."

Tam drops his head a moment as though reflecting on the reality of his experience.

The boys notice. "You all right there Tam?" enquires Stephen.

Auld Tam sighs, "Aye, aye, I'm fine enough, son, sometimes boys, what yie have done in life and war can come back and haunt yie."

William looks at Tam. "You can finish the story another time if yie like Tam."

"Ach naw, am fine son," says Tam. "I need to be telling you about yer grandpa. So boys, when ma spear got stuck, yie've no' got time to stop or think logically in such a fight, so I dived to the shore floor to pick up a fallen sword when I saw that Wee Graham had been badly wounded with almost half his face hanging off, caused by the sheer of a Norseman's blade, but still he fought like a wee lion, never leaving the side of Alexander or your grandfather, who was still tearing the Norse asunder, even though I could see big Billie had been severely wounded too.

"Alain, Auld Stephen, Leckie and yer uncles were wielding their great swords and spartaxes with such ferocity, Norse heads n' arms flew about Largs like ravens in the fall. Your grandfather tried to steady our King when Alexander was struck on the back of his helm by another flying axe, knocking him unconscious. Meanwhile Håkon was being pushed unceremoniously onto a long-ship, that's when he was struck twice in the arse by two Scots arrows. Wee Graham claims the credit for that."

Auld Tam laughs as he thinks of that moment and Wee Graham's claim.

"Anyway," says Tam, "behind Håkon, thousands of his fellow countrymen would never see their *fjords* again. Many *Húskarlar*, *Hirðmenn*, noble *Jarls* and *Lithsmenn* bled the sands of Largs red that day, it'll take the Norsemen a hundred years to recover from that one boys."

Auld Tam reaches for the *craitur* once more before continuing. "As the storm turned to fury William, your father Alain was wounded by arrows in the legs, then he was hit again by another straight through his shoulder. Along with other Guardians, we were all wounded one way or another, but we fought on through the melee with Leckie, Wee Graham, Bryce and your grandfather carrying the semi-conscious Alexander back to a makeshift shelter at the edge o' the dunes. That's when I got struck deep in the chest by an arrow."

The young men gasp.

"Aye," sighs Tam, "There were still many o' the Norse scattered and fleeing over a great distance. There were skirmishes and fights all over the shore and dunes o' Largs. It was just then that about thirty or so dirty big Norse warriors cut off from their ships made a brave but futile rush towards us to get at our Alexander, and being wounded so bad, we knew we couldn't put up much o' a defence, when suddenly, a young mounted Knight from Mauchlynn named Piers Curry attacked the Norsemen all on his own.

"For a youngster, he was a real hero. Young Curry rode straight into the centre of the Norsemen and fought them to a standstill. He stalled them long enough for Hector MacKay, Blair, Boyd and your grandfather with some of the surviving *Gallóglaigh* to make a run at them. But by the time they got there, young Curry had been hacked to pieces, though his sacrifice gave us enough time. I reckon that boy Curry saved not only us but also our King, and maybe Scotland too."

"Feck," exclaims Stephen.

Tam ignores the interruption. "MacKay, Blair Boyd and I were badly wounded. I saw Billy pick up a spartaxe to protect them. He threw the axe with such a force, he embedded it full in the face of the leadin' *Húskarlar* from about twenty feet, then it all happened so fast, with yer grandfather swinging his great sword he hacked into them like a man possessed. He was splitting them from head to groin with one strike or ramming through their skulls till the quillons of his claymore were all that stopped his sword running right through ther' heads. I even saw him strike one with his great claymore on the collarbone on one side o' the fellas body and drove the sword down with such ferocity it left the poor fella at his hip on the other side of his body. What a braw fighter yer grandpa was."

Desperate to know William asks, "So what happened to my grandfather Tam?"

"I'll tell yie son. MacKay, Blair, Boyd, Auld Stephen and Billy fought like heroes of legend," says Tam. "But they kept getting stabbed or slashed and there was not a thing we could do about it, we were all so badly wounded. I saw big Hector, he had two of them by their throats when his skull got split by an Norse axeman. Billy fought on till I saw a spear head come through your grandfather's chest. Feck, but didn't he just snap it like a feckin twig and then he skewered the same spearman in the eye with his very own spear stump, then I saw Billy cleave the fella from brow tae breast. That's when two Norse arrows hit Big Billy about the throat; yet still he fought on to protect Alexander. By the time we reached your grandfather, he and Blair had dispatched all the remaining Norsemen."

As he tells the tale he shakes his head. "We could see Billy would no' survive the wounds he had taken. Your grandfather William, he was a very brave man. Piers and Hector too, all of them. If they hadn't taken to charging those Norse down the way they did, I don't reckon Alexander or any of us could have survived. We found Blair, Boyd, Stephen and Bryce badly wounded, they were the only ones who survived."

Drained, Tam stops a moment for a breather.

William says, "I never knew of the circumstance o' ma grandfather's death Tam. So Billy, Hector and Piers gave their lives for Alexander?"

Auld Tam recoils, "Naw, no' just Alexander, but for us too. Didn't yie know that Big Billy is who yie get your name from, you're the honoured embodiment o' your grandfather? Aye, he was a fine man William, a very kind and generous man indeed."

"Aye, Wee Maw told me so, it's an honour and memory that I know I must never tarnish, even more so now that I know the full story."

Auld Tam jokes, "And yie are so like him in so many ways. Maybe I should call you Big Billy too."

William is not convinced. "I don't think I could ever have the courage he had though."

Auld Tam looks down at the deep pool and his baited lines. He says, "Don't you be worrying about that son, courage isn't something yie think about, it comes to you when it's needed, or yie die."

William laughs nervously, "Feck, I don't know Tam. I've played at fighting, but I like the lassies more."

"Aye, just like your auld grandfather." chuckles Auld Tam. "But then there's yer Wee Maw. Now there's the only person I ever knew who could tame Big Billy. I've seen that wee woman chase him round *Ach na Feàrna* with a hazel switch many a time, and Billy showin' more fear o' her than ah ever saw from him in any battle we were ever in."

"What happened after the battle?"

"Well son, we had to pull back from the impossible weather conditions on the beach, that allowed the surviving Norsemen to get their ships back to sea. Morrison mòr and his fleet of blue angels were beached, as was MacDougal's fleet of Jura. What was left o' the Norse fleet was about to suffer its biggest defeat at sea from mother nature's wrath as the Norse army had suffered its biggest defeat on land at the hands of the Scots. Those Norse fellas claim in their Saga's it was because o' witchcraft that their invasion fleet got feck'd." Auld Tam sneers. "Aye, sure, it had to be something else to blame for ther' defeat. Those Norse storytellers needed something heroic to be writing in ther' feckin sagas to make them look good."

"Aye, ma Dá told me something similar about the Romans,"

Stephen asks, "And what about me Dá Tam, how did he fare in the battle?"

Tam responds warmly. "Oh, the fine fightin' boys of auld Erinn. Brave men Stephen, and yer father, well he was something else to behold too. He led the Irish *Gallóglaigh* forward and right in to the thick of the fightin', man he was fair like the embodiment of Brian Bóruma MacCennétig at the battle o' *Cath Chluain Tarbh*, to be avengin' the death of his son Murchad and grandson Toirdelbach…"

"Brian Boru o' Clontarf," exclaims Stephen. "Jaezuz Tam, that's sayin something very special about me auld fella."

Tam's eyes glint. "Yer auld Dá *IS* special son, and as yie well know, the memories o' you Irish run deep, and it showed that day on the beaches o' Largs. Yer auld fella and his men covered Big Billy's *Gallóglaigh* and fought till there were se' few o' them left alive, very few. I saw your father gettin' struck by four arrows as he ran to fight beside Big Billy. And if I remember rightly…"

"Aye," interrupted Stephen, "Two in his back, one in his chest and one through his stomach from the side. I've seen the marks on his body, but he never was to be telling me how he got them, the auld feckr."

For a moment, Auld Tam says nothing, then he spoke quietly but with solemn purpose, "Stephen, listen to me, and you too William. Many men will not speak of their experience of war for as many reasons as there are dead men. But men like your father Stephen, and your father and Uncle Malcolm too William, they'll ne'er speak o' such things, for when in a battle, it's all about senses you cannot imagine exist till you're there, the stench, the sights, the sounds of men dying, ordinary time as yie would understand it ceases to be during war.

You know you're connected to all humanity down through the ages that has ever fought to live. For to recall incidents in time of war is bad enough, but to try and construct that experience into words that make some sort of sense from another time to any listener, then the story becomes a lie from the very beginning, and men like both your fathers are not and never will be liars."

William is confused. "I'm not sure what you mean Tam, how can you be telling us about it now then, ah mean…?"

"Ach William," sighed Auld Tam, "You two fella's mark my words, men like myself will tell you of what we've seen and about the heroism born in others, for I'm simply a reluctant witness who would have ran for my life if I could have. I'm a simple man who only recalls legends for others as a warning from history. And I have to be lying to make understandable what happened, but the incidents I told yiez about are all true, and even by me embellishing it to make it an understandable story will never truly convey the heroism of man, nor their brutality. But now you know all about your grandfather Big Billy."

Auld Tam sits up "Well, me boys, back to the end of ma story. So, apart from dispatching the Norse wounded, the Battle was all but over when Wee Graham decided tae fire one swan song arrow at the last Norse ship fleeing from the shore. But in him being se' blinded by his own blood pouring down his face and running into his eyes, he fired the feckin arrow straight into ma back."

"He did what?" blusters Stephen.

"Aye son, Wee Graham shot me," replies Auld Tam. "Here, let me show yie the scar." Auld Tam lifts his léine, and there on his back is a perfect scar matching that of an arrow strike, and also the severe welt-mark of the arrowhead's hot blade removal.

"It's the only time I have ever been shot in the back." says a nonchalant Tam as he straightens his *léine*.

"So lads, we were all wounded that day at the battle of Largs, and Wee Graham certainly played his part, and I should know." Tam laughs as he throws his good arm over his sore shoulder and pulls at a stiff muscle in his back.

"Boys, Scotland had repulsed another attempt to be overthrown by misguided invaders and Wee Graham played a mean part in it."

"It sounds to me like it was some battle yiez had there," says Stephen.

"Aye, but then a funny thing happened," recalls Tam. "A strange young fella named True Tam arrived on the beach bringin' his healing magic with him. He sowed Wee Graham's face back together with the blackthorn needle by fixing it to his head with catgut when we reckoned he couldn't survive his wounds. True Tam tended him, yer father, Auld Stephen, the King, most of us right enough. His blacksmith water and healing potions saved many lives that day, I'll tell yiez. And it was after that battle that the King retired Wee Graham with honour. Alain asked the Alexander for permission that Wee Graham could reside with us in Glen Afton, and he's been here ever since."

Impressed by the story, William sighs, "Aye Tam, he's some man. Feck, you are all some men,"

Stephen agrees. "Yer right there. I wish the Irish could put aside ther' differences and unite like you fellas did."

Curious, William still wants to know more. "When I was studying an account of the battle o' Largs, I read a volume called the Håkon Håkonsson Saga, and those accounts state that the battle was only a skirmish, maybe about a few hundred, and the Norse were outnumbered ten to one, ah even read that Alexander wasn't there?"

Tam laughs out loud. "Me boys, for fecks sake, it wasn't Håkon himself who wrote the bloody Saga, it was penned on the behest of his successor Magnus Lagabøter, for auld Håkon Håkonsson died o' embarrassment on his way home. Or maybe a sore arse, courtesy o' Wee Graham. It's more likely though, that enemies within sent him to Valhalla. Anyway King Magnus, he's no' going to memorialize in their famed Sagas that Håkon Håkonsson fucked up and lost the largest fleet the Norse ever sent to sea, but they would never admit that would they?"

"I suppose not," agrees Stephen.

"The Norse claim a tempest took the lives of over twenty thousand of their warriors. Aye, right, for fucks sake boys, it was the biggest feckin fleet the Norse ever put together for an invasion o' anywhere. They even forced the fleet o' Angus óg o' the isles to join them in ther' foolish enterprise. Do yie think the Norse fleet would sail near a thousand empty boats over to Scotland for just a wee look-see then only drop off a couple of hundred visitors after all that effort? Feck off. If yie believe the battle o' Largs was a mere skirmish, then more fool you." Auld Tam sneers with utter contempt and disdain in his voice.

"The Norse didn't call dear auld Alexander the Tamer of the Raven for nuthin'." Tam wags his finger, "And do yie know the worst part o' the Saga's version boys? Folk will read the Norse accounts for a thousand years and they'll believe that shit. But yie will find a much truer account in the Melrose chronicles, aye, a lot different to the feckin Norse Sagas."

William says, "It sounds like the Norse had the same type o' lyin' scribblers recording their history as the Romans did…"

"What Romans?" Auld Tam asks.

William and Stephen laugh, resisting the temptation.

"Well, boys," says Auld Tam. "I was there, and I'll tell yie that the Norse lost thousands o' men."

Stephen grins. "Twenty thousand to be precise Tam."

"Aye son. Yie just have to look at all of the many great grave mounds around Largs now overgrown with sea grass and gorse to see that. Those Norse were fairly beaten and thrown back to the sea, includin' the wee fleet that sailed up to the Lennox. Mind you, those Norsemen were ferocious warriors who had fought many a heroic battle against legions of well-armed priests, wee boys, auld men, women, milkin' cows and flocks o' sheep."

William and Stephen laugh out loud at Auld Tam's vivid description and his version of Norse warfare. Tam continues, "When yie really think about it, the Norsemen were in a league of their own for raiding monasteries, wee farms, remote islands and places nobody had ever feckin heard off, and then writing great sagas about themselves doing it. Aye, they were all heroes in their own wee Norse world right enough." He finishes sarcastically

Tam points at William. "But it was a different story when those same fierce Norsemen had tae face a real army full o the finest o' Scots and Irish warrior blood. We broke them that day and that was the beginning of the end o' the Norsemen, for they never attacked us again after that."

Stephen says, "That's near the same end to the story as what little me father ever said about the battle Tam. He also told me about the Irish bein' gifted some of the finest long-ships o' the Norse by King Alexander, in gratitude for standin' wit yiez that day."

"That's right," says Auld Tam with a smile, "some o' the long-ships were also given to Morrison mòr and MacDougal o' Jura too." Auld Tam pulls at his fishing pole and sups some *craitur*.

"So how is it that the Norse gave over most o' the isles back to Scotland?" asks William.

Auld Tam replies, "Not long after the battle, a treaty was made with the Norse who were then allowed to reclaim their dead for burial. But there were too many dead and scattered all over the place, some whole, but most in bit parts. The most o' them were sanctified in great fires on the beaches, but the rest are buried in pits around Largs. Aye boys, after that scrap the Norse were a spent force, auld King Håkon Håkonsson sure rued the day he attacked Scotland."

Auld Tam stirs. "Boys, it's time for me to be away to another spot for me fishing. There is a big salmon in a wee pool that's been hauntin' me for years. I hooked him once and he was this big." He stretches his arms and extends his fingers as far as he could in each direction.

"D'yie have any more battles scars Tam?" asks William.

"Do yie mean other than those across my face or them that Wee Graham left me with?" Auld Tam proceeds to pull up his *léine* and turns a full circle.

"Holy feck Tam," exclaims Stephen. "You're looking like a bad seamstress' blanket."

Amused, Tam responds, "Well yie should o' seen the state I left the other fellas in then."

Without further ado, Auld Tam packs his fishing gear and makes his way towards another part of the riverbank, leaving William and Stephen reflecting about the story he had spun for them.

"He can sure tell a fine story," says Stephen.

William stretches his arms, "No' half. I never really knew the Scots account of the Battle o' Largs, and I don't know why I never asked before now. It just seemed ma Uncle Malcolm never wanted to speak of it, and I always thought it was because he lost his father there. But am grateful to now know so much more about grandpa Billy."

Stephen ponders, "I wonder what it's really like to be in a battle as fine as that one."

His friend thinks about the story then replies, "It must be something else and a feckr on yer senses to fight in a battle like that. I'd like to know more about my grandfather though, he sounds like he was some man."

"I don't know if I could do what those fella's did, I'm a lover not a warrior."

William thinks another moment then speaks, "I am glad they did fight like heroes, for it's left us with peace in this realm. I hope we never know a battle like that."

"Did yie see all those scars on Auld Tam?"

"Feck aye," says William. "To have such scarification and walk with the peace of nature in him like he has…"

Stephen nods in agreement. "Sure now, yie could never tell when yie look at some o' those old fellas what they've been through, what they have seen or ever experienced in their lives."

"I don't know if I could do what they did." He stands up and looks at Stephen. "Anyway ma fine Irish brother, do yie fancy some scran for I'm feckin' starvin' especially after all that fighting in my head?"

"Feck," says Stephen rubbing his stomach. "Ma guts are thinkin' ma throat must o' been cut. Let's be goin' to see ma bonnie Katriona for she'll have mighty fine and nourishing delights awaiting to fatten me up for later, if yie get ma meaning."

William laughs as they both raise themselves from the riverbank and walk up to Wallace Castle to find some refreshment and vittals. As they approach the kitchen doors, Katriona comes out a side door with a large basket.

Stephen grins, "Ah, Katriona me bonnie darlin', is that something nice n' sweet like yourself you will be having for me to be nibbling on, other than yourself now?"

Katriona replies, "Well me fine Irish rogue, I do have something here, but it's for both of you." Katriona sits down on a large round boulder in front of the Keep and uncovers a platter of hot wrapped bannocks.

"These are for you Stephen, and these are for you William, and all just freshly made for I thought you two might be hungry."

"You're no' wrong there," replies William. He continues casually, "Oh, Katriona, have yie seen the Maid Marion about anywhere?"

Katriona replies, "Everyone left just a little while ago."

She notices the look of instant disappointment on his face.

"Is it a little heart's flutter you've got going there for Marion?

"No, naw, eh, I was just wondering, that's all."

Stephens' face beams with delight, "I think our big friend here is been gone and falling in love there me darlin'."

"Feck off," growls William. "It's no' that. It's just… well, I do like her a wee bit I suppose."

Katriona exclaims humorously, "A wee bit?

Katriona and Stephen turn their passionate attention toward each other, while William turns away to look towards the southern pass.

He mutters. "For some reason I don't feel so hungry anymore? I think I'll be leaving you two lovebirds alone and I'll go a wander through the Glen."

Saying his farewell, William strolls down to the river and sits beside the Afton flow as dusk begins to creep over Glen Afton. He thinks of everything that has come to be in the last year, moving to the Glen with his father, Stephen's friendship, the hunt, even learning more about his namesake, Big Billy, but no matter what he thinks or tries to think off, he cannot get the Bonnie Maid Marion out of his head. He feels a sickness in his stomach at the thought of not seeing her or knowing when he will ever look into her beautiful dark eyes again. It causes him an angst he has never felt before, but the unknown is almost worse. *'Does she even like me?'*

Suddenly wee Graham comes rushing out the kitchen doors and sees William. He calls out "Wallace, quick boy, yer da wants yie to go to him right now."

"What's up?"

"No' sure, but it sounds mighty like trouble."

"What kinda trouble?"

Wee Graham's concern is obvious. "There's reports comin' in frae the doocots o' armed English troops gatherin' at Carlisle and it looks like they're waitin' to be crossin' the border. And we also read there are some high and mighty lookin' English Knights and ther' entourage makin' their way towards Turnberry castle."

"That's the castle o' the Bruce 'o' Carrick?"

Wee Graham replies, "Aye, that's it is, but it gets worse, there are also reports comin' in, the Red Earl o' Ulster has a Birlinn fleet headin' straight across the sea from Rathlan just off the coast o' Ireland, other longboats are sailin' down from the Lord o' the Isles, and they're headin for Turnberry too."

William is confused as to what this all means. "Graham, is Scotland being invaded, are we at war…?"

To be continued

in

Book 2 - Youngblood

WALLACE
LEGEND OF BRAVEHEART
BOOK 2

SEORAS
WALLACE

YOUNGBLOOD

The second thrilling instalment in
Wallace: Legend of Braveheart

For more information
www.seoaraswallace.blogspot.com